262.5

Laity --
Lutheran Church--
Missouri Synod

Gift Lutheran Laymen

UNCERTAIN SAINTS

UNCERTAIN SAINTS

*The Laity
in the Lutheran Church—Missouri Synod
1900–1970*

Alan Graebner

Contributions in American History, Number 42

GREENWOOD PRESS

Westport, Connecticut   ●   London, England

Library of Congress Cataloging in Publication Data

Graebner, Alan.
  Uncertain saints.

  (Contributions in American history; no. 42)
  Includes bibliographical references and index.
  1. Laity—   Lutheran Church—Missouri Synod—
History. I. Title.
BX8061.M7G7   262'.5   75-1573
ISBN 0-8371-7963-7

Library of Congress Catalog Card Number: 75-1573
ISBN: 0-8371-7963-7

First published in 1975

Greenwood Press, a division of Williamhouse-Regency Inc.
51 Riverside Avenue, Westport, Connecticut 06880

Manufactured in the United States of America

For M.K.G.

CONTENTS

Preface

This is a historical essay on the adult laity within the Lutheran Church—Missouri Synod, one of the three major Lutheran bodies in America. It is not a theological disquisition on the proper place of the laity in the Lutheran church, nor is it a sociological investigation of the present lay community, valuable as those studies would be. Instead this is simply a historical introduction to such work, though I have occasionally drawn from both theology and sociology when it seemed appropriate.

There are at least three general themes intertwined in this book. The first was obvious at the initiation of this study; the second and third became apparent as the story unfolded. The first theme is the gradual emergence of the laity in the Missouri Synod as immigrant laymen became more Americanized, more integrated into the culture and society surrounding them. The second is one of search, the continuing search for the most proper, meaningful, and complete role of the laity in the Lutheran church. The third theme is the determinative factor in this search, the synod's view of the world. The first theme was sounded early in the century and its echoes gradually died away in successive decades. It did, however, help set the key and tempo for the second and third: what is the laity supposed to do? And where is the laity supposed to do it? Here variations and improvisations gained steadily in elaboration and importance.

Writing on the laity has its problems and pitfalls; in fact this study was begun at least in part to explore such difficulties. One of the most perplexing is a precise definition of the subject. My working definition of the laity is most quickly stated negatively: the body of communicant members who are not ordained clergy, deaconesses, or parochial school teachers engaged in full-time professional church work. Theologically this is quite unsatisfactory and is potentially crippling; I have retained it nevertheless, mainly because of its convenience. Even given such boundaries, questions of limits, often troublesome in historical writing, were particularly harrassing in this investigation. The penumbra of the history of the laity proved unusually large and often vexing. I occasionally found myself ranging more widely than I had at first anticipated in order to make intelligible both lay life and thinking about the laity. Sometimes, too, I found myself investigating more deeply than I had expected topics that are ordinarily relegated to a few lines. Usually it seemed best not to impose a priori proportions more sanctioned by church history, but to follow the track of the laity where it led.

There is a serious temptation when writing about the laity to engage in what might be termed scorecard history, pitting the clergy against the laity and tallying the goals of each in successive encounters. In some situations, the clergy and laity *were* on opposite ends of an ecclesiastical seesaw. And the historian in such cases has no choice but to record the motion and its direction. It seems wise, however, to guard against an unconscious and automatic application of this paradigm to the whole of the twentieth century.

A further problem is the lack of uniformity even within a church body long praised—or denounced—as being unusually monolithic. Even when some highly Americanized congregations were moving into prosperous suburbs, traveling pastors were calling together desperately poor, inexperienced German immigrants for the first time in the cramped quarters of a crude shack in Montana or Saskatchewan. Later, attacks on the clergy for not permitting more lay initiative bewildered some pastors who were only too well acquainted with the stolid passivity of their own local congregations. And more recently, demands made by some laity that traditional positions be reevaluated clashed with warnings from other alarmed laymen against deserting the true faith. Few meaningful generalizations would cover every congregation in the synod. It is possible, though, to outline the most significant and pregnant characteristics and trends in light of what came before and what followed.

The thinness of American Lutheran historiography and sociology has proved a continuing frustration. As a result, while investigating matters tangential to, but bearing upon, the laity, I repeatedly found myself in relatively uncharted waters. I tried to

lessen the perils of dead reckoning by taking soundings from time
to time, but navigation was complicated by a related problem, the
difficulty of ascertaining what the laymen were thinking. With a
few notable exceptions, they were not very articulate in print and
their letters are not extant. Archival policy in itself says a great
deal about the role and status of the laity. The silence certainly
makes the historian's task more difficult and leads to an at times
untidy and misshapen result. To paraphrase Winthrop Jordan,
were it possible to poll German immigrants on their attitudes, I
would be among those at the foot of the gangplank and at the
church door, questionnaire in hand. Since this is not possible, one
is perforce reduced to inferential reading and deductive logic,
drawing on the statements usually made by official—clerical—
spokesmen. One must also reverse the cliché, in this case sifting
through a mountain to produce a molehill. All too often, nevertheless, one finds oneself discussing not the laymen and their attitudes but what clergy thought about the laity. Clerical statements may be divided into the reportorial, often shrewd and
penetrating, and the prescriptive. Both are essential to a study of
the laity. The prescriptive expecially forms an important part of
lay role parameters, and I have tried to follow the zigs and zags of
ideas about the laity and to estimate the degree of their applicabil-
ity and their application. It seems clear that the next step ought to
be a painstaking parish reconstitution study of a representative
sampling of Missourian congregations. Pending that, no one is
more aware than I how tentative many of the following conclusions must be, though I have eschewed continual qualification as
a stylistic irritant.

Problems such as these persuade me to term this an essay and
to stress its exploratory nature. Mistakes in the following pages
may at least serve as wrecks that mark rocks and dangerous
shoals. To change the metaphor, as Richard Vann remarks, "new
light casts new shadows." Comparative studies of the laity are
badly needed to even the illumination.

No historian is without commitments that in some measure
color his judgments. Readers deserve to know that the author is
of the fourth generation in his family to be born into the Lutheran

Church—Missouri Synod. The question whether a layman of the Missouri Synod can view his denomination objectively is a legitimate one. But so too, I think, is whether someone *not* a member of the synod can write impartially about Missouri. Admitting affiliation is not the same, of course, as confessing conscious suppression or distortion of evidence. My disagreements with previous generations of laity and clergy are many, but I have tried in all cases not to be condescending and not to divorce men and decisions from their context.

Some explanation of organization may help guide readers most efficiently through this book. After an introductory chapter which sketches the situation at the turn of the century, Part One discusses organizational expressions of lay life up to about 1929, as well as the whole course of twentieth-century fund raising. Part Two turns from the synodical and organizational to the parish and individual level beginning early in the century until approximately 1945. Part Three focuses again on synod-wide organizations from the Depression through the 1950s, and the three chapters of Part Four concentrate on lay life since World War II.

One of the most pleasant duties in completing a manuscript is to acknowledge one's manifold obligations to others. Paul Friedrich, then executive director of the Lutheran Laymen's League, played an important part in launching this study and was a great help in its early stages. I owe much, too, to August R. Suelflow and his staff at Concordia Historical Institute in St. Louis, official archive of the synod. CHI was an exceedingly congenial and rewarding place to work, the sources there rich, and the people endlessly accommodating. Librarians at Concordia College, Moorhead, Minnesota, and at Concordia Theological Seminary, St. Louis, patiently endured my demands on their resources and traced hard-to-find volumes through interlibrary loan.

When written records failed and I turned for information to participants, I almost always found a cordial reception. Busy people made time in their office schedules or entertained me graciously in their homes. Space precludes an individual acknowledgment of their courtesies, but a bare listing of the individuals will be found in the bibliography.

James and Eleanor Haney, Dorinda Knopp, Dwight Culver, Charles Vandersee, and Paul Schuessler all allowed me to take advantage of friendship; they read various drafts with salutary skepticism and impatience, often forcing me into more careful thought and expression. Errors and infelicities which remain are the result of my obstinance, not the lack of good advice.

Part One

In his perceptive study of the American Roman Catholic laity, Daniel Callahan suggests prerequisites for significant lay activity. "A lay renaissance," he says, "will depend upon lay leaders . . . who have achieved some general social status and acceptance, some economic stability, some sense of identification with society." Furthermore, a layman who becomes active in the church will "reflect not only his dedication to the church, but also the influence which the values of society have had upon him." The more freedom he has in the community, the more autonomy he will seek in the church.[1]

The emergence of meaningful lay activity within the Missouri Synod fits this hypothesis nicely. It was delayed until significant numbers of the constituency integrated themselves into American society. When it did appear, it was led by wealthy businessmen, and by those well along in the transition from German immigrant to American. The lay activity reflected American ideals in its emphases on publicity and on financial efficiency. Finally, the laymen quietly but persistently pressed for as responsible a role in the church as they enjoyed in secular life.

1

1

Laymen in a Clergy's World

I

The bulletin handed to worshippers every Sunday at most congregations in the Lutheran Church—Missouri Synod by the 1950s usually included the week's schedule for a long list of church groups that depended upon the resources and time of members. All this was so predictable, established, even standardized, that it was hard to imagine things had ever been otherwise. But only fifty years earlier, the church building—which then included no parish hall, gymnasium, banquet room, or well-equipped kitchen—was usually dark from Sunday to Sunday. The congregation might have a *Frauenverein,* or Ladies' Aid, which probably met in some member's home. But there was no men's club, no scout troop, no parent-teacher league, no young people's club, no married couples' club, no Sunday school, probably no adult choir. And, perhaps needless to say, no Sunday bulletin.

Pious, God-fearing Christians there were in every congregation. But the lay activism later generations took for granted simply did not exist in 1900. In fact, synodical leaders resisted it stoutly wherever they saw it. The *Lutheran Witness,* the synod's official English organ, heartily endorsed denunciation of a lay missionary movement in other denominations. "Let the church ask the men to come. If the men will not do it, they will not come if some organization within the Church asks them."[1] Facilities in the church building to promote fellowship and recreation were

3

considered "a pious bribe."[2] As late as 1917, the *Witness* described the pastor of a congregation boasting six lay groups as "surely inviting a case of nervous collapse and premature old age."[3] Probably most of the laity at the time would have agreed. These expressions illustrate an attitude typical of the synod at the turn of the century. In fact it may be misleading to speak of the synod's view of the laity, for this implies conscious consideration of the status of the laity—a rare commodity indeed in the Missouri Synod of 1900. Synodical leaders did on occasion refer to the Lutheran emphasis on the priesthood of all believers, but the doctrine was dutifully reaffirmed rather than creatively explored. In the laboratory analysis of the church's contents, the laity was the proportionately large but chemically inert ingredient. And nearly all clergy and laity took for granted, probably desired, things this way.

II

Such a situation was not typical of American Protestantism at the turn of the century. In fact, New World conditions produced a startlingly active laity in most American churches. The frontier forced fresh beginnings for the church as for other institutions. The voluntary nature of the church in the United States often made these beginnings dependent upon the laity. Laymen who accepted the responsibilities necessitated by the freedom of disestablishment were more independent and assertive in their relations with clergy. The rich American societal life furthered the same development, for laymen became active in a wide variety of extra-denominational organizations with religious or quasi-religious ends. The theological egalitarianism of revivalism and the social equalitarianism of democracy also served as important leveling influences at the expense of clerical prerogatives. Finally, the theological currents predominant especially in nineteenth-century America set up few barriers to an expanded role for the laity; in fact, they promoted such a development. As a result, even ecclesiastical traditions with strong clerical establishments were hard pressed. Anglican clergy had to reckon with assertive colonial vestries, Roman Catholic clergy had to contend with trusteeism, and Methodist bishops were confronted with demands for lay representation.[4] The Missouri Synod necessarily also encountered these sources of change in the role of the laity. But its accommodation to them took a distinctive course, partly because of Lutheran theology which held the priesthood of all believers in tension with sacramental and other emphases assigning a high place to the ordained ministry. But equally important in shaping the Missouri Synod's response to American conditions was the synod's immigrant origin and certain peculiarities of its history.

Between 1832, when large-scale German immigration began, and 1900, some five million Germans uprooted themselves and came to America. Not all of these—not even a majority—were Lutherans, but many were, and one German Lutheran church body after another was established here to gather this wandering flock into the fold. The fold, however, had less secure walls and the shepherd a shorter staff than in the state church of Germany. The governments of the German states provided by law for the financial support of the pastor and the maintenance of the church property. In some of his duties, such as baptism, marriage, and burial, the minister had both religious and secular functions. Officials sanctioned by the state licensed the clergy, appointed, and, if necessary, removed pastors from their congregational posts. One spoke more of a parish—with its geographical connotations —than of a congregation. The average German citizen had as little a decision-making role in the church as he did in the state.

The German experience was not very useful for the American conditions of voluntarism and separation of church and state. In America the clergy did not have the sanctions of the state to force either moral or financial support. The state was not concerned with who called himself a clergyman, much less with what group pretended to be the true Christian church. The laity was not automatically counted as Lutheran. Instead, laymen had to make the choice and ratify their decision by providing financial resources for salaries and buildings.

Yet some early immigrant groups attempted at first to reckon with the implications of the American free church environment by deliberately ignoring them. The Missouri Synod was one of these. *Die Deutsche Evangelisch-Lutherische Synode von Missouri, Ohio und andern Staaten* had its roots in several groups of German immigrants that came to America separately but shared an insistence upon orthodox, confessional Lutheranism.[5] One fairly large constituent was a colony of Saxons led by Pastor Martin Stephan from Dresden to Perry County, Missouri, south of St. Louis. Another was a group of missionaries and colonists sent by the German churchman Wilhelm Loehe to convert the Indians and serve the burgeoning German-American population.

The role and position of the laymen in the union of these groups were strongly influenced by the disillusioning experience of the Saxon immigrants. The colony had submitted itself fully to the clerical autocracy of Martin Stephan, only to charge him guilty in America of financial and sexual profligacy. Stephan himself was summarily banished across the Mississippi to Illinois, but confusion remained in Perry County and in St. Louis, where some of the party had settled. The laymen were smarting from economic losses and embarrassed that they had believed they were doing God's will by following Stephan to America. Many gradually swung from their earlier veneration of the clergy to the opposite pole of stressing the powers of the laity and questioning the pastoral position. Some became explicitly anticlerical; one baker, F. Sproede, denounced the clergymen in the colony as "spirits of the devil, thieves, robbers, murderers, and wolves, false brethren."[6]

A less choleric lay position was stated first by Dr. Carl Eduard Vehse, then by his brother-in-law, Dr. Franz Adolph Marbach. Both men were well educated lawyers, men of social and professional standing in their native Germany. These laymen reemphasized the priesthood of all believers. Vehse asserted that, "as spiritual priests, laymen had the right to judge all doctrine and to supervise all the activities of the clergy," a direct attack on the position Stephan's former lieutenants attempted at first to maintain.[7]

Gradually the clergy gave way. Under constant pressure of the laymen, one of the pastors, C.F.W. Walther, drew from Luther and the Lutheran Confessions a church polity which, as he himself acknowledged, was influenced by Vehse's ideas.[8] In the atmosphere of American religious permissiveness, Walther recognized the fundamental authority of the laity. He argued that the church exists wherever there are God's Word and the Sacraments. The local congregation has the right to call its own pastor; in fact, insisted Walther, it is the seat of all church power. Walther agreed that the minister may not dominate the church, that the laymen have the right to vote in church courts and councils, and even to pass judgment on matters of doctrine.[9] Here and later as pastor of Trinity Congregation in St. Louis, Walther in effect made a virtue of necessity and in a creative way provided theological sanction and ministerial support for the moderate lay demands in church government.[10]

This experience was decisive when the Saxons and the Loehe men made contact and began formal organization. As Walther analyzed it for the Loehe representatives: "The West is full of German demagogues who leave no stone unturned in their efforts to create suspicion and to make every form of synodical organization appear dangerous." Even well-meaning people were affected, Walther believed. "There is a general fear and timidity over against such an institution [as a synod]; people fear priest rule. Furthermore, our immigrant congregations view with alarm every institution that even faintly resembles a hierarchy, because of their terrible experience with Stephan."[11]

The Saxon episode occurred within an engrossing and intensely serious ecclesiological discussion on both sides of the Atlantic. Debate centered, however, not on the laity, but on the nature and role of the ministry, that is, the clergy. "The former, in Missouri at least, was viewed only in terms of and subject to the limitations set by the latter."[12] Between the controversy's two extremes—focusing on the clergy or reacting against it—Walther and his colleagues attempted to formulate a middle position. The Missourians rejected the conscious elevation of the clergy by Wilhelm Loehe and by J.A.A. Grabau, immigrant pastor-leader of the Buffalo Synod; they stressed instead the rights and powers of the congregation, and thus of the laity. Yet, faced with the laicism of some other groups and with what seemed like a cavalier treatment of the clergy by many American denominations, the synod upheld the ministry's divine institution.

The synodical constitution, adopted in 1847, expressed Missouri's position by granting membership to both ministers and congregations. Each affiliated congregation was entitled to send one pastor and one layman as its representatives. Pastors present from congregations not yet formally members were given nonvoting, advisory membership; comparable laymen were not. In formal franchise the lay delegates thus were equal to the clergy; they also insisted on a clause through which the local congregation could nullify any synodical resolution not in conformity with God's Word or unsuited to its circumstances.[13] Yet the constitution did require that the president, vice-president, and even secretary be clergymen. The post of treasurer was alone open to laymen, and it became traditional for a layman to be elected. This distribution of offices was not surprising, given the situation, though in time the precedent would feed the misconception that the layman's duty was chiefly financial.

In sum, as is usually the case, reflection on Scripture in this matter was heavily influenced by contemporary developments, and, willy-nilly, pastors and laymen agreed that the laity might have an active role in church affairs as long as the clergy maintained a fatherly, guiding hand on the synodical reins of power.

III

The mid-nineteenth century formulation is important because it allowed, but did not necessarily encourage, a substantial amount of lay activism. Its possibilities long remained unexplored, for by 1900 the actual, working relationship between pastor and people had reverted to a highly paternalistic one. Official synodical polity aside, the laity was decidedly subsidiary and secondary to the Lutheran *Herr Pastor*. The metaphor of the shepherd and his obedient flock came to include not only the pastoral functions of the shepherd, but in many cases, the sheep-like nature of the flock. For the clergy, the absence in America of an established church and the possibility of virtually unlimited religious choice seemed to protect the layman's rather than the pastor's role. Unhappy experiences with imposters and frauds caused the clergy to inspect their ranks closely. The very freedom in America probably made pastors guard against new and spontaneous lay activity more rigidly than than they would have in a less volatile atmosphere.

Yet pastoral paternalism at the turn of the century was not a stealthy conspiracy by the clergy to regain privileges lost in the 1840s. In fact the laymen often expected, perhaps even wanted, a paternalistic clergy. Not all the laity were entirely docile, to be sure; congregations feuded, divided and strayed, harrying their pastors and synodical officials all the while. Yet the obstreperous were a minority in the synod and they led to a negative selection. Those who seriously challenged their pastor and the prevailing stereotypes of the layman's role were most likely to leave the synod; those who stayed tended to feel most comfortable with the status quo. Furthermore, the synod was not a ministerium. No short tether continually reminded the laity of its subordination. Instead the congregationalism of the constitution was roomy enough that, as long as certain pastoral prerogatives such as tenure were respected, restive laity had space to move about without immediately crashing into fixed theological or constitutional barriers and being encouraged by their bruises to become self-conscious about their position.[14] Most of the clergy recognized that America was not Germany. They tolerated with surprising restraint the situation in which almost half of the congregations served by synodical pastors were not themselves members of the synod; apparently these congregations feared encroachment on their autonomy in finances and authority.

Linguistically it is wise not to imagine the immigrant in an either-or situation, facing an absolute choice between his mother tongue and English. His language was instead a continuum—added to at one end and gradually eroded at the other until the main body was neither the old tongue nor the new, but a way-station easing the strain of adoption. Similarly in religious life, the immigrant did not face an absolute choice between a European and an American model.[15] The continuum held intermediate points. Militant lay suspicions gradually diminished after the Stephan affair; a complex of interrelated sociological factors and Missouri's theological preoccupations then combined to limit the inducements of the American environment toward lay activism.

The nature of the immigrant community and of personal needs within that enclave; the social composition of the Lutheran immigrant group and expectations brought from the old country; the attitudes engendered by a conservative orthodoxy: all these reinforced one another in the latter nineteenth century to create a situation in which the clergy led and the laymen followed. Both expected things to be that way. Both had lost their grasp of the implications of the synodical constitution and of America voluntarism.

First, the laymen were prone to accept a subsidiary role simply because they were German immigrants.[16] Almost until World War I, the fortunes of the synod depended on the exodus from Germany. Leaving behind a familiar world rich in associations and memories, the immigrants entered a new, alien, and sometimes quite hostile environment.[17] Naturally they attempted to recreate the aspects of old world life most precious to them. They could not reconstruct everything, of course. And like their increasingly archaic vocabulary mixed with sauerkraut English, what the immigrants did manage to build was not fully German. But whether they really thought (or persuaded themselves to think) it was *echt Deutsch,* or whether they saw clearly enough that it was not, they treasured the more anything they could reconstruct that bore even a semblance to the past. For at least some, the comforting assurances of religion took on deepened meaning in America. Here, in a strange land, religion was both a tie with the fathers and a hope for the future. The religious rites of passage—baptism, confirmation, communion, marriage, and burial—took on added value, especially when observed in old, familiar language. And, because of his central role in such ceremonies, the German-speaking pastor held high status among the immigrants.

Of course, the *Reiseprediger,* or circuit rider, who moved into new territory searching out German settlers, could not *always* expect a warm welcome. As we shall see, the immigrant community included a number of mutually exclusive persuasions. Some immigrants wanted nothing more to do with the religion left behind in Germany. "We don't want to let ourselves be caught by you deceivers again, for we are in the free land of America and are finished with religion."[18] Thousands of immigrants "from our former fatherland," acknowledged C.F.W. Walther, "count freedom from compulsory church-membership as one of the great advantages that America offers over against other countries, and they consider great fools those who become church members of their own choice in this free land."[19] Others received the pastor with the respect due him as an educated German, but gave no further cooperation. Some missed Lutheranism and a pastor at first, but as time passed they forgot their loss or joined an American denomination. Yet as the statistics of the phenomenal synodical growth indicate, thousands of immigrants received the *Reiseprediger* with joy and thanksgiving. Scenes of a crude but heartfelt worship in a new area were repeated again and again. Even after the turn of the century, reports from the *Reiseprediger* frequently mentioned the tears that glistened among the small congregation as the stanzas of some German Lutheran hymn rang out for the first time in a settler's hut or the local meeting hall.[20]

Numerous congregational histories record appeals by some man or woman longing for Lutheran ministrations which resulted in a candidate setting out from St. Louis. But such lay initiatives, where they occurred, do not seem to have contributed a great deal to subsequent lay self-consciousness. Instead, most laity seem to have deferred to the shepherd who sought them out, organized them into a congregation, and continued to serve them. The pastor tended to gather the people together, and it was the pastor, often with the help of the German language, who kept them together.[21]

World politics also furthered clerical leadership and lay passivity. German immigration of the late nineteenth century reflected Bismarckian nationalism and a tendency to merge religion and patriotism. For such people, the immigrant Lutheran pastor led not only a religious institution, but also an agency that could help perpetuate German culture in this country. The Missouri Synod was particularly vulnerable because of its strong school system, which, in spite of the efforts of educational leaders, often seems to have inculcated Germanism and Lutheranism in roughly equal parts.

Another factor contributing to the absence of lay leadership was the privileged position of the clergy in status-conscious old world society. The German pastor was a *Standesperson,* literally, a person of standing in the community; he might be from the upper classes, was set apart legally from ordinary citizens, and relatively well paid. These origins and prestige did not, of course, transfer in toto to America.[22] Many immigrants had left Germany at least partly to escape just such class distinctions, but such people were not the most likely to join the Missouri Synod. Surely the shoemaker or farmer who had bowed with sincere respect to the *Herr Pastor* in Germany was likely to do the same, at least mentally, in America.

IV

The social composition of the nineteenth-century Lutheran immigrant community helped insure this respect. Within a few years after arrival, the clergy and teachers were the only well-educated professionals in the first Saxon contingent in Missouri. They served a constituency composed chiefly of farmers, craftsmen, and tradesmen.[23] Generally speaking, the same was true for the next fifty years. When the tide of immigration ran especially heavy in the 1870s and 1880s, rapid German industrialization threatened the pattern of life that the independent small farmers and the village shopkeepers and artisans serving them enjoyed in the agricultural north and east of Germany. Rather than move to German cities, many of these people chose as families to reestablish their lives in America. Interestingly enough, this immigration may have winnowed to produce conservatives rather than progressives, for many of these people came to preserve a way of life increasingly difficult in the old country.[24]

In this country, they remained farmers and tradesmen: the butcher, the baker, the cabinet maker.[25] By confirmation at age twelve or so, boys had finished their education and chosen a vocation.[26] When confronted with the bitter warfare between capital and labor during the nineties, synodical writers could condemn both sides because the largest mass of their readers in the synod belonged to neither group.[27] As C. C. Schmidt, an old pastor of wide contracts, recalled in 1922, the synod had consisted of "farmers, mechanics, and wage earners. . . . The rich and educated were rare exceptions."[28] Farmers and men in the crafts and trades did not guarantee deference to the clergy but may have respected the average pastor more than would have a congregation of wealthy urban industrialists and government officials.

Educational disparities reinforced class distinctions. The founders of the synod, largely graduates of German universities, insisted that a well-trained minister have behind him nine years of "college," plus three years of the seminary. The clergy studied in Latin, Greek, and Hebrew, preached in German, and could converse in English. By comparison, among the laity, German-educated parents thought in terms of the trade-oriented *Volks-schule* rather than the college-preparatory *Gymnasium*, and a fortunate American-educated child might finish sixth grade.[29] It is no surprise that, as Mundinger puts it, "the immigrant Lutheran on the frontier knew that his pastor was smart."[30] Few other professionals—even lawyers or doctors—had comparable training. One naturally took one's problems to such a man. One minister recalled that in an immigrant parish, the pastor "was their counselor in all major decisions, their interpreter in important business matters. He wrote their letters and other official documents and translated those they had received. He made their wills, assisted them in finding employment or a place to live."[31] Given the lack of professional specialization within most Lutheran immigrant communities, the pastor assumed he should solve most problems.

Synodical periodicals frequently referred to the minister as

Seelsorger (freely, soul-healer), emphasizing the pastoral role with the individual layman. In this role, the laymen apparently expected, or at least accepted, a directive counseling, even an authoritarianism, the clergy was prepared to provide. A knowledge of the pastoral guidance provided the laity at the turn of the century is essential to an understanding of the evolution in lay roles.[32] Demonstrating an amalgam of orthodoxy, middle-class conservatism, pietism and Biblical literalism, the clerical expressions are striking for two characteristics: breadth of concern and militance of rhetoric.[33] Missouri Synod leaders insisted that life insurance was sinful gambling with one's life, a sign of small faith in God's providence. They warned repeatedly against the theater; in case some might misconstrue this to mean cheap vaudeville, *Der Lutheraner* explicitly condemned *Figaro, Carmen, Romeo and Juliet,* and *Tannheuser* as unfit for a Christian audience. Even discriminating play-going could not be indulged in by Christians, urged William Dallmann, for "if you as an exception witness a clean play you thereby support the institution having an evil influence."[34] Virtually all fiction was proscribed. Novels, declared the *Witness*, "pollute the heart in the recesses of the closet, they dangerously inflame the passions at a distance from actual temptation, and teach the malignity of vice in solitude." The nude in art was similarly condemned.[35] Dancing, another snare of the devil, lured young people inescapably to ruin and a vile end. Clergy spelled out in painstaking detail the laws of Leviticus 18 prohibiting marriage between people of certain blood or family relationships, and pronounced engagement the equivalent of marriage according to the Old Testament (a broken engagement thus constituted divorce). Birth control was militantly denounced as a loathsome interference with the blessings God bestowed on married couples.[36]

All this was on top of repeated admonitions to stand clear of secular societies such as the *Turnverein* or German choral and debating groups that might lead to godlessness. Groups such as the YMCA and secret fraternities, on the other hand, were to be avoided because of their essentially syncretistic religious nature.[37]

The style of these pronouncements is also noteworthy. Impressively certain of the infallibility of their position, synodical spokesmen were quite prepared to break up a romance between a widower and his sister-in-law, as forbidden in Leviticus, or to treat a broken engagement as a divorce case.[38] Some historians have pictured German immigrant Lutherans as the group devoted to "personal liberty" as opposed to the pietistic meddling in private affairs favored by Scandinavian Lutherans and native Protestants. But the sheer mass of proscription in German Lutheran literature at the turn of the century must be taken into account along with German Lutheran theorizing to defend German beer and the continental Sunday. In that context German immigrants seem marked off less by the absence of pietism than by a few specific lacunae in their behavioral code.

An emplasis on New Testament passages dealing with church discipline was entirely characteristic of synodical periodicals at the time. When under siege one dare not tolerate the lukewarm or the dissident. Editors spent many pages explaining how the congregation should secure public repentance from the erring, or, if that were impossible, cast the sinner from its midst. Writers carefully instructed the clergy how to gather evidence for an excommunication.[39] Laymen, too, were involved. When a Milwaukee pastor wrote a pamphlet to help guide elders in their duties, he spent most of the space advising them how to correct and admonish their fellow Christians.[40] True Christians, synodical leaders agreed, have an obligation to reprove erring brothers; proper discipline will strengthen rather than weaken a congregation.[41] Thus did faithful pastors raise and patrol the wall between church and world. The laity was to remain inside these walls ministering to each other under the solicitous care of the clergy.

V

All these factors—the composition of the immigration, the needs and expectations of the immigrant community, and attitudes of orthodoxy—combined to insure that as the twentieth century began laymen had not yet become the self-conscious entity they were to be within two decades. Small, telling signs abounded. For example, until 1904 the annual publication of synodical statistics listed congregations by their pastors' names, not by the names of the congregations or towns.[42] Unconscious contrast of active and passive roles came in the description of the personnel on a synodical board: "one from the preachers and two from the audience."[43]

Constitutionally, laymen had a voice equal to the pastors in district and national conventions. Yet, to judge from the published reports, the laymen were notable chiefly for their silence. When Franz Pieper, the president of the synod, chose in 1900 to comment on the participation of lay delegates at the district conventions he attended, he emphasized chiefly their close attention, and quoted such incisive lay comments as, "How important that is," "I never thought of that before," or "Our pastor should continually remind us of that."[44] Der Lutheraner admonished the pastor, not the lay delegate, to inform the congregation of convention action.[45]

Most impressive is the resounding silence about the laity at the beginning of the century. Much was written for the laity, of course, but the overwhelming bulk of this material was devotional and edifying, Biblical instruction, or proscriptive warnings against the world. Seminary commencement addresses printed each spring in Der Lutheraner repeatedly reminded the clergy of its important calling and the full range of its work. But no equivalent for the laity existed. Furthermore, reflecting the search for order in the church of half a century before, clerical spokesmen still stressed that in the church God had established but one true office: the holy ministry, occupied only by men properly called, ordained, and installed. Any other positions in the church were subsidiary and flowed only from this office.[46] Thus, neither clergy nor laity seemed conscious of the unexplored dimensions of lay activity established decades earlier in the synodical constitution. The avalanche of nineteenth-century German immigration had buried an early promise.

VI

One apparent exception to these generalizations about lay inactivity in the church is the women's auxiliary. Frauenvereine were organized within the synod already in the 1850s, and urban congregations especially took them for granted by the turn of the century.[47] They apparently met most often in members' homes and devoted themselves to sewing projects, support of ministerial students, and other charitable works. Sometimes women even organized a *Jungfrauenverein,* a sort of junior auxiliary. These women's groups were usually the only organizations for adults within the congregations. They are not evidence of incipient liberalization, however, but resulted from the synod's conservatism on the role of women.

For the Missourian clergy, human physiology, the natural order, and Scripture all bore witness that male and female had complementary but quite different spheres in life. A woman fulfilled her calling in domestic and maternal functions. Her role was a subordinate one. The Genesis account demonstrated that woman was created for man, not vice versa. Furthermore, Eve was the agent for the introduction of sin. "She had emancipated herself from his [Adam's] guidance in listening to the tempting words of the Serpent, and therefore she should be constrained ever to be mindful of the evil results of this false step. This is a fact, and no amount of resentment can change this fact."[48]

Lutheran exegetes uniformly chose to emphasize and absolutize the Biblical directive for the silence of women in the church (1 Cor. 14:34 and 1 Tim. 2:11-15 were the favored passages) rather than the egalitarianism of Galatians 3:28. The synod steadfastly refused to consider ordination for women and excluded women from speaking, holding office, or voting in congregational affairs.[49] Some spokesmen thought that there was no harm done if women were present (though, or course, silent) when a congregational meeting was held immediately after morning worship service. But as far as Franz Pieper, Missouri's most respected theologian, was concerned, women should not even appear at congregational meetings, for they had male relatives as their natural representatives.[50] The exclusion of women, the *Lutheran Witness* wanted to make clear, was simply *"because they are women,* not because they are always and necessarily inferior to men in mental capacity."[51] As the century drew to a close, many—if not most—Lutheran congregations still adhered to the custom of seating men on one side of the church and women on the other. During the communion service, the women went forward to receive the elements only after the men were finished. In such a context, the *Frauenverein* was a useful, perhaps even necessary, agency. St. Paul had specified that women could instruct and edify each other without infringing upon the natural order, and the ladies' auxiliary provided such an opportunity.

Not content, however, to restrict discussions of the woman's sphere to congregational affairs, pastors sought to inculcate quietism among Lutheran women in secular matters as well. Looking back in 1896, even the *Concordia Magazine,* a pioneering effort in an Americanized family journal, thought that "woman's ambition in the past decade has tended more or less manward. That is, having grown discontent with her divinely ordained sphere, she has been endeavoring to overstep her bounds and pose as that she is not, nor ever can be."[52] *Der Lutheraner* emphatically agreed. When a girl gets a job in a factory instead of as a maid, or when a woman is admitted to the bar, the paper declared, she is moving out of her proper sphere. As more women become involved, they begin to demand equal rights and equal pay, and then to dress more like men. The result is a repulsive caricature, a creature that does not want to be what it should be and cannot be what it wants to be, that has thrown away its own crown to seize another, but has caught a dunce cap without noticing it. *Zeitkrankheit* and *Unordnung*—this is what the editor thought of the feminist movement and female suffrage. *Der Lutheraner* advised readers to vote down the latter whenever it appeared on the ballot.[53] Only a bit more subtly, the *Lutheran Witness* recommended a Lutheran juvenile novel, *Her Place Assigned,* the plot of which followed two girls. "The one, reared in a Christian home, grows up and marries, and her children are reared in the same manner as she was. The other, her cousin, reared in a non-Christian home, believes in the emancipation of women, lectures for a time, but is finally converted and joins the Lutheran Church."[54] Synodical spokesmen found congenial the triad of *Kirche, Kinder, und Küche,* and defended it in face of feminist assaults.[55] As W.H.T. Dau summarized the synod's position, "Woman is never safer, more honored, more affectionately treated than when she remains in the domain and relationships which the creator designed for her as wife, mother, daughter, sister."[56] Fueled by fears for the future of the home, such conservatism influenced the position of Lutheran women in the church and, to a lesser extent, in the world for decades to come.

VII

As the nineteenth century gave way to the twentieth, Missouri's conservative, immigrant heritage was so strong that the synod at first rejected lay activities elsewhere in American Protestantism. In the early nineteenth century, prompted theologically by evangelical revivalism and sociologically by a rising and prosperous urban middle-class, American lay men and women became extraordinarily active. With the clergy, they organized, funded, and administered a cluster of national, interdenominational benevolent and reform organizations. Through mid-century revivals, laymen took an active part in evangelistic and visitation programs; the YMCA movement begun in the 1850s saw further flowering of lay activism, particularly among businessmen in their twenties and thirties.[57] Early in the century, too, the Sunday school emerged in American denominations. Opposed at first by many of the clergy as irregular, this institution received its main support particularly from the laity as the movement spread prodigiously during the century. In the 1880s, the formation and rapid growth of the Young People's Society of Christian Endeavor and the Epworth League furthered denominational youth work.[58]

In the early twentieth century, there was a resurgence in formal church organizations for men. Perhaps associated with the emphasis upon virile leadership in the Progressive era, one group after another sprang up to organize the laymen in the church.[59] The interdenominational Laymen's Missionary Movement began in 1906, followed in 1910 by another national crusade, the Men and Religion Forward Movement. Through much-publicized mass meetings and conferences across the country, these campaigns sought to enlist men as active church workers, to arouse their zeal for missions, and to educate their financial steward-ship.[60]

On the congregational level, the heightened social concerns particularly of liberal Protestantism helped produce the so-called institutional church. What the minister most likely referred to as his "plant" came to include not only facilities for worship, but rooms for a wide variety of activities: gymnasiums, theaters, kitchens, and club-rooms. Very often one of the groups using these facilities was a recently formed men's club. "Bring the men back into the church" was a popular slogan at the time.

Comparable stirrings occurred within more Americanized Lutheranism. In 1907 laymen, mostly businessmen irritated by chronic church deficits and anxious to introduce better fund-raising techniques, organized in the General Synod of the Lu-theran Evangelical Church what after 1911 became known as the Laymen's Missionary Movement. Much the same progression took place within the United Synod in the South beginning in 1910.[61]

VIII

In spite of its linguistic and theological isolation, the Missouri Synod was well aware of all these movements. Yet it adapted itself only slowly to the American pattern. Church leaders at-tempted to limit to the compromises of the mid-nineteenth cen-tury the synod's accommodation to the American tradition of voluntary associations. Of course, the *Frauenverein* was in line with American expectations, but there was no hint of federation until the 1920s. C.F.W. Walther and others experimented with young people's groups, but these gained no permanent footing for decades until losses among confirmed youth became alarmingly high as they moved out of the immigrant enclave. A number of pastors then began to pay more attention to a young people's society in their congregations.

But a national young people's group, men's activities, and the Sunday school all encountered stern rebuffs within the German

synod. Missourian leaders refused to bend to the prevailing
American tradition of volunteer church society. Antagonism to
the Sunday school stemmed in large part from the synod's investment in an extensive parochial school system and in teacher-
training institutions to supply that system. Parochial school
teachers were issued divine calls instead of contracts and held
special (non-voting) individual membership in the synod. Certainly lay volunteers teaching in Sunday schools were not to dis-
place all this.

Federated youth societies and men's activities ran into opposition for other reasons.[62] The Reformed source of such innovations was the first strike against them. The New Measures of a
former day—the camp meeting, revivals, the anxious bench—
which orthodox Lutherans once fought, may be a thing of the
past, observed *Der Lutheraner* in the nineties, but we must now
resist a fresh group of measures—among them the lay society—
hailed as new means of grace. Criticism of the past implicit (and
occasionally quite audible) in the organization of these new
groups did not sit well with churchmen convinced that the old
ways were the best ways: worship services, *Christenlehre,* the
parochial school—these were methods proper for the Lutheran
Church.[63] A further stumbling block was the disregard in lay
crusades for essential theological differences, the ease with which
these groups crossed denominational boundaries.[64] The Men and
Religion Forward Movement in particular was strongly oriented
to social reform, and this, too, guaranteed enmity from the Missourian clergy. "They have no inkling whatever of the true nature
of Christianity. . . . Christianity and educational or cultural progress are practically identified," complained Franz Pieper.[65]

Also involved was devotion to congregationalism that had by
then become absolutized. Even if we need a lay renaissance,
synodical newspapers said again and again, we do not need a new
organization to accomplish it. We are already admirably organized; the individual congregation is the divinely established
ecclesiastical unit and must remain such.[66] "*Die Christliche
Kirche ist Aggressiv*" insisted a *Lutheraner* headline: of course it
is easier to get a few zealots into a society to push something or

other, as is the American custom; but the congregation as a whole should be involved, if for no other reason than to engage weaker members.[67] Furthermore, an emphasis on fellowship and organizations, it was said, opened wide the possibility of forgetting that the church's true task is to preach the Gospel. It might also endanger the home as the proper Christian social center.[68] "Over-organization" became a favorite whipping boy. The *Witness* dismissed a plan for a loosely structured men's club by stating that only abnormal conditions in a congregation could justify this. "This work as outlined . . . for such a men's organization ought to be in the hands of the voting membership of the congregation."[69] Thus, curiously, congregationalist polity, often so helpful to laicism in America, had at least for a time a negative effect in the Missouri Synod.[70]

Pastoral defensiveness and fear of the laity, too, played a role in clerical antagonism to lay associations. The traditional hostility to church union combined with apprehension that laymen might construct something beyond the control of the local minister. The *Lutheran Witness* articulated this most clearly in 1912: "We fear that the 'Laymen's Movement' is being given credit which it does not deserve, and that it is being used to disparage the long and faithful work of the many Christian pastors who regularly urge men to perform their missionary duties." The editor emphasized that clergy and laity were to labor hand in hand for the church. God's work did "not require a special and separate organization of our laymen, as though our pastors were remiss in their duties as missionary teachers."[71] Pieper pronounced unnecessary the idea that laymen organize a group limited to Missourians.[72]

A certain ambivalence in synodical rhetoric still remained though. One could not really reject the central goal of lay activity. Occasionally a hint of envy at the apparent success of the movement surfaced, even if, writers often hastened to add, the methods were wrong.[73] The agitation among American denominations undoubtedly produced statements emphasizing the role of the laity that would otherwise not have appeared.[74] Yet many of these comments only illustrated the limited horizons and conservatism of the clergy on this subject.

The most extensive and authoritative consideration of the laity in the light of the laymen's movement came in a long essay by Franz Pieper.[75] In his introduction Pieper admitted the need for more lay activity among Lutherans and made a ritualistic bow toward the priesthood of all believers. But he then hurried into a sixteen-page discussion not of lay activity, but of the high and holy office of the ministry. Within this context, Pieper spoke explicitly about the duty of all laymen to proclaim the Gospel, but he then spent most of his time emphasizing only financial stewardship. For a man of Pieper's gifts and attainments, the essay was a sorry one.

Even had church leaders been receptive to lay activism, the lay reaction would likely not have been very impressive. The feebleness of the response was suggested at the 1911 synodical convention. One lay delegate's remark that he felt responsible to help carry out convention resolutions was promptly hailed as a proper Lutheran laymen's movement and the attention of the press was requested.[76]

IX

Over the years the Missouri Synod has frequently modified or changed completely what were apparently immutable positions. Rarely has this occurred with such dispatch, however, as in the case of lay activity. Within a decade of the most militant opposition to the Men and Religion Movement, the synod had its own movement, or better, movements, attacking a whole range of questions within the denomination. And before two decades had passed, church leaders actively backed a strong impulse to form congregational men's clubs. Even while Missourian writers lambasted the American laymen's movements, a significant part of the constituency was undergoing rapid social change. Many laymen no longer fit the old classifications and felt correspondingly restless with traditional lay roles. The real emergence of the laity depended on the Americanization of the Missouri Synod and this was still surprisingly concealed until shortly before World War I.

2

A New Cast in Search of Roles

I

An age unused to scientific surveys and polls did not produce systematic evidence on the metamorphosis of Americanization in the synod. The task of sampling would have been difficult in any case, for the rate of accommodation to American life varied in time, location, and activity in daily life. Precisely because it was so uneven, the early phases of assimilation were enormously expensive and influential for the laity. Those who led the way out of the immigrant ghetto were also those most prone to leave the synod as well. Unlike the Americanizers in immigrant Catholicism who really had no alternative to Rome, the progressive layman in the Missouri Synod had a number of options that were not revolutionary. A place in one of the American Lutheran bodies (to say nothing of a Presbyterian or Episcopalian congregation) was always open to the Missouri Synod layman who was most comfortable in English, who married an "American woman," whose expanding business or social contacts made embarrassing his affiliation with the backstreet "German" church, or who found uncongenial the Missourian jeremiad against the world. From the predestination struggle of the 1880s through the military chaplaincy controversy of World War I, Missouri failed to establish any contacts outside of the most unbending Lutheranism. All the attrition that resulted from a posture on ecumenism therefore occurred on the progressive wing. Those most likely to stay in the synod were the conservative, the orthodox, the deeply committed.[1]

This was somewhat less true when the tempo of change quickened, as happened in the years before World War I. In the two decades before 1914, there was no doubt that the Lutheran constituency was no longer the same; increasing numbers did not fit the pattern of farmers and small tradesmen with provincial taste and agrarian outlook. One simple but important fact was the decline in German immigration. The figures at the turn of the century were the lowest in sixty years.[2] New arrivals from the old world no longer continually reinforced ingrained attitudes in the synod. The stage was set for more rapid assimilation.

In some instances change came when the younger generation brought it home. "The tone of many families undergoes a remarkable change when the older children get into their teens," observed a resident of the south St. Louis German community. "The rag-carpets are replaced by ingrains, and the ingrains by Brussels." Not only decor was affected: "The old family Bible on the center-table may have to make place for an illustrated edition of Paradise Lost, or even of Shakespeare and Byron or The Count of Monte Cristo, and the portraits of Luther or scenes from the Bible, at least on the parlor walls, for works of modern art representing Roman baths and Turkish harems."[3]

Occupational expectations also shifted. Many times this was unspectacular, as when a girl decided, against her parents'—and pastor's—wishes, not to become a maid but to work in a factory, where the wages were better and leisure time greater. Sometimes the new generation went much further. In growing numbers young people from rural Missouri Synod churches moved to cities to look for work; they also began to enroll at colleges and universities across the country.[4]

The middle generation, too, made gains particularly in economic status. Quantifiable data are not readily available, but sometimes subjective observations came at anniversary celebrations, when a backward, comparative glance was in order: "Twenty-five years ago our congregations consisted mainly of poor, simple-living people; now we have doctors, lawyers, big businessmen and public officials as members.'' More frequently the realization came in the widening efforts to provide for Lutheran high school business training: "The time is at hand when our German Lutherans are no longer hewers of wood and drawers of water for others; our congregations are composed for the most part of prosperous people who want a good education for their children.''[5] They wanted it sufficiently to establish five new high schools between 1903 and 1916.[6] In addition various people repeatedly attempted to introduce education for secular occupations into the synod's preparatory schools and colleges.[7]

At least in some cities, the residential mobility of the foreign-born had long been high, but about the turn of the century the Germans joined the trend toward the suburbs, sometimes with results for congregational growth that were premonitions of a half-century later. Jehovah Congregation began in 1908 with 360 baptized members in a newly opened area of Chicago. By 1919 it had more than 2,000 members.[8]

Accessible evidence of shifts in taste, occupation, education, and residential distribution, though widespread, is most often fragmentary, impressionistic, and subjective. The apparent absence of change in one important index of assimilation, political behavior, therefore raises the possibility that the evidence cited here for other changes may be misleading. Recent studies sensitive to the religious commitments of voters demonstrate that for German Lutherans two matters long had political salience. One was the power—real and alleged—of Roman Catholicism. The other was the cluster of moral reforms that threatened the German way of life: Sabbatarianism, Prohibition, and, especially where they could be seen as aiding the latter, woman suffrage, initiative, and referendum. Both Catholicism and these moral reforms were negative referents for the German Lutherans. The best estimates are that prior to the turn of the century, Midwest German Lutherans gave a slight edge to the Democrats. But comparatively, the German Lutherans were more Republican than the Catholics and more Democratic than other Protestants, including Scandinavian Lutherans. In areas or elections where

Catholicism was perceived to be particularly strong, the German Lutherans were likely to move toward the Republicans, or at least away from the Catholic Democracy. In areas or elections where distasteful reforms were gaining, German Lutherans tended toward the Democrats. Of course, a contest, as in 1896, in which a Democrat could be associated with moral reform, or, as in 1928, in which a Catholic could be associated with repeal, might reverse or seriously qualify these tendencies. But in any case they seem to have persisted.[9]

Does this continued Missourian political distinctiveness compel a different reading of other assimilation indices? Probably not, for the very point of concentrating in political studies on denominational affiliation is that these offer the strongest correlations with political behavior and are relatively independent of factors such as income, occupation, and place of residence. We may conclude then, that early in the century, though still politically distinguishable, the Missourian constituency in much of the country was otherwise increasingly difficult to differentiate from American neighbors. As this occurred the laity's role in the synod changed remarkably.

II

About the turn of the century a problem in lay activity was apparent which is still wrestled with today. Granted the laity prepared to be active, what should their activity be? The problem has been posed in different ways at different times. More recently, the question asked has been what, out of an enormous diversity of possible action, is to be classified as truly the sphere of the Christian laity? In the first decades of the century, such range was not the problem. It was not, because, outside of the preaching and teaching reserved for the ministerial office, the activity of the Missouri Synod was itself severely restricted. Missionary work of the time precluded much personal lay involvement, for the nearly exclusive orientation was toward gathering in the immigrant diaspora, even though that potential was dwindling rapidly with declining immigration.[10]

Besides, how could you invite your American neighbor or office colleague to church when the services were in German or when the sermons were delivered in a heavy guttural accent? How could you quote Scripture to a fellow worker outside the church when all the verses you recited so well in confirmation class had been memorized from the German Bible rather than the King James Version? No, effective lay participation in missions would have to wait until at least the late twenties and thirties.[11]

Support of foreign missions had in other denominations been a means by which laymen became active in church affairs beyond the congregational level, but synodical opportunities here, too, were few. Adequate precedents for innovation existed; the wing of the synod originally sent from Germany by Wilhelm Loehe had been a colony devoted to missionary work among Michigan Indians. But few found this an inspiration later in the century. When Missourian missionaries entered India during the nineties, some pastors drafted *Frauenvereine* for support, but the prevailing antipathy to extra-congregational voluntary associations prevented a concerted effort. To initiate a mission to China in 1911–1912, E. L. Arndt formed an independent missionary society, but this included mainly clergy and teachers. Arndt preferred this, believing it the most efficient entry at the time to congregational treasuries. Thus foreign missions opened few doors for lay activism.[12]

The synod itself operated no charitable enterprises. This very restraint, though, when coupled with the needs of the immigrant community, opened the way for more local, possibly lay, initiative. Still at the turn of the century, as the congregational registers showed, illness and death did not wait for old age to legitimize their work. With numbing swiftness, a husband or a wife or a child—so frequently a child—would be gone. And pastors had another entry to lengthen the column *Gerstorben,* Died, with careful compilations of the years, the months, and days that had been the allotted span. Understandably, orphanages were established early. Aside from these, however, it is interesting that the years between 1895 and 1920 included a great expansion of organized charitable effort on the local level. At least twenty-two separate hospitals, home-finding societies, and homes for the aged were established in this period. The impulse was so strong that a Lutheran Charities Conference was founded in 1902.[13] Clergy apparently led or inspired many of these charitable institutions, but more laymen sat on governing boards and participated in decision-making, and increasing numbers of women were prompted to organize ladies' auxiliaries to mobilize their support.[14] But little of this attracted much attention on the synodical level.

To gain such attention and build momentum for more lay effort, lay activity would have to be connected with a synodical project. In the early decades of the century, the major enterprise of the synod as synod was the system of schools to educate pastors and teachers. Laymen sat with clergy on boards of control for each school and as more preparatory schools were established, a synodical Board of Control was set up to coordinate affairs at all institutions.[15] Composed of two laymen and one pastor—a clear indication that it was to limit itself to business matters—the board was the forerunner of the synodical Board of Directors begun in 1917, a group including even more laymen.

The former board came on the scene in the midst of two battles over college locations in which the laity took an important part. In 1907, at the suggestion of a New York layman, Henry F. Ressmeyer, eastern Lutherans organized a Lutheran Education Society to aid synodical higher education there. Laymen were unusually visible among the officers of this group; in fact, Ressmeyer was president. To gain a new campus at Bronxville, N.Y., for the synod's eastern preparatory school, the LES did extensive lobbying, bought the necessary land itself, and also raised substantial amounts of cash for the new building.[16]

Chicago Lutherans borrowed the same techniques in a more bitterly fought struggle over removal of the teachers college from poorly located and worn-out buildings in Addison, Illinois. Another Lutheran Education Society was organized in Chicago during 1911; again the president was a layman, William Schlake, a brick manufacturer and Chicago politician. The Chicago society, too, bought a new site for a campus (at River Forest) and otherwise successfully lobbied for the change. The association lived on thereafter and by 1914 had as many as 900 members.[17] The success of these groups attracted attention and emulation all over the synod.[18]

These education societies were not, strictly speaking, a layman's movement. In fact, during the Addison episode, the most outspoken leaders of the standpatters were laymen.[19] Pastors were easily as prominent in the various societies as the laymen. But to put it that way inverts the significant relationship. Here finally was an activity in which laymen gained as much prominence as clergy, in which laymen received extensive public credit for debating issues. Men experienced in big city politics likely felt at home at synodical conventions; once having been aroused to take hold of the levers of power, they found things moved in gratifying manner. In these Lutheran Education Societies laymen got acquainted with each other, with techniques of religious organizations, and with the potential of collective action inside the synod.

III

After exhaustive casting and dress rehearsals of a scene or two, the Missouri Synod laity assumed new roles about the time of World War I. Younger adults and women especially turned in large numbers to Sunday school teaching, as will be explained in Chapter 5. Particularly the men settled on a renewed interest in synodical business affairs as their proper sphere. One can fix no single debut for the Sunday school, but opening night for the men came on June 22, 1917. That evening twelve laymen attending the triennial synodical convention then in progress met at the Milwaukee home of Fred C. Pritzlaff to discuss synodical finance.

Three years earlier a St. Louis businessman, August G. Brauer, had made a private effort to raise enough money by $1,000 donations to cover a burgeoning synodical debt. He was acutely aware of the church's dismal financial situation, for his brother-in-law and business associate, John F. Schuricht, Jr., was then treasurer of the synod. Since he was able to raise subscriptions for only a quarter of his $100,000 goal, however, he released all pledges.[20] When he told the story of his efforts to a small group of laymen at the 1917 convention, Theodore Lamprecht, a woolens merchant from New York, suggested another attempt. Through one of Brauer's brothers-in-law, a pastor, the men secured an introduction to Pritzlaff, a wealthy hardware wholesaler in Milwaukee, and arranged a meeting at his home. Invitations to the meeting must have been carefully calculated, but came informally: a tap on the shoulder and a few words sufficed.[21]

Nevertheless when the men gathered, things were at first a bit stiff. Pritzlaff was so nervous he forgot to pass cigars. "Everybody seemed to sense that it was to be a 'holdup' party—everybody was afraid of everybody else."[22] A fledgling lay delegate, A. H. Ahlbrand, explained his ideas for improving future fund raising; then the group turned to the immediate problem, the stubborn debt of $100,000 causing much convention talk of retrenchment. Someone started a sheet around the room and pledged contributions soon totaled $26,000. Late in the evening, an unusually heavy thunderstorm struck Milwaukee and the irrepressible Benjamin Bosse raised his subscription, remarking the next morning that "the Lord thundered another thousand out of him."[23]

In order to secure the balance needed, the men formed a temporary organization, chose the alliterative Lutheran Laymen's League as a name, and agreed on Theodore Lamprecht as president and A. G. Brauer as secretary. In rapid succession the group won the approval of the convention, the endorsement of the synod's president, and set out to complete the fund. By December the $100,000 was in and a surplus left over—this at a time when regular synodical annual receipts totaled only $575,000.

Nothing comparable to this had happened before among the Missouri Synod laity. The element new in 1917 was aggressive lay leadership. The twelve men who met in Milwaukee were in the forefront of the progression away from the previously typical constituency. Of the twelve, only two were born in Germany; ten of the twelve were over fifty.[24] Not exactly young turks, many of these men were the descendants of antebellum German immigration. All were at home in the English language. As A. H. Ahlbrand later recalled of an early financial presentation, "I started to talk in the German but it was not easy as finances were difficult to convey the right understanding by the use of German. Rev. Fred Wambsganss, Sr., called out to me in the convention —'Ahlbrand sprechen sie English sie koennen sich besser ausdruecken'. [Ahlbrand, speak in English; you can express yourself better.] This was the thing that pleased me as I was pretty fluent in English."[25]

Business success reinforced this longer exposure to American ways. These were relatively wealthy men with wide contacts in American business circles. They dined at the Missouri Athletic Club in St. Louis, wintered in Florida, or made extended European trips. An individual contribution of five or ten thousand dollars to some cause was not unusual among them. They had succeeded well enough in their main enterprise that they could turn, as many did, to other investments or to politics.[26] Because of their background and experience, these men stood in awe neither of the clergy nor of synodical machinery. In fact, two were trained as pastors and another was once a parochial school teacher; a fourth had broken off in preparatory school. Others were related to pastors. At least half of the men had been active in the church on a national level before 1917.[27]

The twelve men and the resulting league were led by two laymen whose pictures appeared frequently in the following decade, the elegantly goateed, aristocratic Theodore H. Lamprecht and the honest, square-faced August G. Brauer. President Lamprecht was born in 1858 of immigrant parents. Following their wishes he completed a ministerial education; he married a pastor's daughter. However, after preaching once, he returned home and announced, "I have preached my last sermon today." Unable to conquer what was apparently pulpit-fright, he achieved remarkable success in the dry goods business and returned to church work as a layman. Among other things, he was active in the campaign for the River Forest move, served as president of the American Lutheran Publicity Bureau, was central in founding a seminary in Berlin for the German Free Church, and chaired the synod's European relief board following World War I.[28]

Brauer was an equally dependable workhorse in the synod. The son of a pastor, he was born in 1857 and was the only one of six brothers who did not go into the ministry; he had in addition three clerical brothers-in-law, including synodical president Frederick Pfotenhauer. In St. Louis he prospered in a stove supply business. Within the church he was prominent in the Lutheran Publicity Organization, the founding of radio station KFUO, St. Louis institutional missions, and as a member of the seminary Board of Control.[29]

These two men, like the other ten founders, were not typical laymen in 1917, but self-made, highly successful businessmen. These were no longer penniless, deferential immigrants willing, even anxious, to accept the multi-faceted direction of the Lutheran pastor; instead they were accustomed to assuming leadership in competitive circles. It might be possible, given the familial and educational ties of the LLL founders, to interpret their actions as those of men who were in effect frustrated clergy. But perhaps more fair-minded speculation is to explain these men as having two primary reference groups. They were drawn both by the clergy and by the business community, and their actions were in part attempts to reconcile the resulting tensions.

The catalyst for the evening meeting in Milwaukee came in pessimistic convention speeches—speeches, Lamprecht specified, by pastors—occasioned by the recent American entry into the war against *Das Vaterland* and by the synod's debt. The sentiment was "we must cut and save everywhere; there is little money among our people, and it is hard to get!" Such ill-informed crepe-hanging at what was supposed to be a Reformation centennial celebration nearly insulted these laymen and so alienated them from traditional clerical leadership that they embarked on independent action.[30]

One might still inquire, though, why such disgruntled laymen seem to have gravitated so automatically toward financial matters rather than, as among some nineteenth-century Protestants, toward theological concerns. In the revivals of the previous century, clerical preeminence was challenged when lay testimonials and prayer meetings became as valued as sermons and worship services.[31] In conservative Lutheranism, however, the definition of the means of grace (Word and Sacraments) resisted such incursions. Stress on the correct administration of the means implied, moreover, a trained corps of practitioners, all the more so given Missouri's accentuation of *reine Lehre*—to safeguard the purity of doctrine demanded competence in its exposition. Furthermore, as the denunciations in synodical organs demonstrated, Missourian laity knew of recent lay movements in other denominations and these precedents also helped channel Lutheran lay orientation toward business affairs. The LLL founders felt such a course congenial; often self-taught, they were of a decidedly practical, rather than speculative, bent. Finally, as explained in Chapter 4, synodical financial affairs *were* in horrendous shape, a galling fact for men with proven business acumen.[32] Once involved in fund raising, the laymen broadened their assault on the clerical tradition to include all of the church's business matters. In this, reform-minded clergy aided and abetted them. Far-reaching change in synodical affairs and lay attitudes resulted, although the business orientation of the laity proved in time difficult to escape.

IV

An organization that could raise $100,000 in nine months was obviously (at least obviously to the laymen) not something to disband quickly. Early in the fall Lamprecht presided over further meetings and began referring to the debt drive as the goal "for the year 1917."[33] Finally, on December 3, 1917, a laymen's meeting in Chicago organized the league on a permanent basis, opening membership to women as well as men. The *Witness,* instead of the more established, prestigious—and German— *Lutheraner,* became the league's official paper, carrying a regular LLL column.

The permanently organized league confirmed a number of earlier limitations. First, this had been and continued to be a movement of well-to-do laity. It was not a federation of local men's clubs, and deliberately discouraged the participation of many laymen by beginning the league scale of dues at $6, and asking for involvement at a much higher level.[34] A *Witness* editor quite openly remarked of the league, "as never before in the history of our Synod, its wealthy men have recognized their opportunity."[35] Secondly, the league constitution severely restricted its activities by pledging the LLL to aid the synod "with word and deed in business and financial matters."[36] Because of clerical resistance and lay orientation, early leaders of the league took these words literally.

Even within such limitations, however, the early LLL was an exceptionally powerful force in the synod. As a second project, the constituting convention settled on a fund of $250,000 for a church pension fund. The league's decision to aid improvements to a scandalously casual system for the care of retired clergy and their dependents was based upon previous advances by American denominations; laymen explicitly referred to Episcopalian leadership.[37] The campaign required full-time administrators and in June of 1918 Charles Cramer, a former school teacher, was hired as executive secretary. Milwaukee, where Cramer resided, became LLL headquarters. Tellingly, the campaign to raise membership from the 155 when Cramer took office rested heavily on letters to all pastors asking for names of potential candidates. By October the league could boast 482 members in 22 states.[38] Though hardly massive support, this was a credible beginning.

The league had adopted its goal of $250,000 as "seed money" for use at the 1920 convention, where, it was hoped, the synod would make provision for further additions. However, as things progressed, the dazzling success of campaigns by the Red Cross and by other denominations raised Lutheran financial expectations.[39] The league responded at a December 1918 meeting by agreeing to ask for war bond donations and to raise the original goal of $250,000 to $3,000,000, designated as an endowment for the pension fund.[40] To arouse enthusiasm and support, the league initiated its drive with a meeting of district presidents and influential laymen, itself an extraordinary step in the synod. By June

1920, when laymen gathered for the triennial convention of the synod and the first regular convention of the LLL, they had gathered about two million dollars, said to be the largest amount of money ever collected by a Lutheran body in America.[41]

V

The league did not continue the campaign to reach its goal immediately because synodical officials gave precedence to other fund drives, a decision not adequately explained by extant documents. But at least the league's effort had introduced the LLL to the synod on a grand scale. As Henry Horst judged it in 1919, the drive "has been worth while no matter what sum we get. That has been proved by letters from pastors which show the value of the drive cannot be measured by dollars and cents."[42]

In advertising its goal, the league was of course advertising itself. What a later age would call penetration was remarkable for the time. The LLL shrewdly extended membership to anyone who contributed six dollars or more to the endowment fund, thus producing a "membership" of more than 60,000 by June of 1920.[43] Local branches were established in at least St. Louis, Fort Wayne, and Cleveland; in 1921 the league was extended to Canada.[44] One can explain such growth partly because few clergy could argue publicly with a movement to aid retired ministers. In fact, the *Witness* was almost ecstatic. "We have been one of the last bodies to have a laymen's movement," stated Theodore Graebner, apparently forgetting earlier synodical polemic. Now, however, "Our laymen have at last found their voice." Of course, they had never been denied their voice in the past, the editor hastened to add, but how little of what they said "can be classified as being a teaching and admonishing of one another. . . . The minister did that . . . it's his business!" Usually, if laymen spoke at all, it was on business matters. "We have heard members instruct each other with considerable warmth on the relative merits of competing bidders for a steamheating contract and on similar questions." And even then, "it has been a habit of old standing to do most of the speaking on the church-steps after the meeting had adjourned." Suddenly, the paper reported, laymen are admonishing one another in Christian love. "One speaker actually pounded the table with his fist in order to emphasize his demands that we repent of our past sins" of parsimonious giving.[45]

The league also contributed much to denominational self-consciousness and pride among the laity. Early in 1919 when Ludwig Fuerbringer noted in a *Lutheraner* editorial that various other denominations were beginning victory fund drives, he reported that people had written him inquiring, "what is our Lutheran Church doing?" He promised *Lutheraner* readers the LLL had big plans afoot.[46] Assuredly, some of this was using denominational competitiveness to put Lutherans on their mettle. Still, whether on the conscious or unconscious level, the pension fund endowment was a symbol of status to many of the more advanced laity. It reassured laymen that they were part of an up-to-date, American church. Psychologically and socially, the laymen's campaign was comparable to a congregation's moving to a bigger, more beautiful church in a better part of town. This was particularly important among the well-to-do group that the LLL cultivated. The LLL put into contact with each other men of similar status and opinion from congregations all over the country.[47] When the constituency generally was in the lower rungs of the middle class, it was especially important to provide a society of equals for laymen of greater affluence.[48] Making men of comparable means and abilities aware of each other was most likely to spur them to gifts of time and money commensurate with their endowments. By doing so, the league drew men progressively further into church work, deepening their interest and broadening their commitment.

What was observed in 1920 about the Walther League and young people was also important about the LLL and adults: many people, "especially those from smaller congregations, think of their Lutheran Church only in terms of their own local congregations, and imagine it to be a weak and struggling church body. In consequence, they sometimes feel ashamed of the outward appearance their church presents to others." However, participation in a national extra-congregational organization broadens horizons. Members return home from conventions "with renewed enthusiasm and with gratitude toward God for having led them into the Lutheran Church." They are proud of belonging to a denomination that has such people and "at home will show new interest in matters pertaining to the congregation, the society, and the Kingdom of God in general. In short, they will become better Lutherans."[49]

Thus, the early LLL and its campaign contributed much to developing a lay self-consciousness. With a goal ahead of them and an organization behind them, some laymen became active leaders almost in spite of themselves. To the appreciative laughter and applause of his colleagues, one layman at the 1920 convention told of his experience raising money in his congregation for the endowment fund.

> I have never talked much before the public. I went to my minister and asked him to prepare me a kind of speech that I should make to his congregation. He did, and he made me a good one. . . . My heart was beating when I was in front of that congregation, gentlemen. There were a lot of German people there so it was half English and half German. I took the English hymn book and I opened it and the first song I came to was 'What a friend we have in Jesus.' I said that is my song. . . . After the hymn, I just talked. What I talked, I do not know.

As another layman put it, "this movement has developed men in our organization right along. It is making a concrete and crystallized body. . . ."[50]

True, great masses among the synod's laity were left untouched by this movement and many more were doubtless simply uninterested. But there was now a vanguard leading the way, taking up advanced positions. Further assaults on tradition were inevitable.

3

Auditions and Casting

I

During the first quarter of the twentieth century in the Missouri Synod, the laity's major church involvement outside the local congregation followed a surprisingly orderly progression. Since each stage usually included continued participation in those preceding, the range and volume of lay activity grew steadily. Lutheran charitable institutions were the earliest to receive extensive support from Missouri Synod laymen. Then the laity moved on to unprecedented organizational backing for most of the synod's colleges. This, in turn, merged into a great deal of lay activism that flared up in 1917, continued at a high level into the early twenties, then gradually died down by the Depression.

II

The Lutheran Laymen's League was one expression of this ferment. Another, to be taken up in the next chapter, was associated with a long-term effort—partly in conjunction with the LLL, partly independent of it—to improve the general financial system of the Missouri Synod. Still another illustration of the lay ferment was the participation in the organization of an unusual number of associations during this period. The formation of any new organization is usually an implicit criticism of the status quo.

In the Missouri Synod this was true of groups begun in the period from World War I into the twenties.

One type of new society was led by the American Lutheran Publicity Bureau, organized in New York by pastors and laymen.[1] The ALPB really came to life in 1917–1918 with a program to advertise Lutheranism in the United States. Through its periodical, the *American Lutheran,* it also tried to educate the Missouri Synod in various techniques of public relations. In 1917 St. Louis activists formed the Lutheran Publicity Organization to engage in both local advertising and business district evangelism especially during Lent. Other, even less formal, groups followed in additional cities.

Another organization that admitted both pastors and laymen was the National Lutheran Education Association. This was founded in 1917 and had its main strength in Minnesota, Iowa, and adjacent areas. Although the NLEA did not get as much notice as other groups—one writer referred to it as the "half-mythical society"—its goal was Lutheran higher education for the laity.[2]

The American Luther League, organized at Fort Wayne in 1919, combined a dedication to education and a drive for publicity. Its immediate purpose was to repel attacks on the synod's parochial school system that came in the era of hysterical Americanism following World War I. For what it claimed were tactical reasons, the ALL excluded pastors and teachers from regular membership.

Much lay unrest was behind this quickening of the associational impulse between 1917 and 1920. The reason the synod is in debt, said the Lutheran Laymen's League, is that the pastors have not properly informed the people of the synod's needs. The reason the synod is not known outside Lutheranism, said the American Lutheran Publicity Bureau, is that the pastors have not taken the initiative to bring Lutheranism to general public attention. The reason the synod is losing its parochial schools, said the American Luther League, is that the pastors have not inculcated adequate devotion to the schools nor led in their defense. Instead of sitting on the sidelines and urging the pastors to do better, at least some of the laity now became involved.

Their comments and actions did not, however, betray an anti-clerical spirit. This was not a case of laymen on one side and clergy on the other. Rather, usually a coalition of energetic, Americanized laity and reform-minded clerical leaders attempted to activate an old guard among the clergy that was backed by the sheer weight of conservative and apathetic laymen. As outspoken as the laymen occasionally were, their expressions of discontent and frustration were matched by statements from men such as John H. C. Fritz, dean at Concordia Seminary, Walter A. Maier, editor of the *Walther League Messenger*, Theodore Graebner of the *Lutheran Witness*, and the *American Lutheran*'s Paul Lindemann.

III

Attempts to change the traditional relationship between clergy and laity inevitably provoked friction between progressive clergy and laity and the old guard. The reformers identified three main irritations: clerical inefficiency, conservatism, and unwillingness to grant the laymen an active part in initiating and carrying through various projects.

First, many laymen felt caught between the recognition that the local pastor was the key to the congregation and the conviction that they as laymen could do as well in the business and financial affairs of the church without the clergy. "My own experience has been, if I could just get in contact with ordinary people instead of working through the Pastors, I could always enthuse them and get results," wrote A. H. Ahlbrand to August G. Brauer.[3] A Cleveland layman noted in 1919 that he had frequently been asked during the endowment fund drive, "how are you going to tie it [the endowment fund] up . . . so those fool preachers don't spill the beans and spoil all the work we have done?"[4]

The limited horizons of some of the clergy also exasperated lay leaders. "I have almost lost heart in trying to induce the Pastors to systematize matters and get out of the old channel," wrote Ahlbrand in 1915.[5] The *Lutheran Witness*, not an altogether neutral observer, noted that the difference between lay and clergy delegates at the 1917 convention was the financial courage possessed by the former and lacking in the latter.[6] One speaker at a 1919 LLL meeting summed up attitudes of both laymen and clergy; in a synod, he said, "that has from its very infancy been run on a policy of economy, as has no other organization that has ever been organized, . . . when we had the nerve to come out here and talk about $3,000,000 it absolutely broke the backbone of half the ministerial force of the church. Half of them are scared to death and they haven't got over it yet. . . ."[7]

Finally, laymen complained about the hesitancy of some pastors to delegate authority and to permit autonomous activity. The rule, "the minister makes everything his business," is especially true among the older German congregations, one writer exploded. "I daily come into contact with prominent Lutherans . . . who would gladly take hold of the business end of our church, but who continually cry, 'How can we do anything, when they [the pastors] do not give us anything to do?' "[8]

The situation was complicated by disagreement over the relationships between the national association, the synod, and the local congregation. Despite official endorsement, even the LLL, whose national membership was not based on local congregational units, fell suspect by individual congregations highly jealous of their independence. The American Luther League did well on the local level but had a dreadful time with synodical officials. The national groups undoubtedly aroused some memories of the earlier American laymen's movements, which had tended to ignore the boundaries not only of local congregations, but even of whole denominations. In such a context, the aggressive attitude of laymen anxious to get things done clashed with the reservations both of synodical officials concerned with proper channels and of local pastors comfortable in their autonomy.

LLL fund-raising activity focused these differences; even questionnaires the LLL sent to congregations were viewed by some as an infringement of congregational integrity.[9] President

Pfotenhauer was deeply concerned and warned the league repeatedly against usurping rights of the synod or of the congregations.[10] His attitude was so pervasive that, in a league discussion in 1922, John Boehne bluntly remarked that general changes in denominational officials would be very beneficial. As late as 1926 league officers had to admit that "we have not yet succeeded in selling the LLL to the majority of our pastors."[11]

Such friction between clergy and laity was to be expected, for the maturation of the laity almost inherently involved strong antipathy to an outmoded pattern of authority and leadership. Occasional overstatement contributed to lay self-consciousness and hence to redressing the imbalance between laity and clergy. Besides, the synod *did* desperately need reform and regeneration. The new attitude among the laity and some clergy that helped produce difficulties also did a great deal to revitalize the synod. Consideration of the church's problems frequently drove laymen to get involved to solve such difficulties. And their attacks on clerical incompetence in business affairs helped bring to the fore clergy interested in and capable of efficient administration. Gradually, more of the clergy learned the benefits of active, aggressive laymen, and the laymen learned that some pastors shared their concern and even their aptitude for organization and administration.

IV

The formation of the LLL and its early fund-raising efforts seems to have helped channel much of this early tension among the synodical constituency between 1917 and 1920. The best documented instances occurred in Cleveland and in Fort Wayne, where branch associations of the LLL were quickly set up. Very likely much less developed movements existed elsewhere.

The Cleveland episode is a classic illustration of a familiar problem in lay activity—a vague longing for action but no program and little leadership. The laymen there had a strong, if poorly articulated, sense that things were not what they should be in the church: the parochial school was not supported adequately;

financial stewardship was hardly what it should be; there was insufficient evidence of Christ-like love among congregations. In their inchoate frustration, the laymen wanted to do things. They wanted to help improve church life. But they were not quite sure how to accomplish this. They seized on a branch society of the LLL as a promising structure, only to be warned off by synodical officials in St. Louis; the only correctly Lutheran course, they were told, was to work through the congregations. This in effect killed the movement, for local pastors were unwilling to let the laity act as the church, yet were incapable of turning the diffuse lay drives to really productive and positive ends. No strong leader appeared from either laity or clergy to take the helm, and after some aimless tacking back and forth, the movement sank quietly out of sight. All that remained was a book of study topics for meetings of lay societies. These were in German and never translated.[12]

In Fort Wayne, unlike Cleveland, capable local leadership emerged strong enough to ignore synodical disapproval. Lay ferment in Fort Wayne was connected, as in some other places, with the attacks on Lutherans during and after the war against Germany. At their worst, these assaults included arson, bombing, and personal intimidation. While a few looked upon the persecution as something to be endured in Christian martyrdom, the average layman was unhappy and unsettled about the attacks on his church.[13] Matters came to a head when Indiana, like a number of states at the time, passed a law forbidding the use of the German language in elementary education, a direct blow at Lutheran parochial schools. In Fort Wayne, the center of a German Lutheran stronghold in northeast Indiana, the laymen decided that collective action was necessary.

They at first hailed the LLL as an appropriate vehicle and organized the "Fort Wayne Council of the L.L.L.," though their constitutional purposes were at variance with the league's and they had a lower dues schedule.[14] A lay organization was necessary, the laymen said, because the council would not hesitate to take direct political action—something prohibited the church itself in Missouri Lutheran circles. To quiet suspicions of mixing church and state, pastors and teachers were not accepted as regular members. The emphasis on lay activity was not, however, entirely because of political strategy. "They say," reported a Cleveland visitor, " 'the preachers have had their chance and failed. Now the laymen are going to take hold without the preachers.' "[15]

Apparently national LLL leaders had not been consulted, for their reaction was a surprised and ultimately negative one. By August 1919 the Fort Wayne people had changed their name to the American Luther League, though they evidently proposed amalgamation of the two leagues in pretty aggressive terms. "They are playing a hold up game with us," complained one LLL member. "They are virtually saying to us unless you do give us your name, we will do you up."[16] LLL officials were nettled by the dedication of the Fort Wayne leaders. "They think that they are doing a wonderful work, much more important than the work of the L.L.L." But no one could deny success. "At a meeting at the gym, they had about 4,000 people present. They had a picnic where they had about 7,000 people present." Rivalry was inevitable. After a meeting in Fort Wayne, an LLL member returned to the league with the news that "one person said we will make you fellows look like two cents when we get through with you. You can get memberships at a dollar a great deal easier than you can at six dollars or twenty-five dollars and one hundred dollars."[17]

The ALL was as good as its word. It fared especially well with farmers and country congregations—precisely the class the LLL had trouble arousing.[18] Early circulars of the ALL did not shy from including appeals to those who wanted to preserve the German language.[19] In addition, the whole strategy of the ALL was a mass movement instead of a selective, elite campaign. Explained one LLL official, "They come to these country congregations, and the people join in a body and put up a dollar a head."[20] By late 1919 the ALL was stressing it existed to encourage lay activity and fellowship among Lutherans.[21]

The Lutheran Laymen's League, however, would not be budged. League officials understandably opposed any distractions from the endowment fund campaign they had just begun.

They also feared the reaction of church leaders. Having opened a Pandora's box of lay associations by endorsing the LLL, clergy officials now wished they had put a safety catch on the lid. Caught in the assumptions of the late nineteenth century, synodical leadership thought the maintenance of institutional structures more important than encouragement of spontaneous lay activity. In a private discussion of groups such as the two leagues, President Pfotenhauer hoped that as a rule their lives would be short, for soon the congregation would be left with nothing to do. Theodore Graebner agreed with Pfotenhauer, at least about the ALL. The sects (i.e., virtually all Protestant denominations), he wrote back, put all their faith in organizational machinery and we have borrowed this. There is no other Lutheran synod, he thought, so troubled with "parasites" as the Missouri Synod at the present time. Since it was under no form of synodical control, the ALL could cause serious embarrassment.[22]

The synod's secretary expressed still stronger sentiments in a bitter letter to an official of the American Luther League. After stating adamant objections to the league engaging in political activity, the letter continued, "as to all the other good [ALL] aims and purposes, let us not declare our bankruptcy as churches and a Synod by turning over these matters to a league of our good laymen, who even now, so early in the game, feel themselves called upon to get up in the churches and, with the authority of the League behind them, lecture, not to say preach, to the pastors and the people on their shamefully neglected duties toward church and school and Synod." The writer concluded, "I would be the last to deplore that laymen are becoming more active and aggressive in business matters of the churches and Synod." But this must be done in good order. "What ever is good in the League is, or can be, taken care of by Synod or its lay-delegates. . . ."[23]

The two leagues never merged. But this only gave the ALL complete freedom from synodical sanctions. Official formulations of the league's purpose permitted it practically any activity it desired.[24] At its first convention in Fort Wayne during August 1920, the league adopted a permanent constitution that opened membership not only to individuals but also to local societies. The ALL could thus generate and sustain a good deal more activity at the grassroots level than the LLL. By 1920, too, the ALL hired a dynamic executive secretary, John C. Baur. Soon it was involved in major campaigns.

V

The American Luther League was the only serious competition the Lutheran Laymen's League ever faced. The two leagues had a remarkably similar development after 1920. We should trace these parallels partly to see why the LLL lived on while the ALL failed. It is important, too, in order to illustrate some of the problems common to lay associations within the church. The perils of organizational inflexibility became obvious. And even more striking is the consuming search for adequate goals. Usually the threat of imminent collapse produced a goal not very satisfactory in answering the central question of the proper role of the laity in the church.

Once past the birth pangs of covert anticlericalism, the American Luther League turned out to be less radical than it at first seemed. Having a pastor—even as independent a man as J. C. Baur, *sui generis* in the synod—as its chief spokesman helped solace some. Partly through Baur's leadership, the Luther League soon drew back from the original proposals to engage directly in politics; instead it turned to lobbying and public education.[25] Probably its most effective contribution was to assign its indefatigable executive secretary to run major defensive campaigns, most notably in Michigan and Oregon.[26]

Each new attack upon parochial schools was more fuel for the American Luther League. During April and May of 1920 alone, the ALL accepted fourteen societies and 3,826 members. By November of 1921 some 250 societies had organized and the league boasted 32,000 members. The 1922 national convention attracted delegates from ten states.[27] The main strength was and continued to be in rural areas and small towns.[28] As time went on the league added to its field staff, adopted emblems and official colors, and began publications to stay in touch with members. It also diversified its program.[29] The ALL's monthly *Lutheran Layman* urged opposition to blue laws, support for graduate education for seminary professors, and attention to more family devotions. State units of the ALL moved to purchase houses for use as Lutheran student boarding homes at state universities.[30] The search for other projects increased in the mid-twenties as attacks against parochial schools were beaten off or died down. As the wave the ALL had ridden so successfully now receded, the league found itself in danger of being beached high and dry. Membership fell off "due to structural weaknesses in the League organization and to an idea that the League's main business was accomplished now that the schools had won their legal title to existence."[31] In addition a club open to young and old of both sexes seemed too inclusive to work as a social unit without the centripetal force of some emergency.

To remedy these problems, some ALL leaders wanted very much to move the league into the new and untapped field of men's clubs. And at its 1925 convention, the ALL broadened its objectives and attempted to attract such clubs.[32] However, early in 1926 Baur and the league were distracted by the effort to purchase the badly rundown Valparaiso University in northwestern Indiana and remodel it into a Lutheran institution. At its 1926 convention, the league was yet surprisingly strong; it still had 107 societies and 5,100 members—larger than the LLL would be a decade later.[33] But when the Board of Directors suggested restricting regular membership to men's clubs and moving aggressively in that direction, it was rebuffed. Women in the ALL joined those who were convinced the league had completed its work, and the motion failed. The delegates then voted to suspend the league, though they elected officers in case the opportunity for a resurrection appeared.[34] This never occurred. Instead, activists in the ALL moved over into the Valparaiso effort.[35] Local ALL clubs disbanded, died because they could not sustain themselves on their own resources, or in a few cases hung on to enter the reorganized LLL.[36] The last act in American Luther League history came in 1929 when the synodical Board of Directors ac-

cepted $2,600, the balance of the league's treasury, as an endow-
ment for Christian education.[37]

The American Luther League had some of the best leadership
available at the time, it was ahead in its magazine and other
organizational literature, and it gained experience with a base of
local societies. But in driving toward its original goal, it was too
careless of itself as an organization. The league died partly of
simple neglect. In one view, it is refreshing to report a group that
accomplished what it intended, then disbanded. On the other
hand, the ALL might well have served as a vehicle for lay activity
much sooner than the LLL finally did.

VI

The Lutheran Laymen's League itself narrowly escaped the
fate of the American Luther League. Much of the league's history
during the twenties revolved around a search for another way to
repeat the initial focusing of lay dissatisfaction and zeal. The
question on the proper sphere of lay activity remained very much
an open one.

That its support faded so quickly ought not be blamed entirely
on either the league or the laity. The LLL necessarily suspended
its own drive because church officials decided to go ahead at once
when the synodical convention in 1920 resolved to raise large
amounts for building projects. The league's condition suffered
from the delay. Despite strong membership campaigns, actual
LLL membership dropped from 12,447 in late 1920 to an average
of two or three thousand in years thereafter.[38] At meetings during
1922, "it was repeatedly stated that it seemed necessary that a
new objective of the L.L.L. be agreed upon to follow our Three
Million Dollar Campaign as our people were getting tired of being
appealed to on behalf of the Permanent Endowment Fund."[39] Yet
in a sense the league (and particularly its aristocratic and perhaps
somewhat imperious president, Theodore Lamprecht) continued
to live in the past. Already in 1923 President Lamprecht pleaded,
"Let us get back into the spirit of 1919 and 1920!"[40] Much of the
promotional literature in the *Witness* LLL column during 1925

consisted of reminiscences of the early, most glorious history of the league. When the endowment completion drive was finally staged in 1925-1926, two-thirds of the congregations did not even request promotional material.[41] The results so damaged league morale that when helping to survey campaign wreckage early in 1926, J.H.C. Fritz had to reassure league officials that "the work of the LLL was *not a failure* as a few of you seem to think."[42]

He was correct about the past, but in these events the league faced an absolute mandate for change. A number of alternatives were open. The league could follow ALL precedent and simply disband. Or it might search for a new goal. It might shift leadership. Or it might tinker with its organizational framework, even restructure itself. Only the first alternative seems never to have been seriously considered. When the LLL directors met in June 1926, they promptly voted to discontinue future efforts for the endowment fund. Then, after a listless consideration of another financial drive (for the Church Extension Fund), the LLL turned to a project, religious broadcasting on radio, that aroused much more enthusiasm.

In the twenties radio was a marvelous thing. The state of the art and industry was fluid and audiences undemanding.[43] With little regulation and relatively few stations on some channels, a strong transmitter might blanket much of the country, and even a small station had great range. Moreover the financial prerequisites for beginning a station were low. In St. Louis, for instance, local initiative founded a Lutheran station, KFUO, which was widely acclaimed by listeners over much of the country.[44] By the mid-twenties, however, early governmental regulations forced an upgrading of stations that expected to survive. To protect Lutheran radio, KFUO representatives appealed to the 1926 LLL convention for support.[45] The laymen enthusiastically voted to assume full sponsorship of the station and make it the league's official project.

Significant changes in personnel also occurred. As the twenties progressed, some of the league founders retired from active service; others moved into synodical positions of responsibility that consumed much time and energy.[46] In the meantime, the Walther

League was a rousing success among the young people. Boasting more than 1500 societies and its own lively periodical, the Walther League attracted capable lay leadership from men in their twenties and thirties. By contrast, the Lutheran Layman's League had a shaky organization and a reputation as a society for wealthy, established laymen.[47] When Edwin H. Faster was elected LLL president in 1926 to replace the ailing Lamprecht, he represented the relatively few younger men in the LLL ranks. He was only thirty-three at the time and had achieved no great prominence in either business or synodical circles. He and other newcomers had much less wealth and correspondingly less interest in using the league for large donations. Faster illustrated this in 1929 when he informed the group that had traditionally emphasized financial stewardship, "no organization within the confines of the church can hope to exist for any length of time if its sole purpose is to raise money."[48]

VII

Of the three positive alternatives open after the league's debacle of 1926, the last to be scrutinized was LLL structure. Once again, failure forced the league into an extensive reorganization. One structural possibility for an organization in difficulty is amalgamation with other groups. Though this hovered in the air all during the twenties, it never materialized. When the LLL could have, it would not; when it would, it could not.[49] Another, more fruitful possibility was to improve grassroots participation by local units—making the shift the American Luther League rejected. Congregational men's clubs were not entirely new in the Missouri Synod. Despite the opposition early in the century to a "clubhouse church," a few progressive congregations began organizing men's groups shortly before the war.[50] An urbanized, English-speaking congregation was much more likely than a German country parish to participate in this national, American trend.[51] Some clubs were either frankly or covertly prophylactic, anti-lodge or anti-Catholic.[52] Others represented a desire for social contact the quarterly meeting of voters could not satisfy.

Though by the twenties most congregations still did not have a men's group, these clubs seemed to be a gathering trend. Perhaps, some thought, these would further male interest in the church.[53] After all, the American Luther League and the Walther League certainly prospered with local groups.

The upshot was the 1929 LLL convention approval of a new constitution that allowed group membership of congregational men's clubs and lowered these group membership dues to two dollars per individual. The league now included both individual members and local men's clubs. How this decision was made is not entirely clear, largely because the only extended gap in league minutes occurs between early 1928 and June 1929.[54] What is clear is the absence of the spontaneity and lay independence that had characterized the league's founding in 1917. Clergymen were much more in evidence in 1929. Before it finished its deliberations, the committee that recommended reorganization included no less than four "pastoral advisors." The revised constitution also provided new safeguards against untoward league action. The synodical Board of Directors gained the right to appoint two members (one now to be a pastor) of the LLL Board of Governors. Headquarters of the LLL was moved to Concordia Publishing House, the headquarters also of the synod itself.

League personnel also changed. By 1929 A. G. Brauer was the only one of the original twelve founders left as a national officer. In the new St. Louis office, clergymen served in the most central positions of a layman's organization: Lawrence Meyer as part-time acting executive secretary, Theodore Graebner as part-time editor, and Louis Buchheimer, Jr., as field secretary. The growing number of clergy directing the league was not a subversive infiltration. However, neither was it proof that distinctions between clergy and laity had been erased. The participation of the clergy indicated that at least some pastors has grasped the possibilities of active laymen and were anxious to keep the LLL alive. As the *Witness* reflected in 1930, "None of us would want the years of 1900–1910 to come back."[55] There is no doubt that the league looked for the best among the pastors it considered; yet there is no record of a serious search for laymen to assume the ongoing leadership and administration of the league, perhaps partly because it could not afford the salaries of capable lay administrators.[56] The LLL was saved from almost certain death partly by transfusions of clerical blood, but the process introduced elements foreign to the original body.

VIII

The league was not yet in smooth water after its change of course in 1929. It still lacked a compelling goal and it found men's clubs no easier than individuals to recruit as members. Nevertheless, the LLL, after undergoing trials remarkably parallel to the ALL's, managed to hang on. It barely survived a critical period while the American Luther League barely died. But the LLL did remain a foundation on which to build. The LLL—not the ALL—became in time once again a major organizational expression of laymen's activity in the Missouri Synod.

4

Auditing the Father's Business

I

The organization of the Lutheran Laymen's League in 1917 was itself implicit criticism of the current state of church finance. Money and the acquisition of it may be a mundane matter, but, like energy sources, can be taken for granted only when in ample supply. This aspect of lay life, then, deserves our attention for a number of reasons. First, behind the league's stated purpose was a concept of lay roles that was not new—it dated from the time the only layman among synodical officials was the treasurer—but between the two world wars this issue was taken up in a more concerted way than ever before. Louis H. Waltke, prominent St. Louis businessman, put the matter in its most unadorned form: "Would it . . . not be a good idea to separate, as much as possible, theology and finances in our Synod? Let the clergy see to the doctrinal and theological part of our Synod, and let the laymen look after the financial end."[1] Second, the spectacular growth of the Missouri Synod was contingent upon a financial base achieved in large part by lay initiatives. Lay agitation produced the adoption of fund-raising techniques and expectations since taken for granted.

II

In Germany the state saw to the support of the church. Immigrants with this past were slow to learn the habits of voluntary giving necessary in America. As one pastor put it in 1859: "Our congregations are not at all accustomed from their experiences in Germany to make *themselves* responsible for church expenditures. The salaries for the pastors and teachers generally were at hand without their efforts." That congregations would voluntarily support educational institutions "would have been impossible for any member in Germany to conceive of even in a dream." In addition, the immigrants usually lived only a hand to mouth existence themselves. They were, observed the pastor, easy prey for "the unfortunate American disease of wanting to get rich."[2]

Not much progress was noticeable in fund raising in many Missouri Synod circles by 1900. Some congregations escaped the financial predicament of American voluntarism by simply reverting to an ecclesiastical tax system. Others turned to renting pews for revenue. A common misconception among the laity was that only voting members—not all communicants—shared responsibility for the fiscal health of the church and some avoided the duty by never becoming voting members.[3]

Many rural churches employed some variant of the method described by Theodore Graebner:

Once a year the pastor would hitch his faithful nag to the buggy and in easy stages would make the rounds of his congregation. He would call at his farmers, and, as a rule, would commence the proceedings—this was expected—with a general pastoral conversation, conducted in the farmyard with the head of the household. Pretty soon the parishioner would say, '*Nun, kommen Sie mal,*' and would retire with the pastor into the shadow of the barn. The transaction was always in cash, and the amounts were never published.[4]

Native American Lutherans both North and South had made impressive gains beginning in the 1870s by distributing small boxes to members who were to make weekly deposits, contributions to be totalled quarterly.[5] However, from either ignorance or antipathy, such an innovation did not appear among German Lutherans. By all accounts, the custom of a weekly collection during the Sunday morning service was completely foreign to most Missourian churches before World War I. "Four or six collections, later perhaps eight or twelve, were given during the course of the year for synodical and benevolent purposes."[6] An especially aggressive congregation might display in the church vestibule a sign listing the beneficiaries of the widely spaced collection Sundays. Still, if a collection Sunday was blessed by fair weather, a minor synodical enterprise might enjoy—and jealously guard—a surplus, while on a rainy collection Sunday the seminaries might suffer. Collections might well be taken up at a baptism or wedding.[7] Often monies were received in a *Klingel-beutel,* a cloth bag with bell attached, fastened at the end of a pole and passed down the pews by the usher. More up-to-date congregations used a collection basket or plate. Obviously, most congregations had not come very far up the financial ladder described in the *Lutheran Witness*: "the cigar-box system, the *Klingel-beutel,* the quarterly collection, the monthly contribution at the business meeting, the envelope."[8]

The synod itself was not perceptibly better off in the early years of the century. A lapse into English by *Der Lutheraner* revealed that the editor found no satisfactory equivalent in German for "stewardship campaign."[9] The epitome of synodical fund raising may be quickly quoted in its entirety from the back pages of *Der Lutheraner*: "To the congregations of the Eastern District. The Support Fund is empty. The Committee."[10] *Der Lutheraner* acknowledged separately gifts as small as fifty cents. A three-year appropriation of $101,500 for all building projects in the synod was *"Eine grosse Summe!"* It *was* a large amount when the contribution per communicant member in 1900 for purposes outside the local congregation averaged 58 cents.[11] Judging by synodical receipts, fumed Theodore Graebner, "you would think that the Missouri Synod was made up of poor widows whose only sons are employed as freight handlers and drain diggers."[12]

III

In the early years of the century more progressive congregations began employing the envelope system, then the so-called every-member canvass, devices developed by American denominations.[13] Near the turn of the century, the *Witness* reported that in the English Missouri Synod, envelopes were used quite generally by city congregations. German circles were a bit slower, but time and time again writers explained the envelope's advantages.[14] Contributions with envelopes rose to a startling extent: a doubling or tripling of receipts seems not uncommon.[15] Armed with such *Lutheraner* reports, even pastors of conservative German congregations could begin having the collection plates passed in the pew, then cautiously go about introducing envelopes.

The other device, the every-member canvass, was not completely new to the synod; a visiting program had been recommended already in 1866. What was novel was the typical American machinery and hustle. Once again, more Americanized congregations—eastern, urban—led in this innovation.[16] Agitation for use of envelopes and every-member canvasses continued into the twenties, gradually focusing on conservative rural parishes. There is no telling exactly when the regular Sunday morning collection of envelopes became a standard feature, for Missouri Synod congregations lagged somewhat behind national averages. Probably by the late thirties the envelope had come to stay in all but the most stubborn and isolated churches.[17]

Such advances at the grassroots made little impact at the synodical level. By 1905 the synod was bogged down in a seemingly ineradicable debt of $70,000. Beginning in that year, conventions exerted nearly triennial efforts to improve the abysmal situation. Some progress was made in concerted fund raising.[18] In 1906 for the first time the synod collected more than a half-million dollars. Yet success produced little long-term profit; receipts in following years again slipped back.[19] Reviewing financial procedures of the time is something like watching a slapstick movie of the era. Some pastors kept no financial records to report to the synod; others diverted the receipts of the congregation into a favorite project in the denomination instead of toward the operating account. The synodical budget, issued first in 1911, was published only after the first of the year it covered. Some districts did not even have a budget, or at least did not distribute it.[20] Finally, there was a dearth of personnel to deal with finances. President

Franz Pieper was a dogmatician and theology professor, not an administrator. Until he was succeeded by Frederick Pfotenhauer in 1911, there was not a single full-time official in the whole synod. No one had as his job the supervision of synodical finances.

The outcome of this bitter comedy was that the synod hauled itself painfully out of one debt only to slip into another—debts as high as 20 to 25 percent of an annual budget. Yet while the synod wrestled with a deficit edging toward $100,000, the most unadorned of appeals to help Lutheran victims of a flood and a tornado brought in $57,000 (incredibly, *Der Lutheraner* then emphasized that no more was needed). W. C. Kohn, director at the River Forest teachers' college, successfully campaigned for gifts not of ten dollars, but of a thousand for his new campus.[21] Manifestly the synod had not kept pace with financial changes among its laity.

IV

Early twentieth-century synodical business practice, then, was characterized by gross inefficiency, widespread ignorance of needs among the laity, and corresponding passivity. The Lutheran Laymen's League attacked all three when it organized in 1917. Dumbfounded by the fiscal methods in use, the successful businessmen of the league criticized pastors and officials sharply for not educating the constituency better. And they felt that the laymen should assume the responsibility of raising money in the church.

President Theodore Lamprecht articulated well the league's concept of the laymen's responsibility when he explained that the object of the LLL was not only to raise money, but also "to make our fellow-laymen realize that it was *their* duty to *give* and *gather* it." Lamprecht emphasized that "pastors were not educated . . . to become collectors of money in their congregations." Instead, their duty was to preach the Gospel "and the laity, those to whom the pastors bring these riches of Heaven are in honor and in duty bound to provide the means, the money, so that the pastor in his high calling is not forced to divert time and energy to other things.''[22]

Here was the first direct lay answer to the question, what is the laity to do? Laymen must help the pastor by attending to the finances of the church. Once having committed themselves to financial matters, laymen and league made two major contributions. The first came in the endowment fund campaign of 1919-1920. The second was in agitation for better methods in regular money-raising. These two were essential for producing the financial resources that allowed the synod to become what it did.

The endowment fund campaign, as we have already seen, was important in launching the league. It also introduced large-scale fund raising to the Missouri Synod. The league's drive was preceded by what turned out to be a test-run campaign. To raise funds for the spiritual care of Lutheran troops during World War I, a committee of the Board for Army and Navy settled on the new every-member canvass. After distributing a large amount of promotional literature, it specified a Sunday afternoon for every congregation in the synod to approach each of its members for a donation. The cause was a popular one and the campaign quite successful. By the close of 1918, the board had raised $560,000, then considered a prodigious amount for one purpose.[23] This drive also produced for the first time a group of men experienced in raising large sums. The LLL thus had at hand a complete apparatus for its own endowment campaign of January 1919. The league acquired the personnel, equipment, and office lease of the board, and another campaign began. As Theodore Eckhart recalled, to change jobs he simply walked across the office.[24]

The LLL campaign for a pension fund endowment necessarily involved superlatives, for nothing comparable had happened before in the Missouri Synod. The target of three million dollars was beyond synodical imagination. And the campaign itself broke precedents. Obviously those in charge at last realized the necessity of informing the laity of the needs, of arousing an enthusiastic will to give. Finally, too, as a regular *Witness* column indicated, campaign managers understood the advantages of building morale by periodic reports detailing the colossal size of the apparatus, of building suspense over the final outcome of the drive. All this would not have happened without World War I. Multi-million dollar bond drives with high-pressure campaigns, handbooks for speakers, and canned sermons for the clergy had all become familiar to the American people. But such a context was only a necessary, not a sufficient, condition. Equally new now was lay enthusiasm and willingness to support a fresh approach freed from the precedents and the memories of past failures that enmeshed synodical officials. Thus the drive taught lessons as important as the funds collected.

"I have never written so many *millions* as in the past few days," observed Theodore Graebner to W. C. Kohn in January 1919; "a dollar begins to look like three lead dimes."[25] The drive exerted a powerful thrust in raising the whole church's expectations. In other words, church leaders could plan more elaborate programs. The campaign brought home to many as nothing had previously the needs of the synod as a whole.[26] Success bred success. One pastor reported, "At first my congregation thought the whole collection would come to nothing, that it was unheard of to think of raising even one million. But when they read the first report and saw that already $700,000 had been collected and then soon after that over one million dollars was on hand, they would not stand back. We are now at work."[27] Finally, the campaign tested both new procedures and men. Most notably, Theodore Eckhart, the layman who had moved from the Army and Navy Board drive to the LLL campaign, moved on in 1920 to become the synod's first financial secretary and also the first full-time lay official in the Missouri Synod.

V

The second contribution of the Lutheran Laymen's League in finances was its agitation for more efficient methods in the synod's regular business matters. One of the most striking motifs in this agitation was the startling infusion of business terminology and standards into church life. Seeing financial transactions and administrative decisions in the church, these businessmen felt at home, happy to find that the church was, after all, a business. Its product was the Gospel, to be sold to customers. (In times of financial difficulty, the image was varied; the product became synodical need, to be sold to the lay contributors.) Like any far-flung corporation, it required constant attention to lagging branches, occasional shake-ups in administration, and careful cultivation of the work force by internal public relations.[28]

For a time, the appeal of this idiom was so powerful that even the clergy adopted it. "You are the stockholders and you are entitled to know all about the business," Theodore Graebner told a meeting of laymen. Pleading for more exemplary sanctification, the *American Lutheran* reminded lay readers that the non-Christian "is not apt to give the 'goods' much consideration, if the members of the firm are not regular users of the 'goods' and seem to consider them lightly."[29] As was to happen in other areas in later decades, the desire by clerical reformers for improvement (in this case in financial affairs) overcame the fear of blurring the line between church and world.

The most important spokesman for business-like efficiency in collection techniques was Albert H. Ahlbrand of Seymour, Indiana, a Lutheran center in the southern part of the state. A genial unassuming man, a second-generation American, Ahlbrand had spent a few months at the Fort Wayne preparatory school, then decided against the ministry and returned to Seymour where he engaged in diversified business enterprises.[30] In 1914 Ahlbrand was interested enough in church affairs to visit a session of the synodical convention at his own expense. He learned rapidly; responding to A. G. Brauer's private appeal in 1915, Ahlbrand agreed with other spokesmen: people are not giving "simply because they are not in touch with the situation." To remedy this, he proposed a finance board with a full-time manager. "We realize of course, the first thing we are told when we talk of a comprehensive system, that the cost of handling this would represent too much loss to the Synodical Treasury, but I argue that these men will double and triple their expense and salary by the additional money derived for Synodical purposes."[31] Ahlbrand thus summarized the two points that the laymen considered essential to improve efficiency: a better fund-raising plan and full-time officials to administer it. Much of the league's history during the twenties is connected with the extraordinary lay agitation for these two goals.

On hand again at the 1917 synodical convention, Ahlbrand this time had with him a plan he had sketched out at the suggestion of his pastor. In Milwaukee, he quickly got in touch with prominent laymen. As he later confessed, "If a fellow gets hooked up with Mr. Bosse [ambitious Evansville, Indiana mayor], and some of these fellows, he gets to be kind of a politician. . . . You know how to pull the ropes, you know." He addressed both the lay delegates at the convention and also the first LLL meeting at Pritzlaff's home, using language he thought they would understand. "I likened the Synod to a large business corporation with agencies all over the country—a sales-manager and salesmen for each large Dist. and one to cover several small Dist's. These men were to sell the Synod to each congregation in Synod. They had to make daily reports to the sales manager."[32]

The laymen's meeting subsequently adopted resolutions that became known as the Ahlbrand plan. This recommended meetings of representative laymen on the circuit level (the administrative unit between the congregation and the district) to discuss synodical finances. After apportioning the financial share of each congregation, the laymen were to whip up enthusiasm at home. Most of the synod ignored the plan. But the Lutheran Laymen's League offered Ahlbrand both a prominent rostrum and wholehearted support.[33] At a November 1919 LLL meeting he reported that in his district, the laymen, in face of clerical opposition, had insisted upon the introduction of more businesslike methods. Finding that the "ordinary pastor is a very poor bookkeeper," the laymen in the Central District began by developing a standardized form for congregational account keeping. Such a system, claimed Ahlbrand, put real pressure on lagging congregations to produce. "The minute you get a man on record he is going to get busy. Nobody likes to fall down on the job, whether it is a pastor or a layman."[34] Laymen who were embarrassed at the circuit meeting by their congregation's poor showing, Ahlbrand said, vowed such would never happen again.

Under Ahlbrand's leadership, at the 1920 synodical convention the LLL recommended extending lay meetings from the circuit to the district and synodical levels; the LLL also urged the adoption of Ahlbrand's standard reporting forms. By good advance lobbying the resolutions carried by a large majority. The plan for greater lay participation was still not widely adopted, however. Only after heavy pressure did President Pfotenhauer agree through the Board of Directors to permit the league to publish material to advertise the plan.[35] Some individual pastors, too, opposed the plan vehemently. In 1923 a group of Iowa clergy complained especially about the "legalism" of the plan. What they called legalism the laymen called efficiency, and intensive work at the 1923 convention headed off this threat. By 1923, however, even those advocating more efficient fund raising admitted privately that the plan was both cumbersome and susceptible to misinterpretation. The Ahlbrand plan served its usefulness in arousing laymen to action and in giving some blueprint where previously there had been none. In time the plan itself was superseded.

VI

Agitation for the second lay goal, full-time church administrators, was also often phrased in the prevailing business terminology. Wrote Ahlbrand, "Under the present system we select a Pastor for the office of [district] President who is already burdened with all the work that he can do by looking after the welfare of the congregation he is serving. . . . To overcome this shortage on his part we have a number of official [circuit] visitors who are also loaded down with work in looking after their own local congregations."[36] Such overloading "is against all business ethics," Ahlbrand told the LLL with perhaps unconscious irony. "No man would ever try to do anything of that kind in business."[37] The league responded by swinging behind the proposal that in 1920 made Theodore Eckhart the synod's first financial secretary.

Despite Eckhart's appointment, the synod seemed to learn little. The effort to collect a million dollars appropriated in 1920 for a new seminary used traditional methods and failed miserably. Almost as a matter of course, aggressive clergy turned to the

league for help. By this time, though, the laymen were outspo-
kenly angry with the way synodical finances, and particularly the
building fund drive, had been handled. At a May 1922 meeting,
the LLL directors adopted resolutions declaring unanimously
that "the fault lay not so much with the unwillingness or inability
of our people, but rather in the fact that they lacked the necessary
information to an astonishing degree. This in turn was laid at the
door of Synod's officials, the District Presidents, and chiefly the
great majority of our pastors."[38]

The LLL directors recommended still more manpower; a
vice-president of the synod should be given "the sole duty of
impressing upon pastors and congregations their obligation to
promptly raise any monies appropriated by the Synod."[39] Aided
and abetted especially by Theodore Graebner, the league lobbied
extensively for this measure before the 1923 convention. At that
convention, other lay pressure for a centralization of financial
responsibility appeared from a new synodical Board of Auditors,
three laymen elected in 1920. As their report in 1923 showed, they
were scandalized by the way the church conducted its business.
With superb self-confidence they told the convention, "it is clear
that we shall have to suggest and recommend a revision of the
financial organization of Synod's several boards, committees,
missions, etc." The board called for an office of comptroller and
must have raised eyebrows by producing a chart unprecedented
in the synod to show what they considered the proper flow of
financial authority.[40] There was a spirited floor fight, but the convention voted down the office of a financial vice-president by an
extremely close decision and referred the motion to appoint a
comptroller to the Board of Directors, where it died.[41] The delegates did, however, approve an LLL recommendation to appoint
a special committee to handle the drive for a much enlarged
building fund; they had somehow appropriated 3.8 million
dollars.

The simple fact that the convention agreed to raise nearly four
million dollars for building projects between 1923 and 1926 was
itself a tribute to a coalition of LLL leaders and aggressive clergy.
At the 1911 convention, the whole assembly spent an afternoon

debating the construction of a professor's residence for $5,000.[42] Now in 1923 the laymen met repeatedly until league members quieted doubts and the laymen recommended the appropriations.[43] John H. C. Fritz correctly remarked in *Der Lutheraner*, "our Missouri Synod now counts in millions."[44] The Lutheran Laymen's League had done much of the teaching.

VII

More evidence of lay tutelage came in the campaign to collect the money. The drive was entrusted to a committee of three— J. C. Baur, on loan from the American Luther League, Financial Secretary Theodore Eckhart, and J.H.C. Fritz, square-jawed, brusque dean of Concordia Seminary. Fritz had long agitated for better financial methods, and was well known for his authorship in 1922 of *Church Finances,* the first manual on the subject published in the synod. In it Fritz outlined fund-raising theory and practice in a coherent form and with sorely needed emphasis on proper Christian motivation.[45] Here was a team that could function without assistance from the LLL. Interestingly enough, however, this Ways and Means Committee chose to have appointed a large advisory committee of prominent laymen, "to do away with the feeling that may exist that the clergy is too strongly represented."[46] This advisory committee was a mile-post of sorts. Apparently no one ever convened or seriously consulted it. But evidently lay self-consciousness was sufficiently developed that, on the one hand, allowances had to be made for it, and, on the other hand, it could be used by synodical officers to mobilize further lay support. Now that the technique was discovered, this was not to be the last such lay figurehead committee.[47] The Ways and Means Committee's campaign took the basic LLL model and added greater sophistication and some new engineering— including the use of pledges instead of cash contributions.[48] The results justified the work and money. Nearly a million dollars more than the goal was pledged. Such success guaranteed that most subsequent campaigns for the next fifty years employed the same basic pattern and most of the techniques pioneered in the twenties.

Truly, it seemed, the synod had learned to count in millions. Yet some signs warned that the synod had not learned to count at all. While the major drive was booming, the synod's operating deficit jumped from $150,000 in 1923 to more than half a million by 1926. The LLL and clerical critics responded predictably by citing the drive's success as support for more full-time personnel in the fiscal office. President Pfotenhauer forced delay until the 1926 convention where enough support was marshalled finally to secure the second full-time financial officer.[49]

VIII

Although no one realized it at the time, developments in financial affairs during the middle twenties defined in large part the future pattern of the synod's fund raising. The raising of money in the synod after the mid-twenties has four major characteristics: growth, increased expertise, attention to theology, and a curious rhythm. The first and most obvious was steady growth. During this expansion laymen successfully assumed a more active role in this part of the church's life. Steady pressure from laymen and spiraling budgets forced more attention to finances. By the thirties, the *Lutheran Witness,* which during the twenties had printed countless reports of lay activity at conventions, apparently no longer found these newsworthy. This was partly because Lutherans took lay participation for granted.

A second characteristic of the fund-raising pattern, however, also explains less public attention to lay action. By the thirties, lay activity was neither very original nor spontaneous. As an institution, the synod at first resisted its critics. Then by admitting them, by making some accommodation, by actually improving on some parts of their program, it enveloped and virtually silenced them. Lay leaders achieved during the twenties much of what they agitated for. The synodical Board of Control, first elected in 1908 to supervise college spending, was expanded to a much broader Board of Directors in 1917.[50] This included first three and, after 1929, four laymen. In addition, laymen composed a synodical Auditing Committee elected in 1920 (and after 1935 a five-man Investment Board for the synod). The church employed competent, even aggressive, men for synodical finances. Theodore Eckhart substituted a modern, unified accounting system for the old "treasury" arrangement. He and Lawrence Meyer tightened administration on the various levels up to the synod. With the permanent institution of the annual Fiscal Conference in 1926, budget making became a yearly, complex affair.

When their original goals were reached—or apparently within reach—the laymen had very little new to propose. The three consecutive campaigns they suggested between 1928 and 1937 failed disastrously.[51] The limitations of the laity's business orientation now showed in bold relief. Moreover, professionals now worked full time in the synod's financial bureaucracy. The businessman in the LLL was only an amateur. Initiative therefore shifted back to synodical officials. Above the parish level, at least, it became much more difficult to find occasion for the slightly naughty game of playing business father to the spiritual fathers. The gradual withdrawal of the Lutheran Laymen's League from fund raising for the synod was symptomatic of the change. By the early forties, a league staff member could say publicly that the original purpose of the league, to aid synod in business and financial matters, had been basically fulfilled.[52] The Depression, the league's own fiscal needs, and probably most of all, the professionalization obvious in the synod's bureaucracy all spelled an end to the type of lay involvement known in the days of the early LLL.

IX

The 1926 decision to launch an educational effort instead of another major campaign forecast a third characteristic in the synod's fund raising. What we need, said churchmen, is not just another drive, but an educational campaign to show Christians *why* they should give. Such an emphasis upon stewardship became increasingly common, particularly from some pastors. In the early twenties it was repeatedly stated that the laity did not give because, first, they did not know the needs, and second, because they were not given a systematic opportunity. When congregations provided the information and installed the systems, they often found they had, as Paul Lindemann put it, "systematized the parsimoniousness of their members."[53]

The laymen had been instrumental in achieving greater adoption of mechanical improvements in fund raising. Now a vital corrective to their emphasis on business efficiency was added. The major spokesman for the new thrust was Paul Lindemann, writing in the *American Lutheran* (the publication of the American Lutheran Publicity Bureau) and in his extended essay, *Christian Stewardship and Its Modern Implications*.[54] Lindemann was outspoken against a view of stewardship limited to the giving of money. "Stewardship teaching in our own circles has been primarily financial instead of educational. It has busied itself with the raising of funds rather than the building of character."[55] To emphasize man's dependence, Lindemann began with God's creation and redemption and worked out from there the need for careful use of His gifts. In his explication, stewardship became almost a synonym for sanctification, as he himself recognized; as such it touched on so many aspects of life that giving money in church became almost incidental.

Typical of this strain of thought, the essay gave only brief notice to the current financial struggle within the synod. The *American Lutheran* stayed in the same tradition after Lindemann's death in 1938. By 1943 the magazine protested applying the term stewardship to appeals for funds to cover deficits. "That's not stewardship! That's raising money because somebody down the line needs it. Stewardship is not even remotely connected with needs or deficits."[56]

When fund-raising needs and ideals moved in tension, they produced an interesting rhythm. This, in fact, is the last of the characteristic, continuing themes in fund raising apparent by the late twenties. The 1926 decision against a new drive and in favor of educational efforts was in part a reaction against the big-drive, high-pressure technique. The highly successful campaigns of the early twenties, it developed, started the ponderous and apparently inevitable swing of the fund-raising pendulum from high-pressure drive to low-keyed educational campaign and back again. The unavoidable pressure of drives, whether these were successes or failures, usually irritated some people who either disliked the technique or claimed that properly educated Christians would find it unnecessary. Yet no such educational campaign satisfied the synod's needs—partly because those needs rose steadily. The result was always another concentrated drive. Perhaps there is an ecclesiastical law that opportunities for Christian giving will always expand to exceed any level of charity. In sum, a long-term cycle, alternating fund drive and stewardship education, became the norm. The timing of the drives became so predictable that already in 1935 the *American Lutheran* thought that "our people are gradually coming to view the approach of any historic anniversary as the signal for another drive. As one layman cynically asked: 'What kind of festival will be the excuse next year?' Another figured that we ought to be soon running out of dates."[57] That hope was groundless, however, as the 1972 campaign during the synod's 125th anniversary celebration demonstrated.

X

Less significant characteristics of synodical fund raising also remained true in the era after World War II. Lay interest in the church's business illustrated much the same infusion of business terminology as in the twenties, though the jargon had changed. At stewardship conferences "such expressions as 'job analysis,' 'job outline,' 'sales technique,' and others were used repeatedly."[58] Much lay interest in fund raising went into auxiliary enterprises in the synod—educational institutions, the Lutheran Hour, welfare agencies of all sorts. Christmas and Easter seals, patron plans, prestige contributors' clubs, annuities and tax exemptions became common fare, especially in the direct mail solicitation begun on a large scale during the forties.

Budgets and contributions continued to rise spectacularly, especially in postwar prosperity. In 1945 Missouri Lutherans gave about $40 million for church purposes; by 1970 the total was more than $230 million. In the same period the average annual contribution per communicant member quadrupled from $25 to about $100.[59] Individual districts had been employing full-time stewardship secretaries since the mid-forties; more added such officers in succeeding years. In 1949 the synod instituted its own office of stewardship secretary, and, at long last, in 1950 the publicity office was broadened to include stewardship as one of its major tasks.[60] Thus the trend toward professionalization continued.

As he set to work, the stewardship secretary found that the Depression and war had damaged not only church budgets, but also the fund-raising apparatus. Even as late as 1954, only about half the congregations had a stewardship committee; only about a third used an every-member canvass.[61] As a result, many statements in the fifties and even sixties sounded remarkably similar to those of the 1920s, but they came from church officers rather than from laymen. Reintroducing the every-member visit required much work, but by the mid-sixties about 80 percent of the congregations used both a stewardship committee and some kind of visitation program.[62] In the same period there was also increasing consciousness of the need for better motivation behind giving. Concordia Publishing House issued a steady stream of books restating principles brought out earlier by Lindemann and Karl Kretzschmar.[63] Attacks continued against money-making schemes on the congregational level, such as raffles, bazaars, and the selling of dinners. And tithing still aroused a lively debate.[64]

Twentieth-century Lutheran fund raising has thus been characterized by rising financial expectations, growing professionalization in administration, greater emphasis on Christian motivation and an alternation of concerted campaign and continuous education. Laymen were in large measure responsible for establishing this pattern, though once it was fixed they became considerably less active, except of course as contributors. When in the late sixties a layman, in a brash and ill-humored sally, challenged the accounting procedures of synodical finance and suggested at least incompetence, the episode was very different from the twenties. After four decades a layman interested in forcing financial change faced an entrenched bureaucracy backed by certified public accountants, and results were predictable.[65]

XI

In most of these developments, Missouri was not unique, for in the same decades other churches and volunteer agencies (especially in the health field) learned similar lessons to reap the benevolence harvest: mass, concerted drives with unique features such as seals or dimes; the dependence on personal, individual contact that not only secures contributions but confirms the volunteer worker in the cause; the rise of a professional cadre more or less behind the scenes in varying relationships with the volunteer.[66]

Thus the constant exhortations and endless proliferation of gimmicks in Missourian circles owes much to the American context for at least two reasons. One was the attraction of success with these techniques; the other was increasing competition. Good and needy causes abound. To get a share of the philanthropic dollar in the face of pervasive secular appeals inevitably involves competition and competition leads to the search for the eye-catching, the novel. The synod's *Advance* magazine illustrated some of the problems when it replied to criticism for paying attention only to fund-raising technique. The editor emphasized that the synod required his journal to be practical; "to include the whole Gospel motivation" for stewardship would be difficult. "Besides," he added, "we must raise Synod's budget for 1954."[67]

Even the latest in novelty, however, did not seem to improve the indifferent success of church fund raising, at least on the synodical level, in the 1960s. Explanations for this abounded, but the cacophony was a sure sign no one had a conclusive case. It may be in fact that the synod was close to the end of an era in its fund raising. The increasing integration of the Missouri constituency into American society was in large part responsible for the increase in contributions, both through the institution of energetic fund raising and the acquisition of characteristics (higher income, a lower sense of alienation, greater involvement in organizations outside the family and in secular life generally, education, and volunteer involvement in a financial campaign) that are associated with higher levels of contributions.[68] Yet perhaps after a certain level, assimilation may be instrumental in cutting church contributions or at least slowing the growth. Moving freely in the non-Lutheran community and, as we shall see, encouraged by churchmen in the sixties to be active in that community—to be in the world—the layman faced a bankrupting array of pleas for contributions to causes a Christian should support. Sometimes there were Lutheran equivalents to satisfy those with denominational scruples, but often not. That the Lutheran layman by the sixties might apportion his discretionary spending in a way different from his grandfather's should be anticipated. In a sense this was a form of secularization, though in designation of recipient, not necessarily in the motivation of the donor.

Major changes in philanthropic models to the detriment of church support have occurred before. In sixteenth-century England wealthy merchants particularly turned much of their bequests toward secular eleemosynary objects. As W. K. Jordan writes, "the broadening spectrum of social and cultural aspirations . . . simply transcended and overran those areas of responsibility which the church was prepared or competent to undertake. Broadly speaking, therefore, the church and its needs, much less its social services and competencies, came to be regarded as irrelevant. But at the same time the institutions founded by these donors, and the very content of their intense secularism, not infrequently sprang from sources of deep and moving piety."[69]

It is too early to tell for certain and in any case the evidence is fragmentary, but the possibility needs to be kept open that the process Jordan describes was in motion among Lutherans in America by the end of the 1960s.

Part Two

In the early years of the century, as later, most church life of the laity took place not in national conventions or even in local chapters of lay groups, but in individual congregations. Similarly, important developments in thinking about the proper place of the laity were often independent of the lay organizations formed during World War I. These dimensions of lay life are much more difficult to discuss than the Lutheran Laymen's League or the American Luther League or even fund raising, for the record is fragmentary, inconclusive, and contradictory. Chronologically, too, difficulties proliferate, for we must begin again at the turn of the century and look anew at the first three or four decades with a different perspective than in Part One.

We must now focus on developments in parish life and on Lutheran consideration, conscious and unconscious, of the general place of the laity in the church and in the world. In brief, innovations widely accepted in the period between the wars meant that alert congregations reached the point where they prided themselves on having some structured activity within the church for everybody on the rolls. This, however, necessitated no radical rethinking of the laity's position in the church, much less in the world. As far as a more affirmative attitude toward the world was concerned, only the seeds of change were visible by the end of the Depression.

5

Laborers in the Vineyard

I

As the twentieth century began, there was some diversity among the Missouri Synod's 425,000 communicants and 2,100 congregations—and a great deal more by the end of the sixties, when the synod numbered 5,500 congregations with nearly 2,000,000 communicants. Because of this diversity no one can say when all congregations abandoned older forms of parish life. With care, however, one may generalize about the majority of the congregations. One may speak with still greater confidence about the congregations that comprised the cutting edge in the progression toward new patterns in parish life. Activities widely accepted in the period between the wars brought life in many congregations quite close to expectations of the fifties and sixties.

II

Early in the century most Missouri Synod laymen lived in rural areas and small towns under 25,000 population. A significant minority, though, was concentrated in very large cities.[1] In the cities the laity might be closely grouped in a predominantly German neighborhood. One Chicago congregation, for example, had a baptized membership of 2,200, all within a radius of six blocks from the church.[2] A striking characteristic of the synod's congregations in 1900 was the very large number of very small congregations. Nearly a third of the parishes had fewer than 100 baptized members; 80 percent had below 500 baptized members. (This was still true in 1930; in fact, the number of congregations below 100 baptized had grown to 38 percent.) At the turn of the century, the smallest 30 percent of the congregations accounted for only 4 percent of the synod's total baptized membership. Forty percent of baptized membership was in congregations with 100 to 500 members; 70 percent of the synod's laity was in congregations of not more than 1,000 baptized members.[3] The number of men per 100 women was, and according to the federal census continued to be, in the low nineties. In this sex ratio Missouri was approximately midway among the various Lutheran groups, which collectively ranked only behind the Roman Catholics and Mormons among major denominations.

Governing structure demonstrated the simplicity of congregational life. A voters' assembly, male and of mature years, was the main legislative body. Beyond this, a constitution authoritatively suggested about the turn of the century specified only a small board of elders, a secretary, and a treasurer. The pastor was an *ex officio* member of the board and, significantly, also its chairman.[4] When state law demanded it, a group of trustees (often elected from the elders) also functioned. The pastor or perhaps one of the elders acted as chairman of the voters' meeting. The elders were theoretically responsible for everything from admonishing the weak to collecting contributions, from visiting the sick to ushering.[5] In small rural congregations, the elder (or *Vorsteher*) set the pitch and carried the tune for hymns sung in morning worship. Fortunate was the pastor who had ear sharp enough and voice strong enough to help a congregation correct itself in the first line when necessary.[6] Affluence (an organ) sometimes brought its own afflictions. Woe was the organist whose *Vorsteher* set the congregation's tempo by swinging his foot while seated in the front pew on the aisle.

About 80 percent of the congregations early in the century supported some kind of parochial school, though a great many of these were highly irregular. There were so few Sunday schools (and they were so resisted) that they were not even enumerated

until 1910.[7] Many congregations still held to the old custom of
Christenlehre, a catechetical session held during and immediately
after the service or on a Sunday afternoon.[8]

The congregation's membership reflected the insular quality of
the immigrant mentality. Adult confirmations were exceedingly
rare, for few parishes engaged in local missionary activity outside
the German community. Writers directed the Lutheran layman
toward his church for fulfilling his Christian duty. In a revealing
piece, the *Lutheran Witness* urged laymen to consider the
church's business their own. "It is as much your business to see
that the Gospel is preached where the unconverted may hear it,"
said the paper, as it is to engage in your secular occupation.
"What I mean is that you have been given these temporal callings
only that you may perform them to the glory of God." At this
point, however, the paper abruptly converted a promising train of
thought to a plea for contributions. "You do that when, besides
feeding, clothing, and providing for your family, you do the
Lord's work with the money He gives you."[9] Such a restricted
definition of Christian vocation was typical at the time and calls
for personal lay evangelism were relatively few and generally
rather vague.[10]

III

Gradually, however, as seen in Chapter 2, sons and daughters
deserted the farmstead and small town and moved to the city.
And in the city the German ethnic hegemonies broke down as
new minorities moved in. Aided first by streetcars, then still more
by automobiles, the younger, prosperous, more Americanized
laity scattered about the city and especially into the suburbs.[11]
There they organized new congregations and constructed new
church buildings. Neither was quite the same as its predecessor.
They were not because the people were not. Trends with roots
before World War I were discernible in the twenties, even more
generally true in the thirties, and still obvious in the forties.

For example, Missouri Synod laity continued to concentrate in
cities. The birth rate fell steadily in the synod. By 1924 the *Wit-*

ness found it wise to list congregations in major summer resort areas for Missouri Synod tourists.[12] Educational expectations rose another step. "The time is past and will never return," the *Witness* concluded in 1927, "that our boys begin to make a living by carrying parcels for the corner grocer after they have passed eighth grade. The time will never come back when the girl, after her confirmation, settles down to household tasks. . . . Most of our young people, even those of the country (I almost said, particularly those in the country) are eager for higher education. The high school course is considered self-evident; the college, the university, a legitimate aspiration."[13]

The number of Lutheran students increased so fast that the first full-time campus pastor began work at the University of Wisconsin in 1920. Six years later the synod established a Student Welfare Committee. Lutherans also began student associations. About the same time Valparaiso University came under Lutheran control, the first institution in the synod to regularly confer advanced degrees for the laity. By 1939 a synodical census located more than 10,000 Missourian college students about the country, and the Student Welfare Committee finally called a full-time executive secretary.[14]

IV

College educated or not, the Missouri Synod constituency moved well up in the middle class, a class that was itself improving. Observed the *Witness,* "on Middle Street lives—the Missouri Synod, or 95 percent of it. Few of our people are poor, a fair number have acquired great wealth, but the greatest number belongs to the class of the well-to-do."[15] But middle-class life in the suburbs was different from what it had been. The younger generation, the *Witness* said, "had access into circles from which their parents, at a similar age, were excluded and of which, indeed, they knew nothing." Among the older generation the men worked farther away from home and at a greater variety of occupations.[16] The dispersal was so marked that in 1933 the men of one St. Louis congregation set up an exhibit to illustrate their respective work. "The idea was not to sell things and make money, but merely to acquaint their fellow-members and friends with the work they were doing."[17]

In response to this loss of homogeneity, particularly urban congregations remodeled their life styles. As the laity moved out of the immigrant residential and occupational enclave, congregations initiated a more intensive schedule of parish activities. If Lutheran men now rarely saw each other at work, if Lutheran women were now scattered in isolation about the suburbs, other means had to be substituted to hold the church together. For example, in (predictably) urban, English-speaking congregations, little parish papers began to spring up. As one writer artlessly put it, "under present-day conditions most churches, especially those in cities, require a medium of publicity by which from time to time they can bring important notices to the attention of all their members. . . ." By the thirties the practice had spread sufficiently for Concordia Publishing House to offer to busy pastors "filler material" for their papers.[18]

Another means to bring laymen together was through congregational clubs. Beginning in the twenties, social, recreational, and service associations proliferated endlessly in Lutheran congregations. The result was not novel on the American scene. As Atherton has pointed out in his study of the midwestern town, state federations of women's clubs blossomed just before the turn of the century and organizations like the Rotary just after 1900, in both cases spreading from larger cities to smaller towns.[19] For a variety of reasons, associational and club ties usually increase rather than decrease as one moves up the American socioeconomic scale; moving from lower class immigrant to middle or upper class American, the Missourian constituency entered this pattern. Apparently, too, voluntary associations increase in the community when existing forms of institutions and systems of social control are disrupted, when the community at large is too fragmented to act as an all-inclusive social group. In a fluid society, associations arise to help provide stability, cohesion, and leadership. When a congregation is itself defined as a primary group, similar dynamics work within it to produce voluntary associations.[20] If the now dispersed laity could not be together during the day, at least they could be in the evening.

Such lay pressure encountered a receptive clergy. Surveying the religious life of Muncie, Indiana, the Lynds found that "as the informal social life of the churches has declined, the churches are attempting to fight fire with fire by matching the plethora of new outside clubs with new batteries of clubs inside the church."[21] The emphasis within the Missouri Synod at the time was upon protecting the laity, on keeping them within the pale to resist the onslaughts of the world. When laymen began to think of joining clubs—as they did with more leisure and convenient mobility—the progressive and energetic pastor was ready for them with a series of associations to keep them busy at church.[22]

The change was impressively pervasive. The *Lutheran Witness,* which in 1917 had considered grossly over-organized a parish with eight societies, changed its stand during the twenties. By 1935 it reported favorably a St. Louis congregation with twenty-three groups, adding, "there might be ten more without creating 'over-organization' if they do not overlap."[23] In another five years a few congregations found it wise to launch coordinated planning for the multitude of societies.[24]

Inevitably, much of this activity was simply entertainment taking place on church property. Dart games grew so popular that enthusiasts formed leagues and carried them on for years. Complained one Walther Leaguer of the men's club, "they have no Bible-study or topic-study or mission-study. But you can play pinochle or bowl there."[25] It became increasingly easy to fall into the trap of equating activity with vitality, of identifying work in church with church work. At least in tacit fashion, the layman's religious commitment was measured by his involvement in parish organizations. Clergymen fell into the tragic position of setting up programs for the laity, then achieving participation by presenting activity in the parish as having the highest priority for Christians.

Some clergy did protest what Fritz called "Go-Fever."[26] But fatigue of clergy rueing the endless round of church society meetings explains most of the negative pastoral comment. P. E. Kretzmann pointed out in 1934 that "if the pastor desired to be in attendance (as being responsible for all the members of his flock), it means that every evening of the week is taken by at least one meeting.''[27] Manifestly, lay organizations did not automatically challenge the preeminence of the congregation's shepherd and few observers questioned the necessity of the pastor's presence. In any event, the trend seemed irreversible. Supported by many laymen and encouraged by most pastors, the number of groups meeting in the parish hall grew by leaps and bounds.[28] The number of hours and people available offered the only theoretical limits. Until the church was seen as preparation to cope with the world instead of a substitute for it, nothing would halt this movement for more and more lay activity in the congregation. The lure of protective busyness was too strong and too pervasive, as the comments of men such as Paul Lindemann and O. P. Kretzmann, who in other respects were ahead of their time, demonstrated. O. A. Geiseman, surely one of the most progressive parish pastors, presented the case most lucidly before the LLL in 1934.

It is reasonable to suppose that the church . . . will not stand idly by while commercialized amusements, such as movies, races, athletic events, taverns, road houses, and other interests, engage the attention of its members, but that it will rather enlarge its program of activities in such a way as to keep all of its people—men and women, young and old—interested and wholesomely occupied for the benefit of the individual soul as well as for the upbuilding of the Kingdom. This will inescapably call for more organizations, and among these, men's clubs will undoubtedly have a prominent part. Men's clubs, once organized, will need materials to keep them busy, and here the L.L.L. will have an opportunity to be of service as well as to gain ever-increasing numbers of new members.[29]

V

Probably the increase in activities of all sorts helped the synod maintain its traditional stand in one area of lay life, membership in secret societies or lodges. Particularly in the second half of the nineteenth century, Americans, fascinated by quasi-religious ritual and secrecy, automatically included these when organizing everything from farmers' groups to labor unions. Lodges were familiar, too, in the German immigrant community. Missouri Synod leaders insisted, however, that a conscientious Lutheran could not belong to a secret society. Innumerable struggles on the parish level ensued. Countless missionaries—who often used lodge halls as first worship quarters—faced a common dilemma. If they announced the synod's stand on lodges too soon, they risked a barren harvest; if they waited too long they risked having dissenters steal the congregation. Where successful, however, they assured much less competition for church loyalties and time among the laity.

As the constituency became more urbanized and used more English, opportunities and pressures for joining a lodge increased. Many observers feared (or hoped) that the synod's stand on lodges would go the way of its opposition to life insurance, labor unions, and Sunday schools.[30] But shortly before World War I *Lutheran Witness* editor Theodore Graebner continued energetically in English the opposition long stated in German.[31] During the twenties the *Witness* whipped the anti-lodge campaign to fever pitch. Drawing partly on voluminous materials supplied by Benjamin M. Holt, a layman who had left the Masons, the paper pounded away at secret societies. The lodge, charged the *Witness*, involves religious elements, if it is not a religion in itself. To be broad enough for all men, it has reduced Christ to a Buddha or Mohammed; lodge ritual is anti-trinitarian for the same reason. Masonry in particular teaches an anti-Lutheran theology of salvation by works. The oath of secrecy is dangerous for the state because it is taken blindly. The life insurance offered by some societies is larcenous deception, for it is actuarily unsound and rates are later raised to freeze out the high-risk older members. Finally, Masons are frequently the leaders of legislative attacks on parish schools.[32]

Missourian spokesmen conjured up a Masonry more powerful and monolithic than it actually was, and *Witness* articles wearied by repetition. But many laymen and even pastors *were* singularly ill-informed about the synod's position.[33] Gradually, however, the anti-lodge campaign spread throughout the districts until in 1926 the synod itself directed a committee to produce a definitive statement on the lodge.[34] This committee, however, illustrated a basic disagreement. As one pastor put it, "our Missouri Synod lodge-practice is a coat of many colors."[35] Controversy swirled over one central question: how much patience should pastor and congregation have with a professed Christian who remained a lodge member after being warned of its unchristian character? Either sincerely or to get the best of both worlds, some laymen claimed they were ready to be instructed otherwise, but could not honestly see the wrong of their lodges and therefore insisted they be permitted to continue to receive communion.

Many pastors, especially in the central Midwest, answered the question of patience by making short shrift of the whole business. Present the facts, receive those who sever connections, excommunicate those who refuse, and insist upon this procedure as the norm for the whole synod. When some members left for another church, the pastor might quiet self-doubts by saying, as one man did, that "every Lutheran congregation must have a sewer."[36] In the hands of a tactless pastor, this purgative could and did have a debilitating effect.

Many of the clergy in the East and in the English District, however, strongly disagreed with such a blanket rule and insisted that each pastor should be prepared to exercise a great deal of patience in selected cases. To support this contention, they cited the synodical fathers, whose practice turned out to be surprisingly flexible. Though the report issued by the 1926 committee played down past flexibility in practice and emphasized the fathers' unity in principle, the committee could not agree upon a rigid exclusionist policy, and neither would the 1929 or the 1932 synodical conventions.[37]

The intriguing thing about the whole episode is the absence of laymen from the fray. This was a cleric's quarrel over lay life. No laymen sat on the committee in 1926 and apparently no one exerted pressure for such participation. The LLL and ALL hardly considered the matter. Except for B. M. Holt, no layman made really significant public statements against lodges. The best explanation for this silence is that the majority felt the question of lodges not worth arguing further. The lodge issue "was settled by the laymen when the ministers were from sheer loquacity in a fair way of talking the thing to death," reported Graebner in 1928. "I attended the laymen's meeting. I know it was they who finally forced a vote."[38]

Perhaps because of the new congregational men's clubs, the lodges did not attract enough laymen in the twenties to overcome determined opposition. Why, then, was this such an issue in the twenties? In a rapidly changing society (and synodical constituency), here was one area of lay life in which it was relatively easy to hold the line. The test, membership per se, was simple to administer. And since it was, one could readily hold the pastor responsible. But when this was done, incipient differences in theological temperament were revealed, differences that in the forties opened into a wide gap in synodical ranks over the question of relations with other Lutherans.

In the meantime the thirties wreaked worse havoc among the fraternal orders than among churches.[39] From Muncie the Lynds reported, "Lodges, to quote one prominent local lodgeman, 'have been shot to hell by the depression.' The Elks have gone through bankruptcy, lost their expensive clubhouse, and now occupy an inconspicuous upstairs room over a store."[40] The synod was not again to be concerned to the same degree by this question, although during the sixties opponents of proposed affiliation with the American Lutheran Church, which had a somewhat more relaxed lodge practice, attempted to resuscitate the fervor of the twenties, with little success.[41]

VI

Whatever the motivation—and as we have seen, it could be complex—the pressure for more activity within the local congregation burgeoned throughout the synod. To accommodate it, congregations modified both their organization and even their buildings. During the twenties, even modest blueprints were more likely than before to specify a full basement with meeting hall and kitchen.[42] The shift was accomplished before the Depression put a damper on construction. Lutherans had once protested the Protestant trend to make the church building a club house. By 1917, John H. C. Fritz was ready to grant that "the erection of the parish house is an honest effort . . . to meet certain conditions of the time. . . . Years ago our congregations would not have provided a social center for their members by means of the parish house." But that, said Fritz, is a foolish argument for not doing so today.[43] Many agreed; by 1941 the Lutheran Laymen's League held its convention in a Fort Wayne congregation's parish house which contained a large gymnasium, meeting rooms, modern kitchen, six bowling alleys, and recreational rooms, "everything one might ask for to provide the best possible for the members of the church, young and old."[44]

Like the buildings themselves, congregational organization illustrated the changes inside the churches. Model constitutions and by-laws in the late twenties, for example, suggested not only the traditional elders, secretary, and treasurer, but also a board of parish education, auditing committee, publicity committee, board of ushers, membership committee, and a financial secretary. Congregations had begun to elect a "president" instead of a "chairman" as the leading lay official.[45]

Change did not, of course, come in an even fashion either throughout the synod or within all the activities of an individual congregation. For example, public leadership in the church remained a male prerogative. Church leaders resolutely continued their opposition to the steadily augmented pressure on the traditional position toward women. Some St. Louis professors fought national female suffrage to the bitter end—and beyond. In 1913 Franz Pieper asserted that "since woman's suffrage in the State implies participation in the rule over men, it is contrary to the natural order" to which all were bound. "Wherever this order is perverted," warned Pieper, "His punishments are sure to follow." As the suffrage campaign neared success, W.H.T. Dau detected satanic influence: "Just as he [the devil] had caused a great calamity in the beginning by a woman whom he enticed, so he plainly intends again by the feministic movement of our time, to inflict a great injury on the world.''[46] Dau believed that women's suffrage would be soon repealed once statesmen saw its catastrophic effect. Such diehards barely reconciled themselves to the new order; the *Theological Monthly* was still convinced in 1924 that ''neither the Eighteenth nor the Nineteenth Amendment has the backing of the Creator.''[47]

Dire consequences for marriage, family, and home figured prominently in the anti-suffrage rhetoric.[48] Less explicit but also present was fear of escalation: women who voted in secular affairs would seek church franchise, then congregational and synodical office, then ordination. Some churchmen were nevertheless able to arrive at a less logical, but more realistic position than that of Pieper and Dau. Conceding that ''neither God nor nature ever intended her [woman] for politics,'' Louis J. Sieck recognized in 1919 that women would get the vote anyway. Lutheran women should be admonished, this prominent St. Louis pastor told his assembled colleagues, not to spend too much time on politics. Having the vote might lead some to seek office, and they should be reminded that their place was in the home. Lutherans should be warned not to ''soil'' themselves with the company of feminists such as Charlotte Gilman and Margaret Sanger.[49] On this question Theodore Graebner was of the same persuasion and his letters illustrate its difficulties. Supporting the nineteenth amendment, he wrote that ''all politics is concerned, in the last analysis, with taxes. In this women have an immediate interest, even if they are not themselves in business.'' Yet, to a different correspondent, he insisted that ''it is not true that the women of our churches have 'taxation without representation' '' when it came to financial and business matters. ''They are represented by their husbands and by the men generally. . . .''[50]

Paul Lindemann, too, was sensitive on this score. In 1920 he somewhat defensively recalled that his clergyman father had insisted women *were* represented in church business meetings since he believed that ''in the majority of cases the opinion of the [male] voters was formed at home under the clever manipulation of the wives.'' Lindemann, however, admitted that in the modern church there were more widows, unmarried women, and women married to nonmembers; he was therefore willing to concede a sort of straw vote to determine their opinion on some questions. Yet, he concluded, God's law—and common sense—required that women remain in a subordinate position. "We tremble to think of a voters' meeting in which both sexes are represented." Peace is hard enough to maintain among the men alone. "Imagine a mixed council," Lindemann challenged his male readers. "You cannot. It staggers imagination. Imagine women deacons, or rather deaconesses, taking up the collection. What an opportunity to display the dressmaker's art or the latest concoction in the millinery line! But let's stop. The question is not one for levity."[51]

For some, it was not even a question. The status of women was not debated, Martin Sommer recorded after the 1929 synodical convention. Both sexes occupied their proper places. "The men raised their voice in denouncing error and in defending the Truth. And the women saw that the men were made comfortable, both before and after the fray."[52] The question whether a young woman could speak and vote in a young people's society, which had come up in the 1890s, was raised again in the 1920s and settled in her favor. But, disconcerting moderates, President Pfotenhauer ruled that wives of missionaries returning from abroad could not speak before meetings in which men were present.[53] Doubtless individual congregations varied widely in the point at which they trimmed their sails to the winds of change. But sexually segregated seating and communion attendance could still be found well into the thirties.[54] Spokesmen who insisted a theology that supported feminism was invalid because it was influenced by secular thought were unable to see that they were using not a single-edged weapon, but one that cut both ways.[55] And there, on the surface of things, the matter rested.

The men faced no comparable theological resistance to activity in the church, but custom could still be a strong check-rein. Even by the late twenties, a handbook on congregational officers could not find anything really wrong with "the common arrangement of having the pastor preside and the teacher keep the minutes." In fact, "if no suitable timber is found in the congregation, there is no reason why both should not continue their duties as chairman and secretary respectively."[56] The reference to available timber says a great deal about the attitudes of the pastors, perhaps less about the qualifications and expectations of the laity. The handbook did mention, though, "the custom which has lately gained ground of electing a layman as moderator of the voters' meetings." It explained a bit ingenuously that, first, this freed the pastor from the debate restrictions on the chair. "Then, too, it should be our aim to draw the laity more and more into active participation in the Lord's work."[57]

There were really two reasons for this rise in church lay offices: actual need and lay pressure. As the author backhandedly explained it, "Congregational work, particularly in large cities and wherever the missionary opportunity of the Church is being realized, has become increasingly complex. If under these conditions an increasing number of laymen would not have yielded to the conviction that their gifts of mind and speech, of talents and time, are to be placed at the disposal of their divine Lord, the Church would certainly have fallen short of her opportunities. . . ."[58]

VII

Nowhere was this "yielding to the conviction" clearer than in parish education: negatively in the abandonment of *Christenlehre* and positively in the adoption of the Sunday school. *Christenlehre* was a venerable institution in German Lutheranism.[59] Ideally with the whole congregation present, the pastor reviewed for the younger generation Luther's Small Catechism by an interrogatory technique. Synodical educators praised both text and method extravagantly, but already in the 1860s observers had begun to deplore publicly the absence of adults at *Christenlehre,* especially in urban congregations. At the turn of the century writers expressed alarm that some congregations installed Sunday schools, often at the expense of *Christenlehre*. By World War I comments on *Christenlehre* indicated it was being dropped entirely. The institution of more than one service on Sunday morning made it more difficult to schedule catechization after worship.[60] And in an automotive age it was increasingly difficult to persuade the laity to surrender Sunday afternoon recreation.

The most basic problem, however, was that *Christenlehre* was predicated upon an outgrown relationship between pastor and people. Missourian quotations of sixteenth-century references to the catechism as the *"Laien-Bibel"* epitomized the old attitudes. Laymen were considered simple folk for whom the pastor must stoop down and concentrate on essentials; the repetitious review of the basic Christian doctrines could benefit such people. The pastor, as head of the spiritual household, posed the questions in fatherly solicitude, and members of the congregation evinced their childlike faith by the recitation of the eternal verities and brief explanations extracted for them in the catechism.[61] The term *"Laien-Bibel"* rarely appeared in an English article, however, for *Christenlehre* itself could not be translated and Americanized laity and clergy both realized it. An educated laity could hardly be expected to endure the regular repetition of the same material, especially on a level children could grasp. And, perhaps more to the point, an assimilated laity could hardly be expected to tolerate being catechized by the pastor like confirmands, especially not in front of the whole congregation.[62]

Educators who realized this anxiously urged an adequate replacement for the abandoned *Christenlehre*. They specified a session with adults only, the Bible as text, and discussion rather than catechetics.[63] Though the Walther League produced a Bible study guide widely used in young peoples' societies, many adults had other ideas. "There will often be found a preconceived notion," the *American Lutheran* remarked, "that a certain indignity is connected with study on the part of grownups. This idea, although it is usually not expressed, is particularly prevalent among the men."[64] Lutherans had attended services "ever since confirmation and are almost convinced that their knowledge is complete."[65] Through forbearance or oversight, the magazine did not mention that *Christenlehre* had fostered this conviction by its nearly exclusive use of an admirably organized and lucid systematic treatment of Christian doctrine so brief that it could be, and usually was, memorized from cover to cover. The student never confronted the untidiness and perplexities of Holy Writ itself. In steering wide of Biblical literalism among the laity, this course risked the shallows of catechismal fundamentalism. In any event, organized adult education classes on a large scale had to wait for the late forties and beyond.

The Sunday school, on the other hand, thrived partly because it reflected the emerging new role of the laity. The Sunday school was long bitterly resisted in the synod because it was seen as an inadequate substitute (but serious competition) for the prized parochial school, because it was typically a vehicle for the entrance of English, and because untrained laymen did the teaching, compared with the professional teachers, properly called and installed, who taught in the parochial school. Generally, support for the Sunday school came from the most Americanized wing of the synod. As this group expanded in the twentieth century, the Sunday school movement grew rapidly; enrollment doubled between 1910 and 1919 and doubled again in the following decade.[66] Enthusiastic support from the laity explains these statistics. "The laity, in fact, as a class falls for the Sunday school," complained A. C. Stellhorn, the synod's secretary of schools. "More frequently than not, they are the ones that urge the Sunday school."[67] Lay urging grew so strong that even friends of the innovation among the clergy felt the need to remind the laity repeatedly that the pastor held the only true office in the church and that all others were only his assistants.[68]

Attacks on Sunday school teachers revealed an impoverished concept of the laity. As late as the mid-twenties Stellhorn fiercely opposed the institution because, among other things, it used lay men and women as teachers. "It is characteristic of the system. Is this in keeping with the principle that no one should teach unless duly called to do so? The question is not whether the institution demands so many lay teachers, but whether we want to tolerate the institution that demands such wholesale teaching by lay members. . . . These same lay people would never be permitted to teach a day school, unless perhaps in exceptional cases."[69]

While Stellhorn resisted the very idea of training the laymen to teach, Sunday school advocates attempted to improve instruction by better educated teachers. They established Sunday school teachers' institutes in a number of larger cities even before the war to provide evening lectures for the young people who flocked into the teaching ranks. Not until 1938, however, was a teacher training course available on a synod-wide basis.[70]

Sunday school teaching virtually revolutionized lay activity on the local level. The number of teachers jumped from probably under 5,000 in 1910 to more than 25,000 a quarter of a century later, or roughly from one teacher per 100 communicant members in 1910 to one per 30 members in 1935.[71] The Sunday school presented the first large-scale need for lay workers in the individual congregations. Here was something the laity could do on a continuing basis. In the *American Lutheran* one pastor rebuked those who shortsightedly harped on the weaknesses of Sunday school teachers. He told of a colleague who opened a Sunday school experimentally. "He had never realized how willing the people were to help and work until the Sunday School work *created so many demands for workers which had never existed before.*" The *American Lutheran* writer pointed out that "*there is simply nothing to compare to the great possibility which the corps of teachers offers for training a goodly number of our members for constructive work in the vineyard of the Lord!*"[72]

VIII

If the dartball leagues revealed the dangers of the emerging pattern of lay activity within the parish, Sunday school teaching demonstrated that pattern's strength. The congregation and the synod were the better for it. In the meantime the worship service and the sermon remained central in the congregations, but probably not to the same degree as in the nineteenth century. For one thing, there was simply more going on in the church and in the everyday life of the laity. As in national life generally, other forms of entertainment supplanted oratory. As a result of these changes, no spokesman after World War I had the courage to suggest—as did one editor in 1905—that Saturday evening should be spent preparing for Sunday worship.[73] The Sunday evening service already labored in difficulty early in the century, but by the twenties and thirties only artificial respiration kept it alive in most of the congregations where it still continued.[74] As those who traveled about the synod noticed, there was also strong pressure to shorten the Sunday morning service. The *Witness* editor reported being told "that in one of our churches of the Cleveland area they had succeeded in cutting down the service to 45 minutes. ('It's the bee's knees how they do cut down the liturgy,' was the mysterious way in which one of the young ladies put it.)"[75] Preachers curtailed their sermons proportionately until only an unusually determined pastor would speak for thirty minutes, a length his nineteenth-century predecessor might have found sufficient for little more than an introduction.[76] By World War II, despite editorial protests, the sixty-minute service was standard. Urban pastors ceased to worry about the shorter service and began to search for the solution to a still newer problem, substantial absenteeism on summer Sunday mornings caused by easy transportation and more leisure time.[77] One more promising trend did continue, however, year after year. The average number of times a member received communion annually rose steadily over the decades, though without a great deal of public notice. Whatever the causes, once speeded up early in the century, the cycle of change and response in church and constituency seemed to have no resting point.

6

Which Vineyard?

I

Between the wars the parish life of the laity altered greatly. Congregations initiated efforts to provide opportunities within the church for Christian fellowship and perhaps service. Many of the constituency became involved as never before. But what about the general position of the laity in the church, and also, insofar as the church was concerned, in the world as well? Here much was in flux. Laymen and pastors struggled with themselves and occasionally with each other to work out new answers to the broad question of what the role of the laity included. The answers they gave advanced beyond previous formulations (or rather, the absence of such), but were still decidedly limited. Simultaneously, however, the beginning of new attitudes toward the place of the church in the world laid the foundations for more fully rounded formulations of lay roles after World War II.

II

One element in any rethinking of the laity's role was the change in the relationship between pastor and people. Linguistically, *Herr Pastor* became Reverend; but much more than simply language was involved. The layman moving to the suburb or the younger generation migrating to the city left behind not only the ties and restrictions of the German community, but also the proximity that made possible the fatherly, close supervision by the pastor.[1] In the words of one sociologist who surveyed suburban churches in the twenties: "Their constituencies are broken up into so many small social groups that the church infrequently serves them all at once. Their pastors are generally not the oracles that they frequently become in the small town. . . . They find it hard to interpret the whole of life religiously because the group to which they minister knows so little of the major practical interests of the bulk of its membership and because their common community experience is so limited."[2] The increase in mobility permitted the laity to shop around more easily for a pastor and congregation that suited its taste. According to the *American Lutheran*, "the age of automobiles has naturally obliterated all hope of maintaining parish boundaries, and distance no longer is a vital factor in determining church choice."[3]

Rising levels of education also shaped clergy-lay relations. Pastors like the man in a well-to-do suburb who found the number of college degrees in his congregation had jumped from two to sixty likely also found that college-educated laymen permitted and occasionally forced improvements in music and liturgy. They also put more requirements on the clergy's own education. "An increasingly cultured laity demands greater knowledge on the part of the pastors," was to be repeated frequently from the 1930s on.[4] Moreover, especially the urban, more sophisticated laity had ready access to physicians, lawyers, social workers, and psychiatrists; in fact the pastor might face such men in his own congregation.[5] Such service professions had become so specialized that only an unusual minister could acquire comparable competence in any of them. Indeed, growing numbers of the laity knew that the pastor had very little idea of what they did at work. He was fitted to speak only about the abstractions of theology—and some were not even sure of that.

Unfortunately, Missouri's stress on an educated clergy did not prepare the synod for an educated laity. Since the synodical colleges locked themselves into a classical European curriculum of little practical use for non-clerical professions, they could serve laymen only by endangering clerical training. This the synod refused to do.[6] Though the English wing of the synod took the lead in coeducation in the preparatory institutions it founded, the German majority hung back until forced by the need for parochial school teachers. Thus, higher education for the laity came in the synod only decades after other Lutherans had colleges all over the country to train not only lay men but even women.

Fear of the intellectual explains some of this resistance. Early statements on university-student pastors emphasized the advantages of having technically competent laymen who retained "their simple, childlike faith."[7] A survey in the early forties brought a reply from one congregation "grateful to God that none of its members was in college."[8] As Graebner put it in the late thirties, "we have viewed with alarm the entrance of our men, and more recently of our women, into the field of college and university education. Dreadful examples have been cited of brilliant men . . . who entered the halls of learning and gradually rose in their profession as teachers only to lose their religious conviction, if they did not become atheists outright."[9]

Such distrust frequently met disdain, to judge from the impressions of clerical observers. One writer in 1927 feared "that with a smattering of college education in hand many of our young Lutherans have a tendency to belittle the Missouri Synod . . . [and] our pastors and teachers."[10] Even the *American Lutheran*, most open to change, found that "the college graduate in the congregation is usually a busy critic but a poor worker." Editor Lindemann did, however, agree with a reader who pointed out that students coming home found honest questions mistaken for incipient disloyalty and unfaithfulness. Wrote Lindemann, "We know of a very intelligent college graduate who . . . upon seeking light from her pastor in her intellectual difficulties . . . was bluntly told to go home and read her catechism."[11]

Different predelictions led to a confusion of counsel during the rapid transition of the twenties and thirties. Some churchmen indicted the clergy for a *"spirit of cowardice"* in face of lay sins.[12] Others urgently advised against the traditional, bluntly denunciatory manner. The day was past, wrote H. F. Wind, when the pastor's "word was law to the people and his authority was un-

questioned." To many people "the pastor is no longer a counselor and guide in the affairs of life. It is his business to preach
and he is heard with a degree of patience when in the pulpit." But
even some of his most loyal laity "accept his ministrations with a
new air of good-fellowship, of critical appraisal, of employerlike
good will." And among the younger generation, "solemn warnings on the part of the pastor . . . of dangers to the soul . . . result all too often in charges of 'old fogyism.' " Styles of ministry
therefore had to change.[13]

If geographical and occupational dispersion and higher educational expectations put severe strain on the traditional relationship between pastor and people, so too did the economic conditions of the Depression. On the synodical level, the demand for
pastors lagged because of hard times, but the seminaries continued to graduate record numbers. In 1933, for example, only 18
out of 180 candidates received a permanent position.[14] In the ensuing debate over the synod's educational system, for the first
time in the twentieth century the laity could read unsparing public
criticism of the Missouri Synod clergy.[15] On the congregational
level the doctrine of the divine call was hard pressed by the law of
supply and demand. Many times economics won over theology.
Congregations slashed salaries, occasionally without absolute
necessity; gave young men without dependents preference over
maturity and experience (and families); hired on a temporary,
even trial basis; and bypassed synodical officials with impunity.
In addition, some pastors were so reduced that they actively
solicited calls; one congregation received fifty applications for
one vacancy.[16] Caught between the anvil of the Lutheran constituency and the hammer of economic depression, the pastoral role
was differently wrought in the thirties.

If the old relationship between the German pastor and immigrant layman was dying, what new role for the laity was emerging? One possibility we have seen proposed by the laymen who
announced that the laity's role was to take care of church finances. That laymen took their fiscal responsibilities seriously
was undoubtedly an improvement. But a formulation apportioning theology to the clergy and finances to the laity reinforced the

tendency for the layman to find his task completed when he came to worship regularly, contributed generously, and perhaps kept the books for a season.

Fortunately a few leaders recognized such a neat and destructive separation of theology and finances as unworkable and as crippling to the laymen. Some pastors refused to be banished to the pulpit, and Paul Lindemann mused editorially about the "supercilious and patronizing attitude which some businessmen assume toward the pastor when it comes to the business matters of the church."[17] The advance guard became convinced the laity could do more than collect money. The *American Lutheran* admitted that "our laymen as a rule are not straining at the leash, filled with impatient eagerness to get to work for the Church." It warned the laity that the pastor must not be the "hod carrier" to the laymen.[18] But the magazine spoke most sharply to the clergy.

"We remember a case," Paul Lindemann wrote, "where a pastor had made an impassioned plea for laborers in the cause for Christ and was very much embarrassed when after the service a member came and offered himself for any service that might be designated. The astonished preacher had nothing to offer him."[19] Others repeated the same theme. A layman told of pastors who wrote out contributors' names on collection envelopes themselves, and he warned against the tendency to see the layman as a checkbook. "Apathy and antagonism are the best means to build up a wall that shut out the layman's talents and eventually make of him a machine where you pull a crank and out drops a dollar."[20] The *American Lutheran's* lesson was simple: the pastor must if necessary restrain himself so that he can properly utilize the assistance of the people.

III

In sum, progressive thinkers added a further dimension to the lay role. The proper place of the laity was to help the pastor accomplish the work of the church. In ideal at least, the layman had progressed from the inert ingredient in the church to financial manager to general pastoral assistant. He was still subsidiary to the pastor. Essays on the laity still began with an emphasis on the office of the ministry and its incumbent, the ordained pastor. "If the pastor is to be the leader," reasoned one cleric, "there must be others to follow."[21] But at least the verbs were those of motion.

Precisely how the laymen should help the pastor beyond running the physical plant of the church was gradually formulated in the 1920s and 1930s, as the synod shifted its missionary orientation from German immigrants to Americans at large. Urgings to witness to one's faith, long a staple in Lutheran rhetoric, had lacked specificity and practical assistance, sometimes apparently because of fear that zeal would give way to fanaticism.[22] One pastor began using lay canvassers only to be "warned by one kind brother to be careful not to let the men do too much, for they are liable to do more harm than good."[23] In the early twenties, though, the *American Lutheran* began a low pressure effort on the one hand to teach the laity that the church "is not a ferry boat intended to transfer idle passengers to the heavenly shore" and on the other hand to show the clergy how to utilize the laity in the practical work of locating, bringing in, and holding potential converts.[24]

The synod made some progress in the thirties but not a great deal, for it had to struggle to hold its own, let alone launch new programs. The most efficient pressure for lay activity is a shortage of clergy; in fact, the average number of communicants per parish actually declined from 263 in 1900 to 243 in 1930.[25] The synod did sponsor educational campaigns in the early thirties, such as "Call of the Hour" and "Missionary Forward Endeavor"—the very fact that they were given such titles is itself evidence of an Americanized appeal to the laity—but these were designed mostly to convince the laity of missionary opportunities close to home that the church should finance.[26] They did not get very far, given the gloomy financial situation and chronic debt.

The synod staged its most noteworthy effort, "Call of the Cross," in the latter half of the decade. Largely the work of Lawrence B. Meyer, head of the synod's publicity office, its intent was to stir greater consciousness of personal evangelism and, predictably, "sacrificial giving." Though more a thrust toward general lay arousal than a programmatic blueprint, the campaign did propose that an individual family assume responsibility for canvassing a city block and for visiting the unchurched they discovered.[27] Apparently, however, a substantial group of the clergy was loath to leave the established path at the risk of thrashing about in the thorns and brambles of lay activity.[28] But Meyer and others had grasped the possibilities of mass lay evangelism. Preoccupations of war precluded further experimentation, but after 1945 synodical officials were to return with considerable success to the ideas sketched out at the end of the thirties.

IV

Adamant as they were against any apportionment limiting theology to the pastors and finances to the laity, the clergy inched forward only with extreme caution when it came to including the laymen in theological matters, especially when these involved intersynodical merger negotiations. Of course, Missourian writers beginning with C.F.W. Walther traditionally upheld the laity's abstract right to pass on all theological discussions: in the *Witness* formulation of 1944, "Christianity has no doctrine which laymen cannot grasp. . . . The Bible contains no teachings which only a theologian is expected to believe and to understand. It would be placing the layman at a dreadful disadvantage if for his judgment of doctrine . . . he would have to depend on the authority of theologians."[29]

Yet remarks about the laity and theological debate often seem distinctly defensive. Churchmen displayed hypersensitivity to repeated assertions by other Lutherans that the Missouri laity did not share the same mind as its leaders ("a few first-class funerals, and all will be changed"). Though the *Witness* pointed out that one first-class funeral in 1887 (when Walther died) and others since had not changed things, the charge would not down; unfortunately the allegation had sufficient truth to perpetuate it.[30] There *were* laymen impatient with tedious discussion of theological fine points that delayed or precluded cooperative or organic union. One mild-mannered example was a *Laienbewegung* in Wisconsin in 1913 that sought to merge the Missouri Synod and the Wisconsin Synod in that state. Opposed by some clergy as a Peasants' Rebellion—something of unhappy memory for Lutherans—it was short-lived mostly because of the Wisconsin Synod's decision to take another road toward larger affiliation.[31]

Missouri realized its worst fears in 1917 with the formation of the Lutheran Brotherhood of America, a pan-Lutheran laymen's association organized to present a unified Lutheran front in support of religious work in military installations. After the war the brotherhood remained in existence and some of its enthusiasts impatiently blamed the clergy for the continued separation of Lutherans in America.[32] One worried pastor reported the slogan, "if we can't get together with the preachers, then we will get together without them."[33] The initial Missourian panic proved the clergy's awareness of the potential in such groups. But after the brotherhood's adolescent euphoria of the early twenties, it had its own problems of program and support; as it became clear that the brotherhood did not really predict the wave of the future, synodical spokesmen relaxed their guard somewhat.

Almost always, in conflicts over relations with other Lutheran bodies, pastors appealed to or cited lay opinion only behind the scenes. Clergy desiring change warned of lay impatience with obscurantist insistence upon the status quo. Pastors opposing innovation emphasized "how difficult it is to explain this to the layman," meaning in many cases that the pastors had denounced merger in such unqualified fashion for so long they were now trapped by their own rhetoric.[34] The typical attitude toward the laity was symbolized in the failure to include a layman on the standing synodical committee on church union selected in 1934.[35]

A different relationship developed, however, in the late thirties and early forties as conservatives slowed, then balked, negotiations that had promised formal ties with other major American Lutheran bodies.[36] A group of like-minded clergy and laymen then offered each other encouragement and advice in striving for closer union. Frustrated by a synodical officialdom dragging its feet in union negotiations and by much isolationist sentiment among the pastors, some clergy in favor of closer relations with other Lutherans began to appeal openly to lay sentiment. For example, the *American Lutheran,* spokesman for the progressive wing of the synod, and the *Lutheran Witness* promptly reported lay involvement in intersynodical meetings on the local level. Less subtly, both periodicals printed letters from laity favoring church union, something virtually unheard of in the *Witness.* Both also disparaged fears about laymen preparing to stampede the synod into union.[37] The *American Lutheran* did admit some anticlericalism among the laity. "It is, however, not nearly so strong as some clerical Cassandras would have us believe and it is not basic in their thinking." The editorial charged that "in the minds of many well-meaning men the major problem in the entire situation could be summed up in the words: 'Keep it away from the laity. They must not know what is going on, and above all, they must not be permitted to decide on the merits of the case.' "[38]

Even if clergy did not phrase things to themselves quite so bluntly, they may have engaged in some interesting reasoning, as the following letter from a pastor in North Carolina demonstrates. Where there is no competition from a nearby congregation of another Lutheran body, he wrote,

> people know nothing about the differences which divide us, and believe it to be only a "preachers' quarrel and squab-ble." . . . I for my part openly admit, that I have never in-structed any of my Confirmands, adults as well as children, concerning the differences between the different Lutheran church bodies, nor have I preached about these things to my congregation. And, when an United Lutheran family, or one of Ohio [synod] moved into one of my congregations, I have not instructed them first in the teachings of our Synod, but received them into my congregation as 'bona fide' Luther-ans. And I bet, I am not alone in this practice. But when it comes to Pastors . . . I could not conscientiously act in the same manner, as I did with such lay people. For that would indeed involve prayer-fellowship, communion-fellowship, and pulpit-fellowship. . . . I can watch such a layman, and

can put a stop to it, if he would dare to bring false doctrines and false practices into my congregation, but who could stop another Pastor well versed in his persuasion?[39]

As it turned out, however, laymen were not so easily controlled. Involving the laity as ally or appellate judge had its hazards, especially when enthusiastic laymen spoke out with more exuberance than tact. E. J. Gallmeyer's letter to the *American Lutheran,* suggesting that the laymen would have to "take up the cudgel" since the theologians had failed, aroused a storm of objections and provoked reprimands for both writer and magazine from the synod's president.[40] More letters and manifold carbon copies went the rounds when Gallmeyer was reported outside the synod to have emphasized in one speech that unification could come only through the laymen. "The last hundred years belonged to the preachers. The next hundred years belong to us, the laymen."[41] Much grist for clerical fears lay in another layman's letter to the *American Lutheran.* "If we of the laity can't understand . . . [theological] differences because we are not theologians, then let's relegate such differences to the blue law scrap heap. I can't agree that we must be guided entirely by what the experts decide as they have certainly been wrong too often to be perfect."[42]

The potentially embarrassing frankness of a Gallmeyer is one indication that lay opinion was not simply manipulated by clerical leaders. Another indication is the initiative and leadership given laymen by John Sauerman in achieving a union among the charities of the various Lutheran groups in Chicago.[43] A further example is W. C. Dickmeyer's often expressed impatience about the synod's prolonged and sterile preoccupation with the question of prayer fellowship. As the lay member of a committee to consider membership in the National Lutheran Council, Dickmeyer disdained precedent by submitting to the 1950 synodical convention a minority report in favor of membership.[44]

The most outstanding example of lay activism in questions of church union began in July 1945 when five laymen from each of the three major Lutheran bodies in the United States met independently in Pittsburgh to form a loose organization with the name Lutheran Men in America. "One of our main objects is to get the Missouri Synod into the National Lutheran Council," reported one participant privately. "The next most important thing is to get the Lutheran men of all synods to know each other in cities throughout the United States. Finally, to have a national Lutheran voice of laity over against the world at large in publicity, advertising, etc. There is no divergence of opinion at the grassroots. Don't forget that."[45] Most of these goals remained unimplemented, for the LMA was a very loosely knit group, apparently seeking no new recruits and meeting only once or twice a year. Although Lutheran Men in America itself did not grow, it did foster two other lay organizations. In 1945 the Cleveland Lutheran Businessmen's Club led by H. A. Polack urged a federation of Lutheran clubs for business and professional men. Encouraged by the response, the club helped form a National Lutheran Business and Professional Federation in June of 1945, though not much progress was made until 1946.[46] Then, under the influence of Lutheran Men in America, the Cleveland-based group transformed itself into a pan-Lutheran Federation of Lutheran Clubs, interested especially in Lutheran cooperation. The federation hired a Missourian pastor as executive secretary, and laid ambitious plans. Meanwhile in Milwaukee, LMA inspired the formation of Lutheran Men in America of Wisconsin in 1947. It soon had 2,500 members from the major Lutheran groups in the area.

All three of these groups carefully stated that they were not disregarding doctrinal or synodical lines; they proposed to cooperate only in non-theological matters. Such disclaimers, however, did not disarm. All three groups ran afoul of stern resistance from President Behnken and from clergy at every level of the synod. The organization of LMA, apparently a *fait accompli* before Behnken heard of it, brought hostile letters from him. The Wisconsin group was promptly condemned by the local Missourian pastoral conference and, in 1952, by a committee of the Synodical Conference (the most important members of which were the Missouri and Wisconsin Synods). Behnken even put pressure on Missourian clergy invited to speak to the Wisconsin laymen. The official position rested on the long-standing Missouri Synod insistence that doctrinal agreement must precede cooperative efforts. In this discussion laymen could not win. Had they proposed to take up theological matters first in these groups, they would have been accused of bypassing properly constituted authority. Yet their emphasis on other matters with apparent deference to theologians' judgment about doctrine was interpreted as a refusal to recognize essential prerequisites.

Laymen vigorously rebutted the clerical opposition but could not totally block its effect. Lutheran Men of America never lived up to its objectives. Furthermore, within a few years of its founding, a number of its moving spirits died. In response to pleas from Behnken, the laymen decided against concerted participation in the dispute at the 1950 synodical convention over entry into the National Lutheran Council; the convention's decision not to approve entry was a dispiriting blow after years of struggle. Though no single factor was definitive, the movement gradually burned out in the very early fifties.[47] The Federation of Lutheran Clubs and Lutheran Men in America of Wisconsin managed to hang on, though they faced not only opposition but also the familiar problems of lay organizations. By the sixties the influence of the federation was negligible and that of the Wisconsin group mainly local.[48]

Nevertheless, as benchmarks for the maturation of the laity, all three groups were as salient as the organization of the LLL in 1917. The LLL had announced the readiness of the laity to engage in financial and business matters, but carefully avoided any involvement in theological or intersynodical affairs. Obviously things were different in 1945; some laymen desired to move into a new area of activity. Two themes emerge in their motives. One was the businessman's distaste for the inefficiency of overlapping facilities and competition. This desire for efficiency, so marked in early twentieth-century American denominational life, had two sides; it might be a considered judgment on a scandalous waste of resources, or it might be the promoter's delight in sheer size. The other element sometimes apparent was an impatience with abstractions. At its best this represented a positive evangelical commitment opposed to the defensiveness of those more interested in guarding truth than in proclaiming it. Happily the anti-intellectualism latent in this approach did not often at that time find much public outlet.

Though important, neither of these motives explains why laymen became active in finances in 1917 but in theological concerns in 1945. One reason is that in 1917 it was easiest to establish lay activism through financial and administrative matters. By the 1940s church union replaced problems of business and finance as the burning issue. Most important, the ministers were bitterly divided about church union. And as one layman phrased it, "When pastors do not agree among themselves, we laymen must think for ourselves, and act accordingly."[49] Unanimity among the clergy could not eliminate lay dissent, but could drive it underground. Diversity among the clergy could not produce lay dissent, but could make it more likely. A clergy divided against itself could stand, but required lay propping to do so.

How many of the laity were genuinely agitated by these questions one can only guess, but all guesses should be very low. The *American Lutheran* editor encountered "lay officers of the church who thought that the term 'unionism' referred to labor unions."[50] Of those who knew better than that, initiative and momentum seem to have belonged to the group interested in a broadened fellowship. Predictably enough, though, a liberal lay party gave rise to a counter-movement of particular interest in light of later developments. The trend of events and clash of personalities produced a right-wing publication, the *Confessional Lutheran,* in 1940, but this was not edited to appeal to the laity. In fact, the progressives far outdistanced the conservatives in realization of the potential in the laity. In 1951, however, a conservatively inclined Wisconsin layman, Alfred H. Knief, published the first issue of *Lutheran Loyalty*. At the contentious synodical convention in 1950, Knief served on the committee on intersynodical and doctrinal matters. Heated debate before the committee furthered his alarm over Lutheran Men in America of Wisconsin, and he reacted with the new publication, sent gratis to pastors, teachers, and laymen whose addresses could be collected. Only four issues of the paper appeared between January 1951 and June 1953, but these demonstrated the possibilities of the style to be developed more thoroughly a decade later. Very likely financial problems had something to do with *Lutheran Loyalty*'s erratic publishing schedule and demise. But more important was the *Lutheran Witness*, which, after Lorenz Blankenbuehler was appointed editor in 1952, conducted a doughty retreat from the controversial. Knief was zealous, but not a fanatic. The renascent torpor of the *Witness* and a satisfactorily conservative synodical convention in 1953 persuaded him that the situation was disquieting but not out of control.

The indecisive and interminable course of inter-Lutheran negotiations after 1950 reassured conservative laity, as it disillusioned those who had once seen promise. As a result, in this area of lay involvement, the fifties was a trough between the initial crest of the forties and its massive successor in the sixties.

7

Watchmen on Zion's Walls

I

By approximately World War II, Missourian spokesmen had gone about as far as they could in an articulation of the laity's role that presumed the traditional view of church and society. The position designated for the laity coincided with the limits of the local congregation (and through this, of the synod). Naturally, performance did not always measure up to the best ideals, but these ideals were themselves limited. The church-centered concentration meant relatively little emphasis on such key areas of lay life as, for example, Christian vocation.

Lutherans made little progress here until they reconsidered one of the most perplexing questions always confronting the Christian, his position in relation to the world. The classic solution to the dilemma is to be in the world, but not of it. At best the answer is ambiguous. The individual is still left balancing "in" against "not of." Judgment on what constitutes equilibrium has varied considerably from time to time and from individual to individual. Generally, from 1900 to the late 1930s, and in many cases much longer than that, church leaders chose in effect to weight warning against being of the world rather than admonitions to be in it. Their choice shaped the tone and content both of advice to the laity and of reflection on lay roles. Only in the thirties did a small number of Missouri leaders begin to take an explicitly more affirmative attitude toward the world, and so laid the groundwork for attitudes later to support radically new views on the proper place for the laity.

II

To account for the Missourian emphasis on staying clear of the world, one must tease out a number of closely wound strands. One of the most visible is the pietism out of which many of the synodical fathers came. By no means a joyless asceticism, this pietism still included a strongly ingrained predilection to equate the world and sin. These Lutherans tended to regard most activities as worldly unless specifically demonstrated otherwise, and the burden of proof rested upon the accused. Another strand was a certain Biblical literalism that could help produce unusual views on, for example, usury, life insurance, or contacts with other Christians. Biblical authority amply supported views quite at odds with the rest of society or even other Lutherans. Missouri was accustomed to being out of step with the times.

Finally, the Missourian attitude toward the world could not have been otherwise, given the intensely particularist nature of the synod. What Gleason, in speaking of German-American Catholics, refers to as "multiple hyphenation" applies equally well to these Lutherans.[1] The Missouri Synod was German, American, and Lutheran, yet unqualifiedly none of these. Its Americanism was tempered by immigrant experience or parentage, its Germanism was modified by religious affiliation and an adopted home, and its Lutheranism was narrowed by theological peculiarities.

The immigrant and his children could hardly be expected to identify fully with the larger American community. Yet even within their ethnic enclave, the anticlericalism and rationalism of many who came from Germany further separated the faithful. "There were two distinct kinds of Germans in America who had little in common with each other and who did not mix much," one man recalled of his boyhood life in a city with a strong German community. One group was composed of "churchgoing Germans, who sent their children to parochial schools and who centered most of their social life about the church. Then there were the *Bier-deutsche,* the beer-Germans. Not that the other group was averse to beer—but beer seemed to play a larger role in the life of the latter. They were likely to be freethinkers, might have their children baptized as a sort of tradition, but never went to church. They belonged instead to a *Turnverein* and a *Saenger-bund.*"[2] Using somewhat more elegant terminology, other observers agreed in dividing the immigrant community into two main wings: the *Kirchendeutsche*—itself divided among three irreconcilable groups, the Catholics, Lutherans, and other Protestants—and the *Vereinsdeutsche*, primarily oriented to German associations and clubs rather than to religious institutions.[3]

If the Missouri layman or pastor could not easily identify with American society or with the German immigrant enclave, there was also little sense of oneness among Lutherans. After all, Lutherans had had their own "Americanist heresy" led by S. S. Schmucker in the 1850s that helped divide immigrant and native factions. And even among immigrant Lutherans, ethnic peculiarities and endless theological differences, exacerbated by Missouri's often prickly insistence upon thorough-going agreement in both doctrine and practice as a precondition for fellowship, splintered Lutherans into dozens of self-conscious groups.

Truly these were strangers and pilgrims. They carried with them the paranoia of the outsider—as immigrants sensitive to the native's smug condescension, as Germans to the ridicule of the freethinker, as Lutherans to sarcastic references about "pure doctrine." Was it any wonder that they reacted defensively and negatively? There was so much to guard against. Of course being an outsider is not the absence of a status, but is itself a defining characteristic that may lend cohesion. The manifold ways of defining what it was not aided the synod in preserving its identity. Thus both habit and institutional self-interest (expressed, of course, in the concern for the spiritual welfare of members) implied no decline in the siege mentality as the distinctive marks of ethnicity blurred and the constituency merged into American society. If anything, the transition to English and to American ways required more strenuous expression.

"Dangers surround us on all sides," N. J. Bakke reminded a commencement audience in 1894:

Before me I see rationalism and skepticism undermining the very foundation on which faith rests. Behind me is indifferentism with its manifold shades crying: "let us eat, drink and be merry. Let us enjoy life while it lasts!" To my right is the monster fanaticism that has its root and outlet in the numerous sects of our country. To my left is catholicism, the fruitful mother of anarchism, socialism and illiteracy, now appearing as an angel of light, now as a roaring lion, but whether as one or the other, always yawning to engulf us. Towering high above them all I see lodgism, oath-bound labor and trades unions gnawing on the very marrow of the church and the commonweal rising sometimes in their might against "the power that be."[4]

The typical attitude toward contemporary society was negative; the typical response was to attack it. Before World War I, synodical editors kept up a constant barrage against Roman Catholicism, Reformed denominations, Christian Scientists, lodges, and other Lutheran bodies. Summer time was an occasion for strong warnings against vacation sins. Each new development extended the strictures against worldliness: against immodest dress as hemlines rose above feminine ankles, against ragtime music on the new phonograph records, and against early motion pictures. Pastors encouraged Sunday evening services particularly for urban congregations so that people "may not be tempted to spend the time in some frivolous way."[5]

Proscription continued livelier than ever during the twenties and thirties. In his *Pastoral Theology* of 1931 John Fritz flatly informed seminary students that actors were in an ungodly occupation, thus lumping them with drug peddlers, brothel madams, and abortionists. One of Fritz's colleagues at Concordia Seminary, P. E. Kretzmann, was similarly directive about female dress. "It is indecent to expose shapely arms and legs," he advised readers in 1925. "It is indecent to wear waists and gowns which expose the graceful lines of shoulders and bust in a well-developed woman. . . . It is indecent for a girl or woman to wear such shoes or such figured hosiery as calls attention to her ankles or legs. . . ." Whole chapters of philippics against worldliness swelled to more than 500 pages the first marriage manual offered the synod's laity, Walter A. Maier's *For Better, Not for Worse.*[6] In the *Witness,* attacks on jazz and dancing, sex education, evolution, and atheistic professors in higher education joined the long-familiar anti-Catholicism.[7]

These were not the opinions of cranks or hermits in the synod. Voiced by responsible men and widely shared, they illustrate a way of looking at the world that influenced the synod's definition of the proper sphere of the laity. What was the ideal Christian life? Certainly one could not follow the oversimplified Roman Catholic answer of monasticism and withdraw from the world completely. In fact, intercourse with the world is required in business and civil affairs. No one suggested a Lutheran autarky, and from an early date Missourian spokesmen granted the need for Christian participation in government.

But in the typical synodical view, civil government was a negative force in society. The task of government was more to restrain evil than to attain justice.[8] When one seminary professor urged Lutheran involvement in government, he justified this with "lest the scoundrels who are in politics for profit arrogate everything to themselves."[9] Lutherans stressed obedience and duty rather than rights, order rather than progress. In the midst of the labor strife during the 1890s, A. L. Graebner drew a revealing analogy between the Christian in the world and a passenger on a railroad train that begins an impromptu race with another train on a parallel line. Though the passenger is unavoidably involved, he is not responsible for the race, nor for any catastrophe that may occur. Just so, wrote Graebner, the Christian is in the world, but not responsible for injustices that are a part of the impersonal system in which he must live.[10]

In addition, synodical thinkers gradually rigidified the principle of separation of church and state. Just as the state had no proper authority to interfere with religion, the church had no right to positions on civil affairs.[11] In actual practice, synodical officials and editors took very definite, public stands when Lutheran in-

terests were at stake (particularly in legislation adverse to parochial schools) and when questions concerned sex and the family.
But otherwise the synod fulfilled its concept of the church's duty
by protesting against demonstrations of Roman Catholic political
power (unless this happened to be useful in struggles where
Lutherans and Roman Catholics were unaccustomed allies) and
against any attack on the separation of church and state.

The business of the church, as President Pfotenhauer put it in
1911, is to preach the Gospel, not to abolish physical misery or to
gain earthly happiness. The church could speak with directives
on daily life only to the regenerate; to the world its message could
be only the invitation to the Gospel. Santification and justification
were thus put in their proper relationship.[12] Reiterations of this
thought hardened, then ossified, partly because of the theology of
its opponents, particularly that of the Social Gospel. Fearful of
losing touch with the individual soul, Lutherans shied from an
approach to society as a corporate body. Synodical essayists
quoted a single sentence from Rauschenbusch to dismiss him:
"The business before us is concerned with refashioning the present world, making this earth clean and sweet and habitable."[13]
But in reaction to such naivete, Missourian leaders failed to see
the truth for the laity in Rauschenbusch's judgment of the synod.
In theory, he wrote, the synod "leaves individuals free for christianizing activity in society; in practice it leaves them unstimu-
lated, uninstructed, and even sterilized against social enthusiasm."[14] His judgment was certainly correct through the first
quarter of the century. Here and there synodical laymen did enter
politics, but church papers almost never referred to them early in
the century, much less hold them up as examples of Christian
citizenship.

If the church offered very few explicit incentives for laymen to
become involved in government, it positively discouraged penetration of secular society by more intimate personal ties. According to God's clear word, said synodical authorities, the Christian
may have conversation with the non-Christian when business or
courtesy requires it, or where there is some chance of doing
good.[15] But such contacts must be limited to an impersonal level.

Christians who believe they can elevate secular society or improve the reputation of the church by closer contact with the world are deluded and doomed to disappointment or apostasy. Forbidden to the Christian is "first, the conversing with ungodly men, where there is no *necessity,* no *providential call,* no business, that requires it; secondly the conversing with more frequency than business necessarily requires; thirdly, the spending more time in their company than is necessary to finish our business; fourthly, the choosing ungodly persons to be our companions or our familiar friends."[16] As Theodore Graebner admonished his *Witness* readers in 1917, "It matters not whether the occasion be *in itself* sinful or not; if in taking part in such affairs I must fraternize, be brothers, be in fellowship with those who are not united with me in the faith, I must refrain from sharing their society." Friendship with the world is a sin in itself, one pastor warned, and "is no less than *spiritual adultery.*"[17]

As the twentieth century wore on, such uncompromising statements fell off in frequency, but the thought behind them remained. Synodical leaders attempted to maintain a social structure defined by ethnic and religious boundaries that was, save for politics and economics, as self-contained as possible. When secular clubs and societies attracted the laymen, the church developed its own sequence on both the local and national level. When the laity moved into higher education, it was high time for a Lutheran university. When laymen became more affluent and had longer vacations, the church acquired camp sites and fostered Lutheran tours.[18] Typically, a *Der Lutheraner* editor defined his task in protectionist terms: to encourage constancy of Lutherans in the New World, to warn the laymen against the dangers all about, to provide weapons to battle the enemies of the faith. It was no coincidence that spokesmen drew for metaphors from Nehemiah's rebuilding and guarding of Jerusalem's walls after the return from Babylonian exile; this was a defensive reconstruction while under siege.[19]

For many, for a time, the protectionism worked. O. H. Pannkoke recalled the Lutheran head of a Chicago mortgage house who confessed early in the century that he never felt comfortable and at home with non-Missourians.[20] But the centripetal impact of the years 1914 to 1917 was only temporary. American discrimination against Missouri Lutherans was insufficient to counter the mounting centrifugal forces among the constituency. In addition to the actuarily normal attrition among the older generation, American entry into the war and the passage of prohibition and woman suffrage battered the ethos of the immigrant community.[21]

A few laymen spoke out publicly against the concentration on protecting the laity, but most of the laity, as they did so often when a synodical stand proved too uncompromising, voted with their feet.[22] Who could hope to halt the geographical and psychological dispersal of the laity into the American community? Already in the 1890s a St. Louis professor lamented that so many Lutheran young people forgot their schoolmates of the faith and became friends with those who did not know God's Word.[23] Things had not changed by the 1930s. "In the course of years our church-members have become more and more worldly, so that *to-day it is in many cases very difficult to find the line of demarcation between the life of the man who calls himself a Christian and the man of the world.*" This lament evoked a chorus of agreement: "their soul is rotting out through the movies, the dance, cards, and birth control."[24] In 1936 President John W. Behnken opened the year with an appeal for Christian action. "All of us," he pleaded, "should also strive to correct the condition, which surely is not wholesome, that some of our members have dearer friends among the unchurched than among their fellow-members."[25]

III

A corollary to the lay dispersal was the decline in exercise of church discipline. Details are elusive, for the synodical statistician kept no cumulative reports of total discipline cases, nor even of the total excommunications in any given year. But the overall progression is clear enough. In 1895 a professor writing a series on discipline in *Der Lutheraner* was candid about pressure toward laissez faire. The term "church discipline" has a bad ring today, he admitted; people think it is a residue of the Dark Ages that excludes weaker members and guarantees small congregations.[26] Needless to say, Lutheran churchmen never publicly agreed with this, but a handbook for church officers in 1928 gave much less emphasis than earlier to the disciplinary duty of elders. A general discussion in the *Witness* in the early twenties carried a positive title, "Gain Thy Brother," and strongly emphasized the need for caution and tact. By 1936 the *Witness* observed "in all too many congregations . . . an almost complete decay of church discipline."[27] But by then this was an unusual reference, for church papers almost never mentioned the subject, much less instructed the laity on its intricacies. Affirmative discussion continued, but was usually limited to a pastoral audience.[28] Laymen could well be excused for believing, as some did, that church discipline referred to proper decorum during the worship service. According to a survey during the early fifties, although nearly half the representative sample of laity accepted the synod's definition of engagement as binding for marriage, only a quarter was willing to consider any type of discipline in a case of broken engagement—traditionally tantamount to divorce. And by 1970, when faced by the questionnaire item, "Pastors have the right and power to forgive sins and to excommunicate the unrepentent sinner," college-educated laity rejected it by a decisive margin. About twenty percent even called such a claim either unwarranted interference or magical superstition.[29]

The decline in discipline—perhaps demise is more accurate—paralleled or followed similar trends in other American denominations and other immigrant Lutheran bodies, but that makes it no easier to explain satisfactorily, all the more so since so few debated the development.[30] Church discipline was not explicitly rejected by the Missouri Synod. It simply fell into desuetude. Yet people have hardly become less contrary since the nineteenth century.

In this case the etiology can be traced to the general loss of community. The atrophy of a sense of communion in the congregation operated on a number of different levels. In some aspects it involved the process of Americanization. Members of a closed and cohesive immigrant community might risk or endure discipline at least partly because psychologically they had no other place to go. After the language transition in the synod and in other immigrant bodies, it became much easier to find another Lutheran congregation quite happy to receive unaccredited a fellow believer, victim of Missourian narrowness. For a highly mobile laity with a reference group larger than synodical Lutherans, church discipline lost the deterrence it once possessed. On the other side of this coin, less exercise of formal discipline was necessary when the erring could so easily leave upon reproach. The loss of community also resulted in less consensus and dogmatism about what constituted sin. Changing standards of personal morality, or even uncertainty about traditional values, eliminated the basis of much earlier action. Of course sins newly recognized (e.g., racism) might have been the subject of discipline had the institution held firm. But when they lost a sense of community, congregations also lost the assumption that they were as responsible for the sins of their weaker members as they were, say, for the physical needs of their less fortunate members. The heterogeneous, fragmented, Americanized congregation had less sense of the communion that on the one hand sought the spiritual welfare of the brother or sister in Christ by formal admonition, and on the other hand assumed the reputation of the whole congregation demeaned before the world by the sins of a member.

Discipline in the twentieth century also suffered through association with nineteenth-century excesses, real or apocryphal, in immigrant congregations; laity with different standards saw these as pharisaical parochialism, as part of Old World ways having no place in up-to-date America. Ole Rølvaag's bitter account of the discipline case in the rural Norwegian-American parish of *Peder Victorious* says as much about later generations' attitudes toward discipline as about the institution in actual practice. A young girl in the Dakota farm congregation is unjustly accused of giving birth to an illegitimate child and of allowing it to die. Forced to confess in person before the whole congregation, she later hangs herself.[31] Was this the image of church discipline, the *"Stueck Polizei"* reputation, that Professor George Stoeckhardt admitted made the institution unpopular?[32] Probably so, to judge from incidents of required public apology still incredulously retold in Missourian circles to this day.

Finally, when Rølvaag had an aged layman disrupt the discipline vote, raging that "they'd have no popery in Dakota Territory," he alluded to the relationship between pastor and people which helped in perpetuating formal discipline. Laymen happy to see the pastor denounce sin and even pronounce God's wrath in person to the individual sinner were not necessarily amenable to clerical urgings that they, too, should be instrumental in the proceedings. To judge from advice for elders, this was true already in the 1890s, and such persuasion could hardly have gotten easier as laity grew more independent of clergy.

These parts of an explanation may not add up to a whole. Yet whether explained or not, the fact remains that as time went on fewer and fewer of the laity were subject or witnesses to institutional ecclesiastical measures for insuring conformity to godly behavior, however this might be defined.

IV

The silent decline in church discipline was one index to a general metamorphosis in Missouri Synod attitudes on the relationships between the church, the laity, and the world. Successive stages cannot be periodized very neatly, for they overlapped and occasionally regressed. But *Moving Frontiers* correctly fixes basic outlines as "a pattern of statement of conservative position, prudent silence when the position proved too difficult to maintain, and then accommodating restatement."[33] Put in another way, synodical spokesmen somewhat hesitantly followed their laity—but lagged at a distance. Then, in time, some older churchmen changed their minds and new leaders emerged to approach things from a different perspective. The result was usually a theology or a "theologization," depending upon one's perspective, of moderate lay practice.

In the twentieth century, this happened repeatedly on one question after another in lay life. The most notable period of silence and tentative restatement came in the late thirties and forties. The *Witness* did not disavow its earlier crusades, but in the forties fell quiet on matters such as dancing and birth control. The *American Lutheran* criticized Reformation Day sermons that indulged in gratuitous Catholic-baiting.[34] Typically, O. A. Geiseman's *Make Yours a Happy Marriage* of 1946 was less than a tenth the length of Maier's polemical marriage manual of the thirties and was as important for what it did not say as for its positive advice.

As clergy and laity became increasingly restive with the old answers, many social, esthetic, and intellectual questions were readdressed. For this purpose, the avant-garde adapted existing organizations and began some new associations and publications. The most outstanding examples were the Associated Lutheran Charities, the *Cresset* magazine, founded in 1937, and the organization in 1941 of the Lutheran Academy for Scholarship. In their timing and development, particularly the first two mirrored the social anguish of the Depression; all three were predicated upon the emergence of a new generation of leaders.

The Depression had its most immediate impact on Lutheran welfare. Frustrated by their helplessness, thoughtful and sensitive men connected with Lutheran charitable endeavors began to reassess the traditional synodical position on the relationship of the church to social reform. Those who wrestled first hand with the Depression's social consequences or who were angered by the suffering in the country found newly relevant some passages of Holy Writ previously slighted in the Missouri Synod. What now communicated most urgently was not Nehemiah the restorer and defender, but Amos the social critic; not the sexual asceticism of the Pauline epistles, but the primitive communism of Acts; not the God of Genesis, creator of an inexorable order, but the God of the Gospels, whose miracles fed and healed and whose beatitudes disrupted.

The annual proceedings of the Associated Lutheran Charities conventions and the ALC's bimonthly *Review* bristled in the thirties and early forties with what in the Missouri Synod were radical sentiments indeed. New voices insisted that people are not divisible into soul and body, nor the Gospel into spiritual and social.[35] To the question of what the church should do, some Lutheran thinkers now urged a new answer. "The church can no longer wait until the flotsam and jetsam of social wreckage comes drifting to its doors," declared Edwin Glabe. Edgar Witte agreed; it is not only illogical but impossible, he said, to continue to treat the symptoms of a disease and do nothing to cure the disease itself. We are not only an "ambulance corps picking up the casualties of social and spiritual disorganization," Virtus Gloe argued; we should also work to prevent the accidents from happening in the first place.[36.]

The judgmental here was not new, but the assumptions of the suggested solutions and the definitions of worldliness were. Calls for social justice were premised upon a positive, interventionist view of government. And this in turn prompted reassessment of relationships between church and politics. Edgar Witte implied that New Testament or Reformation rhetoric could not be transferred simplistically to a democratic system in which "the state is simply the people in their political aspect."[37] The traditional distinction between speaking of santification in the church and of justification in the world—good works to Lutherans and faith to non-Lutherans—was rarely reiterated in conversations of the Associated Lutheran Charities.[38] Most of these churchmen could agree that if the church itself should not speak, its members must. Here some thinkers began to bring the laity into a different relationship with the church and world.

Definitions of worldliness also shifted. Worldliness within the church grieved the advanced guard of clergy as much as it had the most orthodox *Herr Pastor,* but the charities conferences had a target different from the usual subject of a clerical jeremiad. R. R. Caemmerer and others were disconcerted "to note that when we canvass social opinions of our Lutheran people, they follow the pattern of their class or of their geographical area rather than the divine dimension." We have allowed the world to set our standards of sin, observed O. P. Kretzmann; people are outraged by adultery or a pickpocket, but not about sweatshops or the Memo-rial Day Massacre or Arkansas sharecroppers.[39]

Sympathetic clergy quickly absolved laymen of the chief guilt. As problems crowded in on top of one another, wrote E. J. Fried-rich, the church has not helped. Instead pastors steered clear, "leaving it up to the individual, no matter how weak he may be in knowledge and faith and how deficient in Christian experience, to apply the principles of Christian ethics." Friedrich and others were by no means calling for a return to the womb of immigrant clergy-lay relations, but repeatedly stressed that current social problems were too complex to be dismissed by brief references to the law of love. Ministerial candidates and pastors in office had to apply themselves to serious study and discussion and then refuse to pontificate. In R. R. Caemmerer's opinion, the person who pontificates "is then doing only a police job; he is not applying Christian ethics to a situation at all, but merely announcing that he is ethical."[40]

In embryo here was a strikingly different perspective on the laity. Though still hesitant to introduce the institutional church as agent, social reformers did recognize that the laity was already on the scene—*in* the world—and could be an instrument of change. The church therefore must educate and encourage its lay people to act their faith where they were. And to instruct the laity, the pastors had to assent to the role of accepting the insights and expertise of the laymen.[41]

Both the premises and conclusions were remarkably similar to what was to occur about two decades later in the synod. Why did this thought not blossom into a lay renaissance already in the late forties? One major obstacle was organizational. Something like the Catholic Central-Verein turned to social concerns early in the century when, threatened with dissolution, it was searching for some revitalizing and mobilizing goal. As will be seen, by the forties, the Lutheran Laymen's League was temporarily out of this phase and committed to other tasks. The Associated Luther-an Charities could not serve as a vehicle, for its members and friends comprised only a very small minority in the synod, a minority on the synod's institutional periphery. In addition, as much as these men might decry "ambulance chasing," that, not rethinking the laity's role, was their livelihood. For a time the ALC did manage to hold together the social worker and the social critic. But the war distracted interests and preempted and scattered personnel; prosperity removed much of the sense of urgency about social reform. The growing specialization and professionalization within Lutheran charities gradually dominated and narrowed the concerns of the annual sessions. Those who continued to reflect upon the laity and the world (R. R. Caemmerer is the most extraordinary example) did so largely alone. The results were to surface again in much more mature form by the early sixties.

V

Participants in the Associated Lutheran Charities conferences agreed that Christians should be expressing their views on a broad range of issues. The major experiment to institutionalize this sentiment was the *Cresset,* advertising itself as a monthly review of literature, the arts, and public affairs. Initiatives by Theodore Graebner, editor of the *Witness,* and O. P. Kretzmann, then executive secretary of the Walther League—a curious blend of the older and younger generations—led to the magazine's founding in 1937. For Graebner, at least at first, the magazine's protective role was of great importance; the *Cresset* could warn against bad books that for one reason or another the *Witness* could not consider. [42]

Kretzmann, however, represented a different orientation. As staff head of the Walther League, he warned his fellow pastors that constantly negative preaching left young people unsatisfied. As president of Valparaiso University (1940–1968), he began to articulate ideals for a Christian university in relating faith and the world instead of placing primary stress upon the school's protective role. [43] As editor of the *Cresset,* Kretzmann recognized that the traditional emphasis on the warning against being of the world had been workable as long as sociological factors supported this theological emphasis. When these social props fell, a negative and defensive theological posture was precarious. Unable or un-willing to fit themselves into this mental state of siege, many laymen simply stopped listening. As a result, wrote Kretzmann in his opening statement for the *Cresset*, "it is not unusual for a Christian today to arrange his views in all fields of human en-deavor according to a pattern which is woven by every hand but the hand of the Eternal. His economic views come from the newspaper. His social attitudes are determined by his immediate, often narrow, environment. His literary and artistic tastes are formed by voices from the streets of New York and the boulevards of Hollywood."[44]

This context cast synodical spokesmen in the role of a militia company, rushing out on alarm to put down one civil disturbance after another until this was impossible and the company had either to stay in its barracks or go down fighting. An alternate role was to lead, and thus direct and channel, the revolution. For some, of course, revolution in the synod was synonymous with betrayal. What is binding upon the fathers cannot be overthrown by the sons. The harder the world presses, the more sternly must the good Lutheran resist.

In 1937 most of the *Cresset* staff would have been slow to differ with such beliefs. The editor emphasized that when concerned with moral or religious questions, the magazine would be "frankly authoritarian," the authority being, of course, God's Word.[45] Hardly the Missourian equivalent of something like the *Catholic Worker* or *Christianity and Crisis,* the early *Cresset* en-dured an editorial board that ranged politically "from slightly left of Ickes to slightly right of the late Mark Hanna"; editorials tended to be much less radical on social questions than the publi-cations of the Associated Lutheran Charities.[46] Anti-semitism, the status of the Negro, and the plight of the poor gained no consistent, much less crusading, response. In foreign affairs, the basic pessimism of commitment to the doctrine of original sin, European roots, the bruising experience at home in 1918, and scorn of American liberal shifts from war hysteria to pacifism all distinguished the *Cresset* from most American Protestant opin-ion. Very often through the early forties, no one asked, much less answered, the hard questions. In the arts some of the *Cresset* staff were dismayed when music critic Walter Hansen stuck up for Gershwin and Sibelius. Reviewers decided the early Faulkner had "no message to present" and criticized him because "he does not clean us."[47]

But the *Cresset* was capable of growth, as the review sections first showed. Most illustrative was a protracted debate among editors and readers over motion picture reviews. Only after much soul-searching did the editors inaugurate a section on movies; but once begun, the reviews forced discussion of fundamental issues. Which was to be determinative of *Cresset* opinion: the artistic merit of a movie, or traditional morality and the movie's possible effects on the laity? One reader articulated the familiar position when he objected that the movie column mentioned "murder, divorce, and sin of every description. It is true that *The Cresset* does not approve of some of the films, but in writing about them you are unconsciously furthering the cause of that institution." Besides, "actors and actresses are notorious for their wicked conduct. There are, of course, Christian men and women on the stage today, but as a whole their lives are open to fierce temptations and most of them yield to these temptations."[48]

The *Cresset* rejected this as a "specious argument," but its early defense of the column rested not upon esthetic principles but upon protectionist traditions: large numbers of Lutherans went to the movies and needed Christian guidance.[49] Yet some of the questions the reviewer posed had not previously been as unclear as the *Cresset* now considered them. Must all movies that include drunkenness, adultery, divorce, and crime be automatically condemned? the critic asked with some perplexity.[50] He gave no direct answer, but by the mid-forties reviewers dismissed many more films as dull, poorly done, or tasteless than they rejected as violations of conventional morality.

Progress was speedier in book reviewing, where there were no associations with theater to overcome. Readers of early reviews quickly protested any tendency toward "moral indignation"— what one man defined not as moral commitment, but "ranting" and another reader denounced as zealous oversimplification in order to damn. Early issues some lay readers judged as too "pas-toerlich" with "too much sermonizing."[51] Such protests made reviewers sufficiently self-conscious that one half apologized for stating that there were no morally questionable scenes in a certain novel. Another reviewer reported the "bawdy" language in Steinbeck's *Grapes of Wrath,* but insisted, "If condemnation is in order condemnation, moral and spiritual, should be directed at the conditions which give rise to language."[52] The book review section at first carried the motto "Books—some to be read—some to be pondered—some to be enjoyed—and some to be closed as soon as they are opened"; by 1940 the subhead was replaced by "Read not to contradict and confute—nor to believe and take for granted—but to weigh and consider." As time went on, the *Cresset*'s weighing and considering reflected a position beyond pietism and parochialism, a commitment to the arts and high intellectual endeavor, and a lively curiosity about many aspects of human existence.

Certainly the magazine did not desert a judgmental role over against the world. Few Missourian writers could be as grandly gloomy as the *Cresset*'s editor reflecting on the prodigal-son world of 1939; "The hour of the husks has come."[53] But more than any other synodical publication of the time, the *Cresset* sought to be in the world it judged. Inevitably, such a position was educative in itself. The older generation on the *Cresset* staff mellowed in earlier views; younger men who were co-opted brought still broader perspectives. At the end of its first decade the *Cresset* was far from its early anguish over movie reviewing. As one reader enthusiastically congratulated the editors, "The *Cresset* is more than just another magazine; it is a cause."[54]

The Associated Lutheran Charities spoke for a new Lutheran emphasis on social action; the *Cresset* presented a different judgment of secular affairs. The organization of the Lutheran Academy for Scholarship in 1942 demonstrated a more affirmative view of the intellectual. The idea of the association was to encourage intellectual interests and endeavors among Missouri Lutherans. The war, financial limitations, and the problem of locating Lutherans with advanced degrees all retarded development; the group managed to publish a small quarterly, but annual conventions proved beyond its resources.[55] Nevertheless the academy was the first organization in the synod to encourage research and scholarly interests; even so simple a thing as a list of projects in progress was a mile-post of sorts.[56] Perhaps the best proof of innovation was a certain sense of precocious self-consciousness in the pages of the little LAS journal, *The Lutheran Scholar*.

Initiative for the academy and the *Cresset* and for the Associated Charities' interest in social justice came almost exclusively from the clergy. Lay involvement was guaranteed only when, to the acute dismay of well-to-do laymen in business, a pastor condemned laissez-faire capitalism but condoned labor unions.[57] The locus of initiative in these three ventures demonstrates the extent to which most educated laity had eased the church and theology to the periphery of their interests. When the prevailing climate was so markedly otherworldly and unintellectual or anti-intellectual, laymen could compartmentalize their lives or leave the synod. Doubtless both alternatives were used. To change this was no easy matter. Like the Associated Charities, the *Cresset* and the academy spoke to and for only a tiny minority through the forties. In a denomination with more than a million communicant members and 3,500 pastors, the academy came up with 113 members by 1946, more than half of them clergy. The *Cresset* then went out to about 5,000 subscribers.[58] Nevertheless, all three are important as evidence of social trends and streams of thought that were producing a new balance of "in the world" against "not of the world," and in doing so were to be instrumental in shaping the role of the laity in the church and in the world.

Part Three

In the long run the changes in parish life described in Part Two meant a robust life for national lay organizations, at least for those which survived the harrowing years of the Depression. Of course, at least theoretically, a vitality which rested on inter-war changes could be destroyed or at least called into question by subsequent, further shifts in parish life and in thinking about the laity. As a result the history of lay organizations is bracketed by the Depression at one side and the developments of the sixties at the other. The Depression and the following, more promising years are explored in the next two chapters, reserving for Part Four the breaks with the past caused by the broader changes of the sixties.

8

Oppressed by Depression

I

On the synodical level, the Lutheran Laymen's League was the major lay group to survive the twenties, though by a slim margin. Energetic St. Louis clergy then spearheaded a reorganization of the league to recognize men's clubs and looked forward confidently to a soundly based lay auxiliary. The same group of leaders had visions of establishing concurrently a comparable national entity for Lutheran women. But neither goal was reached in the time expected. In the history of Lutheran lay organizations, most of the Depression decade is a great slough separating fertile high ground in the two postwar eras.

II

The reformed LLL still faced, of course, the related problems of gaining members and finding an attractive program. Only a large membership could finance a major project, yet only a major project could attract a large membership. At least Louis H. Waltke, St. Louis businessman and league treasurer, was engagingly candid about the reasons for the restructuring in 1929: "The old organization was very limited in its sphere of activities, and it was regarded by many as a mere collection agency." Since men's clubs became quite popular, Waltke continued (perhaps a bit dryly), "it was very essential to the progress and life of our Lutheran laymen's movement" that these agencies be developed. Waltke pointed out that the idea had worked very successfully for the Walther League.[1]

Yet as the LLL's field secretary traveled about the country seeking to enlist clubs, he discovered that the men's association did not necessarily follow Walther League precedent. On Long Island, he found a recently organized Federation of Lutheran Men's Clubs. In Michigan a similar association was twenty clubs and 1,300 members strong. These regarded the reorganized LLL as a latecomer and feared encroachment. In a complete switch from the early twenties, the field secretary assured such associations that the LLL "has no thought of interfering with their local projects."[2] If the LLL was tardy in some areas, it was premature in others. The spectre of overorganization in the individual congregation was difficult to banish. In rural congregations qualified lay leadership seemed hard to find.[3] Finally, many groups were simply hard to arouse. One pastor sympathetic to lay activity described his men's club as a "sick organization. . . . I get about a dozen to come. They are vitally interested in a game of cards and lunch."[4]

In fact, however, the league had little more to offer than enthusiasm. The title of the league's publication was changed to the *Lutheran Layman* in 1933, but it was certainly not a league newspaper and hardly even an office organ. Aside from short biographies of laymen to increase Lutheran consciousness and pride, the paper was mainly an unabashed, continuous appeal for membership. The chief advantages of the LLL seemed to be fellowship and becoming part of a projected national organization.[5] The league's main early contribution was a *Manual for Lutheran Societies,* which included outlines to focus educational discussions at club meetings and suggested innocuous local projects.[6]

Society dues in the 1929–1930 fiscal year produced a discouraging $148. Total membership reported at the 1929 convention was 2,823, and by the end of 1930 only 29 clubs were on the league rolls.[7] The national convention in 1930 that approved the first network broadcasts of Lutheran radio evangelism included only 38 members, but 50 guests, mostly clergy.[8] It was easy to agree with a staff member's conclusion in 1930: "I firmly believe that the L. L. L. at present stands in need of a concrete national objective. . . . Nothing will so much tend to unite our laity as the undertaking of some popular specific common task."[9]

III

Since 1926 and acceptance of KFUO as its main project, the league had been involved with radio. But ironically radio's exponential growth created dissatisfaction with sponsorship of KFUO. The number of families with receiving sets jumped from 4.5 million in 1926 to 13.7 only four years later. In the same year that the league took over KFUO, the first major network, NBC, was formed. The networks and increasing commercialization reduced any one station's audience. Increasing government regulation worked further hardships on small stations such as KFUO, indeed jeopardized their very existence. Thus, just about the time the league adopted KFUO the station was losing its national potential.[10]

The national networks provided an alternative, however, by instituting religious broadcasts on free time for each of the three major religious groups. Given such precedent and synodical antipathy to joint worship with non-Lutherans, it required no great leap of the imagination to envision a Lutheran program. The basic idea seems to have been in the air by the late twenties, but who suggested it first in the Missouri Synod is impossible to say.[11] Momentum built up early in 1930 when, upon inquiry, the less prestigious CBS proved receptive to paid broadcasts. The league's annual convention agreed to the idea. In August Walter A. Maier was chosen as first speaker, and a year's contract was signed with CBS. The first Lutheran Hour went on the air for a half-hour on October 2 over a network of 34 stations. The choice of Thursday evenings (to still fears of competition with regular church going) was a happy one, for the Lutheran Hour inherited a huge potential carry-over audience from recently instituted mystery thrillers that preceded it.

For the public, the first Lutheran Hour series was an exhilarating success. Behind the scenes, it was a constant financial struggle. Even though the Walther League promised $50,000—which was substantially more than the LLL could itself produce—a meeting had to be called to discuss the program's fiscal straits only a month after the season began. The league resorted to increasingly desperate financial expedients in succeeding months until an emergency conference on June 11 decided the program that day would be the last.[12]

Although the Lutheran Hour was on the air only eight months, it cannot be cavalierly dismissed. It successfully demonstrated the basic idea of a Lutheran network. And if in any sense the program was a national audition for Maier, he proved himself completely.[13] The first Lutheran Hour was significant both for the laity and for the league. To be part of a denomination with a national network broadcast was heady stuff for a laity only a dozen years from the calumny of World War I. "The Lutheran Hour has 'registered' OUR Church with the American public," trumpeted the LLL *Bulletin*. "It cannot be denied," several pastors observed, "that our members suffer from an 'inferiority complex,' as they consider the standing of our Church with that of sectarian churches that were more in the public eye." Now, though, our people are "taking pride in the fact that they belong to a church which is carrying on its work in such a manner."[14]

The Lutheran Hour was important, too, for the LLL. As was the case in 1919 with the endowment fund, it turned out that the LLL had selected more of a project in radio than it could handle. Yet again as in 1919, the project helped to introduce the reorganized association on a grand scale.[15]

IV

All of this, however, is clear only in retrospect. League enthusiasts had the advantage of no such hindsight and for them the future appeared grim indeed. The Depression was only worsening. As the nation tightened its belt for a hungry time, no LLL officer could hold serious hope for an early resumption of the Lutheran Hour. KFUO, on the other hand, had been dealt a great blow by the experiment with network programming. With one eye on impending deficits, the Board of Governors slashed the KFUO subsidy until it was a mere $1,000 in 1934.[16] To add to its troubles, the LLL had to cope with antipathy from within synodical officialdom. In 1929 the League *Bulletin* reported with considerable satisfaction that the "bugaboo of the L. L. L.'s becoming a church within a church has almost reached the vanishing point." As events demonstrated, the editor was only testing the power of positive thinking.[17] One North Dakota member even requested a minimum of publicity for his club "since we have quite a few here in this District that would like to make it appear that the LLL is unseating the congregation and taking things into their own hands."[18] The attitude of some synodical officials was such that the Board of Governors interrupted the last-ditch campaign for the Lutheran Hour by a joint meeting with the synodical Board of Directors to answer the question why, as Edwin Faster diplomatically phrased it, "a certain indefinable apathetic attitude which in some instances could be called passive resistance was being experienced by the L. L. L." Frederick Pfotenhauer, the synod's president, responded by blaming the league; the shift to local clubs, he said, had aroused fears among local pastors and the dues were too high for the laity. He apparently did not offer to intervene to quiet fears or encourage laymen. Fortunately for the league, its friends among the clergy rallied to the cause of lay societies and the result was inconclusive.[19]

V

If the opposition could not kill the LLL, it was nevertheless lethal to hopes for a woman's auxiliary or a parallel woman's association. Well-developed in many areas of the synod by the twenties and thirties, women's groups included both congregational ladies' aids and ladies' auxiliaries attached to charitable enterprises. For example, the publication of the St. Louis Associated Lutheran Charities regularly reported on the activities of no less than eight different auxiliaries in that city alone.[20] But a larger affiliation garnered little support until the late twenties when a number of independently initiated movements arose in Oklahoma, the Central District, and elsewhere about the country. One alternative was tested in 1928 when women from six congregations in Oklahoma founded the Lutheran Women's League of Oklahoma. Quite another form was utilized in the synod's Central District (Indiana, Ohio, West Virginia, and part of Kentucky) in the establishment of a Central District Missionary Endeavor. This was not really a lay movement at all. One writer recalled in 1941 that it was "an organization that was no organization," operating as it did without committees, conventions, or minutes. It was instead a scheme by the district mission board to generate interest and money for missions among Lutheran women. The local ladies' aid was used as a convenient point of contact only; there was no formal structure and clergy planned and administered the whole program.[21]

Such stirrings at the regional level encouraged the small group of clergy and laymen that set out to rescue—and transform—the LLL. Late in 1929 league officers arranged for a meeting in St. Louis of sixteen Lutheran women to discuss the organization of a national women's group.[22] Reaction was highly favorable and women held larger meetings in the spring of 1930. Some of those most active in the LLL reorganization were extremely anxious to have the proposed women's group as an auxiliary of the new league. (The enthusiasm with which the *Bulletin* offered itself as a spokesman for the women's cause reflected in part the fear that the new women's group might fall in with the Women's Missionary Endeavor and become locked into passive support of foreign missions.)[23] Others felt strongly that the women should have a completely independent organization. The draft constitution drawn up in 1930 for the Lutheran Women's League compromised the issue; it gave the projected organization a name and structure quite similar to that of the LLL and included on the women's board of governors one advisory member from the men's league. Otherwise the two groups were to be separate, presumably parallel, entities.

As events transpired the discussion was purely academic, for influential clerical voices in the church opposed the whole idea.

In the spring of 1930 the *Concordia Theological Monthly* cautioned that large federations of church women's clubs "are in danger of becoming busybodies in other men's matters."[24] Shortly thereafter, the synodical Board of Directors threw up warning signals, and in the fall of 1930 a meeting of district presidents came out strongly against a national women's association. After further meetings to consider alternatives still open, the women refused to throw in their lot with the LLL and withdrew from the field to fight another day.

Probably clerical rejection of the women's league was part of the predictable Missourian reaction to the efforts of some Protestant women in 1929–1930 to establish what became known as the National Council of Federated Church Women, a group that not only disregarded denominational boundaries, but was devoted to social action as well.[25] Certainly the clergy's negativism represented the oft-reiterated conviction that the congregation itself was the proper locus of authority and activity; fear that extracongregational lay groups might infringe upon local (and clerical) prerogatives; anxieties real and rhetorical about "overorganization"; and dogged resistance to change.[26] Central, too, was the traditional Lutheran insistence that woman's place was at home and that in the church her role was a silent one. By the 1930s some writers implicitly granted women equality in mental endowment and in secular suffrage.[27] But supremely unconscious of the similarity, *mutatis mutandis,* between their own strictures and those they had abandoned, certain Missouri spokesmen continued a rear guard action. During the Depression, one seminary professor assured Lutherans that "women in the industries, in business, and in the professions have upset the equilibrium of society and of public life." The woman with both husband and career was said to be practicing "a type of twentieth century bigamy."[28] A wife who had received an education "that lifts women out of her sphere," who could both vote and earn her own livelihood was assumed to be the type raising the divorce rate.[29] Even in Lutheran fiction for the younger generation, though the heroine did go to the city, she went to find a job, not a career. Once engaged to the hero, she retired, to the disappointment of her superior, and devoted herself exclusively to husband and children.[30] In 1930 the *Lutheran Witness* quoted approvingly a warning to men not to marry "a public-spirited woman," for she was likely to "lead a movement for better babies without having children of her own."[31] Lutheran women who traveled long distances and gave much time to plan a national woman's association were perilously close to being public-spirited.

Unlike the men in 1917 and 1918, the women in 1930 could not silence opposition through a contribution the synod desperately needed or to the clergy's personal financial advantage. In 1930 the women really did not have any more or less of an immediate concrete program than the reorganized LLL did. But the men's group was by then more than a decade old; the women's league had yet to elect permanent officers. When it came to lay organizations, the old guard would not sanction murder, but would countenance abortion.

VI

Thus the immediate prognosis for Lutheran lay organizations coincided with that for the nation at large during the early thirties. Small wonder that members of the LLL met for the fifteenth anniversary convention in a somber mood. The league had no projects, few members, and negligible support from some key synodical officials. The only change in the status quo was retrenchment. Sensing hopelessness in the league's future, capable pastors and laymen who had worked to reinvigorate the league now returned to their main concerns and more promising ventures. The only man left at the LLL headquarters was T. G. Eggers. Born in 1888, Eggers went through the synodical educational system to become a parochial school teacher. First active in the Walther League, he was hired by the LLL initially as a field secretary. He became executive secretary in 1931, a post he retained until 1950. A quiet man without unusual gifts, Eggers worked tenaciously through a discouraging period. In later years of Walter A. Maier's hegemony, Eggers was willing to labor in the background and for a long time played the role of the devoted caretaker making repairs and modest improvements where possible.

When he became executive secretary in 1931, however, it appeared Eggers might serve more as undertaker than caretaker. Membership reflected the league's moribund state. In 1932 just three new clubs joined the LLL; by 1934, nearly five years of efforts had resulted in affiliation of only 72 clubs.[32] According to statistical analysis, parishes with clubs in the LLL were quite large and heavily urban, at a time when the mass of congregations was small and strongly rural.[33] Granted the long-term urbanization of the synod, the league might have a promising future, but only if it could stay alive to see it.

The malaise of the league was all too obvious. For instance, when the convention selected Ernest J. Gallmeyer president in 1934, he was not even present and was elected on the strength of Walther League, rather than LLL, activity. In program the national office could offer nothing more serious than energetic promotion of dartball. An attempt was made in 1933 to remedy this through the issuance of a monthly *Men's Club Meeting Program*.[34] The extremely elementary nature of most of this material probably reflects judgments similar to the counsel of one layman: "Remember our societies will be made up of men who have no experience whatever in gathering suitable material for a meeting. This will have to be handed them ready to use."[35] Even so, it is hard to imagine adults being vitally gripped by much of the literature sent out from St. Louis headquarters. Perhaps the most telling indication of the league's precarious health during the thirties was that the church's bureaucracy permitted the appointment as LLL pastoral adviser of a young and untried Springfield seminary professor, O. P. Kretzmann.[36] Theodore Graebner confirmed this in 1935 when he wrote, "the old LLL has passed out and the new will not command any influence for a long time to come."[37] If the synod's officials had little to fear from the league, they had little to gain either.

VII

Thus by the mid-thirties the national men's organization was enervated and national women's work paralyzed. What had been thought a temporary condition became chronic and what had seemed within reach in 1929 receded year by year. Many viewed the illness as terminal and hoped or feared for an early demise of the patients. The malady did yield in time, however, to solicitous care and a change of climate. Recovery was apparent first in the LLL (and will be described in the next chapter), then in the women's campaign.

At first the most important progress was made on a local or district level. In the LLL there was promising activity by city-wide associations of league members, especially in St. Louis and Cleveland.[38] St. Louis was also a center for women's activities above the congregational level. That city had been disproportionately represented in the effort to found a national women's group, and after the negative reaction from the synod's district presidents, sympathetic clergy encouraged the St. Louis women to begin a local federation. The move whispered defiance, for one of the new organization's unstated purposes was to demonstrate the value of a woman's federation. The St. Louis Pastoral Conference was agreeable when the idea of a woman's organization "only local in scope" was presented to it, and in the spring of 1932 women established the Lutheran Women's League of Greater St. Louis. But in the fall of the same year they changed the name to Lutheran Women's League, Missouri Synod and began to accept membership applications from societies and individuals as far away as Texas, Oregon, and Florida. Having failed in an assault on the center of the line, the women were attempting a ladylike, but determined, end-run. The St. Louis organization was unusual in its diversity. Most interesting as an index of social freedom among the Lutheran women was the formation in 1934 of an evening division to serve those who had jobs during the day. Predictably enough, this group became involved in community social-service projects, and in 1940 emerged as the independent Lutheran Business Women.

Other local or district women's groups that existed or organized during the thirties were usually characterized by a higher degree of clergy initiative and control and almost exclusive attention to missions; a nearly universal feature was collection of the small sums a woman could set aside from her household budget.[39] Mission boards desperate for added revenue could congratulate themselves for tapping an additional source of income while at the same time creating a new opportunity for service by consecrated Christian women. References to Phoebe, Priscilla, and Dorcas abounded. But what church leaders had actually done was to develop a structure and expectations demeaning to women and destructive of Christian lay life. In the mission society, the proper role of the Christian woman was to engage in study sessions so endless as to be mindless, and, thus inspired, to support the endeavor as best she could by contributions necessarily modest (were they not to be deposited in her "mite box"?) and by her prayers.

Mission work was an ideal tether for a woman's association. Neither old-guard clergy nor those with a vision of something more inclusive could easily oppose it; who could decry missions? It provided an answer to women who felt they deserved a larger role in the church. And yet it was eminently safe; the work was away from the local congregation, so women could not be tempted to violate the injunction against public speaking. In addition it provided a well-defined channel; one could quickly identify and head off tendencies toward action that did not belong in the woman's sphere. Of course such advantages had their price. The typical district woman's organization did not even recognize the existence, let alone the viability, of a new life pattern for women. Even for "woman's sphere," the home and family, the Lutheran associations were largely irrelevant.

By 1938 advocates of a national federation had deployed for another attempt, though this time by direct appeal to the synodical convention. The two memorials submitted, however, revealed different orientations to women's activities. The mission board of the Central District presented a plan completely conventional in its premises about the laity in general and women in particular. It proposed in effect an extension of the Central District program: no national lay machinery, no conventions, and no lay participation in the selection of (mission) projects to which women were to contribute. In short, an outrageous suggestion by the late thirties. The other memorial, sponsored by the Lutheran Women's League, was more activist in intent and less detailed in specification.

The convention responded by appointing a survey commission—of five men. While the committee studied the question, the LWL agitated more openly by issuing a quarterly, *The Lutheran Woman,* beginning in 1939. The 1941 convention accepted its committee's sympathetic report and voted to sanction a women's organization, albeit one hedged about with all manner of synodical controls.[40] Tension between the confined, cleric-dominated Central District tradition and the more open, lay-oriented expectations of the Western District's Lutheran Women's League persisted at the constituting convention in 1942. Two main points were at issue: should the new group include the restricting word "missionary" in its name and should the women have their own treasurer or use the synodical office? The upshot was an organization identified as the Lutheran Women's Missionary League which had its own treasurer. Its stated objectives were to nurture missionary consciousness among the synod's women and to gather funds for mission projects.

For those who had worked a decade and more in behalf of a national women's association, the formation of the LWML was a signal achievement. Their hopes seemed shortly vindicated, for within five years the league had more than 2,000 societies and was compiling a substantial list of projects completed in domestic and foreign mission support.[41] But the long conflict over the league's organization and then its very success helped conceal how conservative was its approach to the status of women and of the laity in the church. Although founded twenty-five years after the Lutheran Laymen's League, the LWML's answers about lay roles in the church were no more advanced than those the men's group arrived at in its struggle for existence during the intervening years.

9

Conquest by Radio

I

Having once reconnoitered the philistinian territory of network broadcasting, the Lutheran Laymen's League looked forward to radio as the promised land. Yet is was long uncertain whether the league itself would suffer the fate of Moses or enjoy the role of Joshua. The league survived, however, and, in large part through the publicity radio gave it, ultimately grew to be the strongest lay organization within the Missouri Synod. Because of this, both process and results of growth merit study. In addition to the league's intrinsic importance, developments in the LLL's structure, personnel, size, and purposes serve as a case study in volunteer lay religious organizations.

II

After the collapse of the first Lutheran Hour, the league accomplished nothing until 1935, aside from modest subsidies to local programs in areas where few Lutherans lived.[1] Initiatives and prodding for a return of the Lutheran Hour came not from the LLL, but from the Detroit Pastoral Conference and the St. Louis seminary Board of Control.[2] After a successful trial run in Detroit, the LLL moved the program to St. Louis, solicited and received aid once again from the Walther League. The Lutheran Hour began its third season in October 1935, now on Sunday afternoons, over ten stations in the recently organized Mutual Broadcasting System. This time, however, there was no financial emergency. Fan mail contributions plus the efforts of field representatives assured the support of the program. When the end of the season arrived in April 1936, there was no serious doubt about continuing the next fall. Here at last was the pattern of success. Its basic elements were not tampered with for the next fifteen years. Changes, when they occurred, were usually only to enlarge the program.[3] In the early forties, the program became international in scope; the domestic broadcast expanded to a year-round schedule.

Every fresh report seemed to carry news of another station in use, another country covered, another language employed by the Lutheran Hour. Endless extracts from fan mail letters became a trademark of Lutheran Hour publicity. By 1947–1948 the program was heard over more than 1,000 stations, Maier had an estimated domestic audience of 20,000,000 and the Lutheran Hour headquarters was receiving close to half a million pieces of mail a season. There was, in short, nothing to compare to it.[4]

III

This was the golden era of radio. Radio was not carried in a pocket; it was not just background noise. Radio was something you sat down and listened to. It was F.D.R.'s fireside manner and Father Couglin's more discordant tones, Charlie McCarthy and Amos'n'Andy, H. V. Kaltenborn and Lowell Thomas.

It was also Walter A. Maier. Maier entered radio when no other conservative preacher was a regular feature on network broadcasting; he gained public attention as had Billy Sunday before him and Billy Graham was to do after him. Born in 1893 to German immigrant parents, Maier early distinguished himself for his initiative. Well endowed intellectually, he completed both the synodical ministerial training and a Harvard doctorate. After a dynamic period as executive secretary of the Walther League, he became a professor at Concordia Seminary. Gradually his rhetorical gifts were recognized and through radio work he acquired an enormous following far beyond the synod. On the air he had a rapid-fire delivery and a piercing tone; he modulated his voice chiefly in a constant crescendo. Many found it intolerable; a few sent cards like "4 CHRIST'S SAKE, CHANGE YOUR VOICE. IT SOUNDS LIKE HELL!"[5] Millions, however, found their attention riveted to what the man had to say. Through the Depression-plagued final years of the thirties, the anxious time of World War II, and the postwar confrontation with communism, Maier spoke to, and probably for, a massive bloc of the American people. Following the pattern of religious programs generally, the Lutheran Hour had its most enthusiastic audience on farms and in small towns.[6] For these people and for others, as the mountains of fan mail and of mail seeking advice demonstrated, the Lutheran Hour was a habit.

"Bringing Christ to the Nation," the program's motto, was no empty or pious phrase for Maier. Theologically he was not a Fundamentalist as classically defined, but while he scathingly denounced modernism, he refrained from setting himself off explicitly from the Protestant right wing that supported him. Once requested by some of his seminary colleagues to present more of the whole of Lutheran theology, Maier replied that he was teaching people how to die in Christ, that others would have to teach them how to live, an explanation too facile by half.[7] Maier spoke about living in a running commentary on social ills; his choice of subject was predictable. With slashing invective he flayed at disrespect for the Bible, belief in evolution, corruption in high places, movie morality, the Social Gospel. His analysis of contemporary society was obviously what millions of people beyond the synod wanted to hear.[8]

Maier's personality was one of warm enthusiasm, infectious energy, and abundant ego. As an activist by temperament, he assumed that laymen were to follow. And they would best be employed following him. Moreover, Maier was convinced that he was engaged in the greatest work a man could do, the saving of souls. There could be no question, then, whether those who assisted him in this work were fulfilling the proper role for the laity. Assertive, ever ready to think on a bold scale, Maier was supremely impatient with any in the league hesitant to embrace his vision. His influence dominated the league at the same time that he stood slightly aloof from it.[9]

IV

The undeniable success of the Lutheran Hour meant that it quickly became the league's major project. In fact, Oscar Doerr, long the LLL secretary, recalled, "We had actually no other project."[10] Radio programming did advertise the league as little else could have; it opened some doors previously locked to the LLL.[11] But for a long time the LLL found itself in the position of the poor boy hired to water the circus elephants; it was the only way he could get past the gate, but there was not much extra time to see the rest of the show. League recruitment and local organization work, for example, suffered during the thirties simply for lack of staff time. As late as 1944, seven employees maintained the LLL offices while radio administration required fifty.[12] In 1938 the LLL league shifted its fiscal year to conform to that of the radio season and even encouraged local clubs to follow suit. At many meetings of league officials during the 1930s, Lutheran Hour business was the only significant item on the agenda.

The effects of this concentration on radio were strikingly illustrated in 1936. Lamenting the Depression mentality that had conquered many pastors, church leaders worked out a program to put John W. Behnken, recently elected synodical president, in touch with the laity through mass meetings and small conferences. To get names of laymen, the organizers went not to the LLL, but to pastors, though times had changed sufficiently that they were cautioned, "the clergy must be altogether inactive, even unrepresented."[13] Synodical leaders privately stated that the LLL had lost the momentum of its founding, was entirely absorbed in radio, and, more seriously, was in most cities not attracting the new generation of capable leadership.[14] One official explained to some pastors that the lay leaders of the early twenties had died off and the reason there were so few in the thirties was that *"Synod has not developed them."* He did not mention the LLL.[15]

Maier and the Lutheran Hour were as close to revivalism as the Missouri Synod got and in American Protestantism revivalism and laicism have commonly been associated; the revival's regional or ecumenical characteristics may free the layman of his local minister, and the charismatic gifts it esteems may visit a layman as well as the minister. There was an element of this for the LLL and the laity, to judge from the synodical folklore of underground opposition to the league and its project. In arranging a mass Lutheran Hour rally or gaining local publicity for the radio program, the layman might well be free of his pastor. Yet, free for what? Maier's dominance of the Lutheran Hour, synodical opposition to revivalistic measures, and Lutheran stress on the sacraments put severe limits on any laic side effects of radio revivalism.

Partly because of its preoccupation with radio, the LLL adapted itself very slowly to an increasingly well-educated laity. Just as the earlier LLL had been identified with wealthy laymen and fund raising, it was now associated with broadcasting and the simple *Gemuetlichkeit* of the men's club meeting. The tendency was reinforced as people with intellectual interests ignored the league because of its image. Though it had no substantive publication in the late thirties, the league did not become the sponsor of the *Cresset,* nor would it accept responsibility for the *American Lutheran,* the main unofficial monthlies privately published in the synod. In the forties, the LLL was again bypassed in the formation of the Lutheran Academy for Scholarship. Only after the LAS was well established did the league attempt special seminars for professional men.[16] Finally, largely for fear of offending contributors to the Lutheran Hour, the LLL deliberately withdrew from serving the laity as a forum for the serious discussion of theological issues raised in the prolonged controversy over synodical affiliation with other Lutheran bodies.[17] The way was open after World War II for Lutheran Men in America, the Federation of Lutheran Clubs, the Lutheran Men in America of

Wisconsin. Once again the league broadened its own program only under competition from these groups.[18]

Sponsorship of the Lutheran Hour thus prolonged the serious limitations obvious in the league's first years. The league's early answer to the perennial question of the laity's role had been to stress business methods. Now, in practice though not by conscious intent, the league's answer was that the role of the laity was to provide backing for radio programs. The role of the energetic layman was to contribute to network broadcasting and to persuade others to do so; to erect billboards, construct parade floats, and sponsor advertisements to call attention to the Hour; to help plan and participate in the mammoth rallies at which Maier spoke. Thus network broadcasting deafened the league to creative thought by contemporary Lutherans.

V

As the national economy improved in the late thirties and the early forties, the fortunes of the LLL, too, brightened. The coincidence was not entirely fortuitous, for laymen with some economic security could afford both financially and psychologically to involve themselves with other concerns. Further, a great many more men's clubs sprang up; by 1941 at least a thousand congregations had men's clubs outside the LLL.[19] Radio made attracting these clubs not only easier, but necessary, for the advent of foreign broadcasts in 1939–1940 (from which fan mail receipts were negligible) increased revenue needs of the LLL. In response the 1940 league convention adopted a dual campaign for both club affiliation and individual memberships. Voluntary contributions replaced mandatory club dues. The move was beneficial; in 1941 alone, 125 new clubs joined the league.[20]

Progress was also made in staff and program. The league added personnel to boost membership and administer the "seminar" series. This new program followed the precedents of the St. Louis LLL branch and of synodical officials in offering evening lectures about some aspect of the synod or about topics of current interest. The lecture was followed by questions and sometimes discussion, though the limitations of both format and participants were all too clear in the report of a program on business ethics: the questions "were presented by . . . Mr. Walter Schlueter, and answered by Dr. J.H.C. Fritz."[21] Obviously, the traditional clergy-lay relationship died hard. Nevertheless (or perhaps, therefore), the programs caught on especially in small towns and rural areas.

The release of great amounts of time and energy into areas of peacetime civilian life after 1945 showed up quickly in the league. Membership climbed from 19,000 in 1944 to 45,000 in 1947.[22] In 1947, too, the LLL issued its 1,000th club charter. Symbolizing this growth, annual conventions were held for the first time outside the Midwest. Growing size meant greater rewards in developing further organizational structure between synodical and congregational levels. Particularly after World War II, more districts were rapidly formed; 33 existed by 1947.[23] In some cases, clergy led the founding of such units.[24] However, initiative sometimes came from the field with sentiment of lay dissatisfaction reminiscent of the beginnings of the LLL itself thirty years earlier. An active layman from Tennessee wrote league officers, "Since I have been in the South I have seen so many instances where our Lutheran Church has literally missed the boat that the urge to do something about placing our Church on the map has grown stronger and stronger until I came to the conclusion that, if nobody else was going to take the initiative, perhaps I might make the attempt." Taking a group of laymen to the regional pastoral conference, "I persuaded the pastors that we laymen could be of some assistance to them in breaking down the inferiority complex that was the curse of our work here in East Tennessee. They were a bit skeptical at first. However, when we met in Wartburg this fall we had the largest gathering of laymen that was ever assembled in this area."[25]

Martin Daib summarized the condition of the Lutheran Laymen's League as a whole in 1946 when he mused, "Ten years ago it was difficult to interest our membership in the League. There was no enthusiasm. Formerly a District was organized and then people wondered what they would do next. Now the men in the District 'carry the Ball.' "[26]

VI

Thus the late forties were exuberant years for the league. Aided by American influence abroad after the victorious war and pressed by Maier's determination to use all possible stations in the world, Lutheran Hour translations were broadcast by 1950 in thirty-six languages in more than fifty countries and territories. At home the Lutheran Hour began making exploratory forays into the new field of television. Even all this, however, was not sufficient to engross the full attention and self-confidence of a rapidly growing league. In an expansive mood, the LLL experimented in three new areas: motion pictures, a proposed building at Valparaiso University, and a hospital in Mississippi.

Encouraged by the success of a synodically produced film, T. G. Eggers enthusiastically recommended that the league sponsor a film on juvenile delinquency. The league's production of this and three subsequent films was frequently simplistic, didactic, and amateurish. But with the return of peace in 1945, only a backward congregation failed to buy sound projector and screen.[27] Lutheran audiences as yet undistracted by television were willing to spend an evening in the church basement watching a movie they were told was wholesome entertainment.

In the midst of such productions, the league adopted a goal of $500,000 for an administration building at Valparaiso University.[28] And during this campaign three doctors offered to the LLL the hospital they owned and operated in Vicksburg, Mississippi. Walter A. Maier responded enthusiastically. Nearly thirty years before, he had revived Wheat Ridge Tuberculosis Sanitarium in Colorado and turned it into a highly successful enterprise for the Walther League. Now his leadership was seconded by that of a mercurial St. Louis layman, Homer Fitzpatrick, and the convention in 1949 passed a resolution in effect accepting the hospital on the spot. All parties expected financing to come from federal grants.[29] These three projects proved the resurgence within the

Lutheran Laymen's League. At least the last two, though, demonstrated that the LLL was still committed to the traditionalist side in the matter of the laity's role; the layman's job was to finance church work and the league was to help him do it, and in so doing, help itself.

The future, however, did not live up to the league's expectations in any of its projects during the postwar years. In the Lutheran Hour, increasing coverage raised foreign broadcasting costs from $12,000 in 1942 to more than $300,000 in 1950. But unsolicited fan mail contributions began to decline from a peak of $360,000 in the 1945–1946 season. The network ban against soliciting contributions on the air and perhaps greater American wariness, when combined with steady expansion of the Hour, meant deficits at the end of four out of five seasons between 1945 and 1950. These Maier ignored and when opportunity came to use the ABC network in addition to Mutual, he insisted upon this double broadcast. The program's economic position worsened ominously in the fall of 1949. Whether things would eventually have improved, no one can say, for in January 1950 Maier died of a heart attack.

Maier could hardly have had an understudy and the months following his death were difficult ones for the Lutheran Hour and for the league. Factions formed to support one or another candidate as Maier's successor; in the year following his death no less than fourteen speakers preached on the program.[30] Finally the league settled on Armin C. Oldsen, who served for two seasons. He was succeeded in 1955 by Oswald J. Hoffmann. Both of these men were quite different from Maier in personality and speaking style. In addition they entered an established program. As a result the relationship between the Hour's speaker, the league, and the laity were never the same. In the meantime, however, Maier's death encouraged a young revivalist preacher, Billy Graham, to consider a move into radio; in the fall of 1950, aided in part by some of Maier's followers, Graham launched his highly successful Hour of Decision.[31]

To complicate things further, many people felt that before long television would totally supplant radio. The LLL was well aware of these alarms. It wanted very much to man the lifeboat of TV just in case radio did sink, but the league had to move slowly for two reasons. First, it simply did not then possess large enough reserves necessary for TV programming.[32] Second, the synodical environment had changed. The Lutheran Hour began when the synod was deeply in debt, synodical headquarters badly under-manned, and the tradition still strong that new ventures should be left to independent groups. All this was no longer true by 1950, and the synod itself preempted the field of television with the sponsorship of the dramatic series, This Is the Life, which pre-miered in 1952. Temporarily at least, very nearly in spite of itself, the LLL escaped the function of becoming the broadcasting arm of the synod and was free—and forced—to look farther afield in exploring the full role of the laity.

In the meantime, though, television affected not only radio, but also the league's motion pictures. Faced by fierce competition, the LLL withdrew from this area. Similarly, when the lagging drive for Valparaiso did not pick up, it was suspended, and the league terminated the project in 1953 with the gift to the univer-sity of about one-half the original goal. The last of the three non-radio projects, the Vicksburg hospital, turned out to be a horrendous nightmare, for the failure to receive the anticipated federal grant revealed a wide discrepancy in the expectations of the Vicksburg doctors and those of the LLL. By 1953 the LLL found itself bearing a cross between a white elephant and an albatross, and decided to return the hospital to the doctors, who then set terms the LLL considered exorbitant. Not until 1954, five years to the day the LLL had assumed control, was the Vicksburg property returned. The venture had cost the league nearly a quarter of a million dollars.[33]

VII

It is testimony to the strength of the league that this series of reverses and disasters did not wreck the organization. In retro-spect the LLL seems hardly to have faltered. That it came through such trials so unscathed is partly due to the infusion of new blood. Between 1946 and 1951, E. J. Gallmeyer, Oscar Brauer, and Oscar Doerr retired as, respectively, president, treasurer, and secretary, after tenures as long as twenty years. Most notable of the new officers was Emil C. Jacobs, an insurance agent elected president in 1949, who applied himself assiduously to a renewed membership campaign, with gratifying results.

After 1950, too, the LLL finally effected important changes in staff. Within a few years, by retirement, resignation, and additions to the staff, a different group of men served the league full time. Most significantly, the Board of Governors established the office of executive director. No administrator sufficiently strong for the job would have tolerated the autonomy Maier assumed, but after Maier's death the way was open, though there was discussion whether the incumbent should be clergy or lay. The board turned first to a pastor, but when he declined, in 1951 it chose a layman, Paul Friedrich.[34] Friedrich was the son of one well-known clergyman in the synod and brother of another. A graduate of the University of Wisconsin rather than the synod's system, Friedrich taught in private schools until he became executive secretary of the Cranbrook institutions, affiliated with the Cranbrook Foundation. By all accounts one of Friedrich's chief strengths lay in a fine grasp of administration. He managed to be tough-minded without being cynical and set about a rationalization of the league household. Gradually the whole LLL program, including the Lutheran Hour, was centralized and coordinated as it had never been before. This was none too soon in an organization with a budget that reached two million dollars in 1959 and three million in 1966. One observer noted critically that the chart of authority in the LLL strongly resembled the bureaucratic plan of Standard Oil of New Jersey.[35] He was correct in recognizing a managerial revolution; in fact, had he known, he might have mentioned Remington-Rand filing assistance, professional survey service, administrative consultants, and high speed mailing and accounting machines. The much more serious question is whether a large, efficiently structured religious organization is more likely than a small, informally administered group to mistake means for ends, to idolize growth per se, and to succumb to empire building. To this the league gives conflicting answers.

The construction of a commodious and well-equipped headquarters building in St. Louis both facilitated and measured the drive toward centralizing and strengthening the LLL structure; there in 1959 the league gathered all its offices under one roof for the first time. The new quarters housed personnel more numerous and more specialized than ever before. For example, a new professionalism drastically revamped the *Lutheran Layman*. At first not much more than a house organ, it gradually moved to fill the vacuum in the synod created by the drab and dull *Lutheran Witness* of the 1950s.

A highly popular publication and increased staff did a better job of catching the attention of laymen ready to join a men's organization, and the result was astonishing growth. In the decade after 1953 league membership doubled from 69,000 to 140,000. Such expansion was still another mandate for much attention to league structure. Staff members discovered that district presidents were often ill-informed about their own territories.[36] There was in addition a problem in adequate communication. As one local pastor observed, league headquarters seemed to have a revitalizing spark, "but by the time it gets down here, it's a dartball league."[37]

To correct these deficiencies, the staff spent much time fostering the organization of zones, units between club and district.[38] New staff members organized new departments to supply ideas and guidance to the grassroots. They developed a variety of mimeographed publications to educate and enthuse officers at various levels and, beginning in 1955, initiated annual conferences of district officials. Naturally not all of this was uniformly successful.[39] As one staff member admitted after surveying district conventions, some are excellent, some are poor, and "some should not even be held."[40] But there is no doubt that on the grassroots and regional level, these efforts strengthened the league.

On the national level, officers and staff devoted considerable attention to the annual conventions, whose chief function remained engendering enthusiasm rather than the exercise of authority. Since most power rested in the LLL Board of Governors, and the convention was open to any member, the chief duties of the convention-goers were to elect new officers from a previously prepared slate and, more rarely, to vote on major policy decisions. Probably the most accurate description of the league's aim at the conventions appeared in a *Layman* headline on the coming events: "Good Balance of Education, Inspiration, Fun Promised."[41]

The results of all these efforts furthered a long standing claim of the LLL. However poor its record in the thirties, the league did play a role in shaping synodical lay leadership. It provided laymen with experience and training in volunteer church organizations, in the process drawing the susceptible into deeper involvement in church work. Probably much more important, the LLL provided a route of upward mobility that was an alternative to the official ecclesiastical organization. Few Lutheran men looked in their shaving mirrors to announce they were going to be active in the LLL in order to sit on the synod's Board of Directors. But high office in the LLL did provide the national visibility that was necessary before any one layman would be sufficiently known in the synod to be a realistic nomination for election to lay seats on national or even district boards. This explains the frequency with which LLL presidents and staff members were elected to the synod's Board of Directors.

VIII

By the late fifties, then, the league had had an eventful life. Like many a child prodigy, the LLL had difficulty sustaining its reputation as it grew older in the 1920s. After a youth somewhat stunted in the 1930s by a job too demanding for its age and strength, the league blossomed into a more exuberant adolescence in the 1940s. Maturity schooled by reverses came in the fifties. In organization, bureaucracy, and budget, the league was healthier than ever before. But what was its power for? There was no avoiding the old question: given a laity prepared to be active, what was its activity to be?

Radio continued to be a central thrust of the league. Foreign broadcasting expanded until by the late fifties a professional survey gave the Hour a place tied with Radio France, behind only Voice of America, Radio Moscow, and the BBC.[42] However, competition and a more critical appraisal by staff and laymen no longer in Maier's shadow led to revisions in both domestic and foreign broadcasting. Earlier preoccupation with the sheer number of stations diminished. Sponsors of the Lutheran Hour were chagrined to discover that broadcasts in England did not delete Americanisms, that programs for India were beamed from Portuguese-held Goa, that sermons read over the air to Guatemalean peasants were translations of material prepared for the American middle class. In domestic programming, new staff raised artistic, especially musical, standards. The LLL stayed within the realm of public information media with the inauguration in 1961 of a series of advertisements in various combinations of newspapers and national magazines, a project that owed a good deal to the Knights of Columbus.

Whatever their value to the church, these efforts represented no new solution to the dilemma of the layman's proper role. What is noteworthy is not that the league began the advertisement series, but that it refused to adopt a whole new complex of similar national projects. Of course the league had been burned by such proliferation in the late forties, but a decade later the LLL was vastly stronger. The restraint of the fifties reflects a much greater readiness on the part at first of staff and then of officers to grapple with difficult questions on lay roles. Paul Friedrich indicated future developments when he insisted in 1956 that the primary purpose of the LLL was to interest the laity in the church, "and to galvanize them into active participation in it."[43] Granted the maturation of the league in other respects, such a statement was a harbinger of a new era in the history of the league and of the laity.

Part Four

Throughout the twentieth century the Missouri Synod has been shaped by events and forces of secular society much more than it has usually cared to admit. This influence increased inevitably as the great drama of Americanization drew to a close. The postwar last act of that drama was avant-garde theater. There was no final curtain and thus little applause. Instead, ad-libbing, the actors edged off the stage into the audience and, removing their makeup as they went, disappeared into the crowd. Only a few reviewers stayed to watch stagehands slowly remove furniture from the period-piece set. Thus the church was progressively more susceptible to the American ambience. The synod was progressively a more sensitive gauge for changes in what became a steadily more volatile American atmosphere.

However blurred the sequence in Lutheran rhetoric and reality concerning the laity, the years between 1945 and 1970 acquire form by three periods. The first, in the years immediately after the war, was characterized by acute awareness of the potential in using the laity for a great deal of church work previously done by the clergy. Separating this from what emerged in the sixties was a different stance toward the world, that is, a different definition of the locus of lay activity. In their intensity and creativity, the discussion and experiments of the early sixties were easily the most promising and creative for the laity since the nineteenth century. In the late sixties, however, an acrimonious internecine struggle gradually choked off or at least slowed such developments. Debate over hermeneutics and ecumenism came to dominate attention and energy in the synod. The following chapters take up in turn these three periods.

10

Using the Laity

In dramatic contrast to the era of World War I, during World War II the synod and its constituency were relatively untroubled by superpatriots. This was partly because the Lutherans were less German. Writing on the eve of the war, O. P. Kretzmann observed, "in many cases, particularly in urban communities, the process [of assimilation] has already ended. In all the influences which must be grouped under the indefinable concept of culture—language, art, music, education, amusement, recreation, political and social thinking—we are no longer what we were."[1]

Indices supporting this judgment are worth review not simply to demonstrate relentless Americanization, but because they help delineate new characteristics of the laity and its life. The most obvious criterion of assimilation is language. The *Lutheran Witness* passed *Der Lutheraner* in circulation during the twenties, and the German paper fell rapidly in readership during the 1930s. Similarly the graph of language used in worship services, which serves as a rough indicator of relative attendance, shows a widely opened scissors pattern centered on 1925.[2] The proportion reversed rapidly thereafter so that by 1940 the synodical ratio of English to German was about three to one. The English and Southern districts by then used English almost exclusively, though a district such as South Wisconsin had barely gotten past a 1:1 ratio.

157

Actuarial tables predicted much of the shift. Immigrants who had arrived in 1890 while in their twenties had aged to their sixties by 1930. But the transition was more complex than simply attrition of the older generation. Changes came most rapidly at the periphery of the synod in younger, smaller congregations outside the Midwest. Well established urban congregations had to institute English services to hold the younger generation, but maintained German for the old and the scattering of recent immigrants. Often strong rural congregations in long-established midwestern ethnic islands changed the slowest, though weakened demographically by the exodus to the city and psychologically by the advent of radio.[3] By the fifties and sixties a German service was a rarity almost everywhere in the synod, and only occasionally did speakers dare phrase a punch line or proverb in German and then hastily translate it for most of the laymen and many pastors in the audience.[4]

Somewhat more subtle indices show the same course. After 1945 the Lutheran birth rate, which had dropped precipitously during the Depression, followed the ascending curve of the postwar baby boom. Lutheran families suffered the same strains noticed outside the synod and observers commented on the rapid rise in the divorce rate.[5] Missouri Synod Lutherans married outside their church in comparatively large numbers. "The people with whom they associate and among whom they find their friends and future husbands and wives are no longer the neighbors known by all, but strangers whose family backgrounds, character, and ideas are not known to the folks at home," remarked Alfred Rehwinkel in 1948.[6] Warnings against intermarriage especially with Roman Catholics (exogamy known in church vocabulary as "mixed marriage"), long a staple in Lutheran publications, increased substantially, a reflection not of rising anti-Catholicism, but of changing lay practice.[7] When in 1935 the highly urbanized Northern Illinois District suggested a committee to study this and recommend action, it got nowhere. In 1947, however, when pastors from southern California asked for help on marriage and the family ("the lax thinking and practice of the world has made definite inroads into the attitudes and actions of our people''), the convention agreed to what became known as the Family Life Committee, which sought to clarify appropriate attitudes and to aid pastors counseling the laity.[8] The synod also attempted to foster family life with *This Day,* a monthly publication supposedly designed for the whole family. Such a magazine had long been discussed as a means of doing for the laity what the popular German-American journal, the *Abendschule,* had earlier done for the immigrant community.[9] But by the 1950s it was much too late for that; the postwar suburban Lutheran family was too sophisticated, too atomized, and too much involved in the world. The split-level ranch home was too far from the narrow brick flats of south St. Louis or Chicago or Milwaukee, as the eventual demise of *This Day* indicated.[10]

From its founding the synod had had to cope with a mobile laity, a problem not solved by Americanization. Wartime dislocations created a particular challenge, with little respite thereafter. Though the *Witness* typically continued well into the fifties to use pictorial illustrations mainly of rural subjects, this was increasingly an anachronism, for the proportion of congregations in places of below 2,500 population sank from nearly 60 percent in 1947 to below 40 percent by the late sixties. By then only 23 percent of the laity belonged to a parish outside of some kind of urban setting.[11] Between 1940 and 1960 suburban communicant membership jumped 152 percent while rural congregations suffered a small net loss.[12] In 1961 what was termed a reasonably stable urban congregation in Chicago reported only 170 of its 600 communicant members in 1935 still there. In the meantime some 400 members had died. Nearly 1,000 had transferred.[13] When, in a renewed bid to keep track of those who moved, the synodical headquarters began using change-of-address notices to the *Witness,* it discovered that about a third of the laity who moved were destined for the Southwest.[14]

In other words the synod's constituency, like the American population, migrated from country to city, from city core to suburbs, from Midwest to the coasts. Each of these trends presented problems because the synod was not traditionally strong in any of these three destinations. The synod thus had perforce to invest large amounts of all types of resources to provide new facilities for the laity who moved and at the same time look out for the congregations weakened by their leaving. City congregations that saw their memberships moving away did as they had since the nineteenth century; they relocated further out in the suburbs. Few protested what one critic termed such "flight from the blighted" until well into the fifties when forward-looking leaders placed more stress on the need for maintaining church structures in downtown areas, serving whoever moved in.[15] The rural church threatened by mobility was in a more difficult position because possibilities for developing a new constituency often seemed remote. Between 1940 and 1960 nearly 600 congregations outside metropolitan areas closed.[16] Particularly in the plains states, long pastoral vacancies and rapid turnover in clergy added to parish woes. Special pleas and programs were not of much avail against the steady shrinkage in farm population; consolidation of congregations seemed the only answer, no matter how unacceptable.[17]

Language changes, shifts in social behavior, and mobility were trends of long standing that made Lutheran laymen increasingly difficult to distinguish from their neighbors. But in the period after World War II, another important development shouldered its way forward. The synod made a transition in missionary orientation from German-Americans to Americans in general just in time to face the great postwar revival of American interest in religion, and the synod's growth rate was soon the highest of the major American denominations. The number of adults baptized or confirmed—clearly growth from outside—jumped exponentially by decade: 85,000 in the thirties, 165,000 in the forties, 300,000 in the fifties.[18] By 1970 adult converts in the preceding two decades equalled one-third of the synod's communicant membership.[19] As he liked to do at periodic intervals for their exotic sounds, Theodore Graebner in the *Witness* read off the roll call of one 1947 adult confirmation class: "Bronson, Collins, Donahue, Eastman, Fullington, Krympotic, Leapley, Mann, Nichols, Thompson, Isard. And the pastor's name," the editor added, "is Burroughs."[20]

These people were newcomers in an immigrant church. For them the synod had no past; everything was present. Church was not an ornate white and gilded chancel downtown, but a natural-oak cross on an A-shaped wall behind the slab altar. *Reise-prediger* was only a foreign word, and their pastor's name was not Pfotenhauer or Fuerbringer, but Burroughs. They associated a guttural accent with DP's and refugees, not immigrants and steerage. A verse of a German hymn conjured up not an old grandmother, but a language professor in a college classroom, or perhaps no image whatever. There had always been a men's club in the congregation and the Sunday school needed more room. This was something different from the break between genera-tions, for these new members brought with them expectations partly shaped by childhoods in a dozen different denominations or in none at all. They brought with them habits of living and patterns of thought completely untempered by the immigrant Lutheran community.

Did these newcomers by their very diversity foster a growing openness to the world? Or did the synod's dogmatic conser-vatism, otherworldly emphasis, and resistance to change attract those for whom these traits filled particular needs? No one studied these questions systematically.[21] All one may say is that the laity was already changing in the course of an immigrant denomination's evolution, but the postwar expansion vastly speeded and complicated that change.

"We are no longer what we were." Before long, sociologists documented how far the laity had moved away from the expecta-tions of the immigrant parish. By the end of the fifties, Stark and Glock, studying Protestant laity in northern California, found Missouri Synod Lutherans *less* likely than the Protestant average to have as their best friends people who belonged to the same congregation.[22] Responding to such loss of community, congrega-tions continued to employ a variety of tactics. One California church scheduled a "Get Acquainted Month" in 1949. Only *he* knew everyone in the congregation, observed the pastor, appar-ently thinking it worth reporting.[23] This breakup of the ethnic religious community, which, as we have seen, so damaged traditional clergy status and roles, also helped to offset the effects of that damage. Greater heterogeneity in the congregation meant that the pastor, regardless of his theological position, played an increasingly important part as broker, as intermediary, as personification of the congregation.

II

The influx of adult converts is an important key to explain the rise of adult education in the postwar years. The need for further indoctrination seemed more pressing for people who entered the Lutheran church as adults than for those who had grown up in the synod.[24] At the same time, many of the new members did not have the aversion of the lifelong Missourian to Bible classes; some even had experience with adult study in another denomination.[25] In 1946, Oscar E. Feucht became the church's first full-time executive assigned to adult education. As a young pastor, he had drawn from the experience of other American denominations in establishing Bible classes in the various congregations he served and became something of an authority among Lutherans on adult education.[26] The most immediate felt need when Feucht took synodical office was for more formal Bible study. *Christenlehre* had been abandoned but not replaced. The *American Lutheran* and the Walther League championed the Bible class in the twenties, but by the early 1940s only about 5 percent of the communicant membership attended Bible classes.[27] Feucht and others agitated energetically for more attention to the subject, and gradually the synodical apparatus responded. By dint of great effort, Bible class enrollment climbed from about 65,000 to more than 200,000 in the decade ending in 1956.[28]

In the process, adult education slowly evolved into more than *Christenlehre* in English. As laity became better educated and clergy less defensive, more often laymen, not the pastor, taught classes.[29] Yet most laymen still regarded confirmation as graduation and believed that "education is for kids."[30] After two decades of hard work, only about 17 percent of the communicant membership enrolled in religious education classes. The typical layman knew the cardinal points by heart, or he once did, and that was enough for him. He might not have a terribly good idea of what all was in the Bible, but he was pretty well convinced it was true.[31]

Leaders in lay education, however, could be numbered among those beginning to see the laity in a different perspective. Already in 1951 Feucht emphasized that the church should "not look upon its members merely as a *field* to be served (at birth, Baptism, confirmation, marriage, sickness, and death), but as a *force* to be trained." Ahead of his time here, Feucht spoke of training the laity to be "instruments by which the Christ in them still carries on His mission in the world today."[32]

III

"When historians write the history of the Lutheran Church in the 20th century," observed William Hillmer in 1956, "they will surely say that the decade of 1945 to 1955 witnessed an increased emphasis on the use of lay people in Kingdom work."[33] And he was correct, for especially in aspects of mission work the laity was used as never before.

By 1946 both laymen and pastors were ready for large-scale lay participation in missionary endeavors. The laymen's religion was in English and they lived scattered about the city rather than in German enclaves. Synodical leaders had the Call of the Cross experience and precedents from the late thirties. What some had been urging since the late 1920s now became a reality; the synod, like other American denominations, launched major evangelistic campaigns.[34] Although they differed in many details, all these drives shared one essential characteristic: heavy dependence upon the laity. Besides the routine clerical work, laymen were variously delegated to canvass neighborhoods, to call on prospects, to invite or bring them to church, to stay in contact with those who indicated interest.

In the postwar years, the Lutheran press gave a great deal of attention to such lay participation. Some of this fostered old misconceptions, as when in 1950 the *American Lutheran* began a regular column, touted as written by a layman for laymen but whose purview was limited usually to matters of organization and finance.[35] Most public statements, however, repeatedly admonished pastors to involve laymen even if with temporary loss of efficiency, handing over to them especially the routine administrative work of the parish.[36] Changing clergy-laity ratios presented additional incentive. In 1940 there was one parish pastor for every 276 communicants; by 1960 the ratio was 1 to 357 and by the end of the sixties it was nearly 1 to 400. The average size of congregations also grew. In 1930 probably half of the Lutheran congregations had fewer than 100 communicants; by 1945 this dropped to 35 percent and by the late sixties to 20 percent.[37]

The involvement of the laity was valuable both for the church and for the laymen who participated. Some laymen, it is true, still clung stubbornly to old polarities; let the "pastors tend to the shepherding of the flock and [allow] laymen to run the business end of the congregation."[38] But thousands of laymen, after initial hesitation, found themselves articulating their faith in public for the first time. The emphasis on evangelism helped rescue at least some church organizations from futility. Other results were slowly evident on both parish and synodical level. Already in 1948 seminary students doing field work reported many previously open duties filled by laymen.[39] Beginning in 1954 synodical headquarters shipped some literature directly to local lay committee chairmen instead of funneling it through the pastor.[40] Larger congregations increased the number of elders and assigned each to a specific area, making him responsible for maintaining congregational contact with members in his area. About the midfifties the so-called cottage meeting was introduced; these were informal gatherings in homes, used at first mostly for business and instructional purposes.[41]

The church also gave more consideration to full-time lay positions in the church. Laymen were better educated than ever before; they had more leisure time and were retiring comfortably at an earlier age. As the 1950s began, the synod established a Committee on Enlisting and Training the Laity. As the decade closed, the synod was studying proposals for an institution to prepare full-time lay parish workers. The school, established at Milwaukee in 1961, graduated its first class of twenty in 1963.[42] In the meantime some laymen on their own initiative volunteered for a regular period of work at the local church office or found places as full-time business managers or administrators of large congregations. A few retired people went abroad in these capacities.[43] In foreign fields the Walther League took the lead in sponsoring young volunteers to do construction work for a new mission area in New Guinea. By 1964 more than half the people the synod sent that year into foreign mission fields were laymen.[44]

IV

Small wonder that when O. A. Geiseman looked about in the synod during the mid-fifties, he wrote, "anyone who has been in the ministry during the past thirty or forty years must these days pinch himself occasionally to awaken to the fact that the things now happening in the work of the Church are real and not a mirage."[45] After the long, parched journey through the decades of lay idleness or partial employment in congregational work, the period of the late forties and fifties was indeed a pleasant oasis. But it was only an oasis, not the promised land. A clue to the real state of affairs was the entry under "laity" in the 1954 *Lutheran Cyclopedia,* which simply copied verbatim the entry from the *Concordia Cyclopedia* of 1927, with its emphasis on Luther's priesthood of all believers over against Roman Catholic sacerdotalism. Apparently not enough had changed as yet to make expressions of the twenties out of date.

Hillmer reflected the prevailing view of the mid-fifties in his choice of words when he spoke of "the use of lay people." Few Lutherans yet saw the crucial difference between the concepts of using the laity for church work and of preparing laymen to do their work. The publicity for the various lay-worker training programs held up for emulation a clericalized layman, someone in the full-time employ of the church—a layman only in the sense of not being ordained. The typical progression of thought still began with the clergy: "Because the harvest is so great and the day is far spent, our professional missionaries need all the assistance the Church can give them. Hence they must rely in even greater measure on its laity." One essayist illustrated more than he intended when he compared the laity and pastor to factory employees and foreman. The whole rationale was summarized inelegantly but concisely in the title of an article for the clergy, "You Can't Do It All Yourself."[46]

In this atmosphere spokesmen recognized no incongruity in following a discussion of the priesthood of all believers with advice that pastors hand over the routine and mechanical to the laity.[47] Especially the early evangelism campaigns emphasized having the people bring prospects to the minister, who would do and say the right thing. The early programs for full-time lay workers were no more revolutionary. A paid lay worker was simply more efficient in freeing the pastor than, say, occasional volunteer lay canvassing. Using laymen in some capacity was better than ignoring them, and efficiency was preferable to waste, but this was not an innovative approach to the laity. Lutherans eliminated questions about the laity by eliminating the laity. Laymen were made amateur clergy.

Recognition of clerical limitations promoted emphasis on lay participation, but not a resurvey of the locus of lay activity. Essays and manuals of the late forties and early fifties took for granted that the layman did his church work in church. To be a "worker in God's Kingdom" meant to be involved in congregational activities. Missourians did not deny the doctrine that a Christian serves God in his secular vocation, but they treated it in such a cursory and casual fashion as in effect to remove it from the church's concerns about the laity.[48] Most churchmen still operated with an image of the world inherited from early in the century. They regarded vocations, secular clubs, labor unions, and political parties as competitors for lay time rather than as fields for lay ministry.[49]

In sum, here was no basic motive for a serious reappraisal of the pattern of lay activities developed in the preceding decades. What criticism there was generally objected that existing church societies and activities tended to be self-centered or concentrated on secondary ends—an unrecognized confirmation of the charges made by church leaders resisting lay movements early in the century. But by the postwar years the basic system was accepted. Conscientious pastors and laymen who followed the dictum, "in the Kingdom [the congregation] there is a task for every member and a member for every task" found themselves in a quandary.[50] To keep laymen active in church work, jobs had to be found or created; to fill these positions workers had to be cajoled or coerced. There was no dearth of advice given harassed pastors for the achievement of these goals. It ranged from instruction in calculated recruitment and retention ploys (tell the layman that Christ requests this service, commend the worker in front of his friends, organize an appreciation dinner) to suggestions toward rationalizing the whole system.[51] Chief expression of the latter was *Parish Activities,* an annual manual begun in 1947 that suggested a theme for the year, a different emphasis each month, and advised how various study and social groups in the congregation could tie in their activities.

If many congregations found the full package overly ambitious, at least the idea behind *Parish Activities* was a necessity by the postwar years. A survey form of the late forties listed thirty-seven possible groups, societies, and committees often found in the congregations, and a model constitution of 1960 suggested no less than nine standing committees in addition to the usual officers.[52] In this proliferation, the voters' assembly, usually the center of authority, steadily lost standing. Long plagued by poor attendance at meetings, congregations began dropping monthly sessions in the 1950s, leaving business direction up to a small church council, with perhaps an annual open information meeting.[53]

Social activities, however, did not seem to slacken in most parishes during the postwar years. Progressive congregations even organized a new group, the married couples club, a natural addition in years of early marriage and national emphasis on keeping the family together. By the mid-fifties about a thousand congregations, a fifth of the synod's total, boasted such a society, and by the end of the decade this had grown to 1,800.[54] There was a good deal of lay resistance to the parish activism, some of it good-natured rebellion, as when a club in St. Louis scheduled a meeting designated "Stay-At-Home-With-Your-Family-Night."[55] Stark and Glock discovered a less accepting attitude toward the system in northern California; slightly more than half of the Missourian laity in their survey did not in the average week attend any evening meetings at their church. Yet the same survey showed it was possible to get more than a third of the laity out at least once a week.[56] That was enough to maintain and perhaps even expand the pattern of parish life taken for granted by most clergy and likely even by those laity who did not participate in it.

Critics both in and out of the church were to fiercely assail this pattern, of course. It is hard, though, to find in the synod much prescience of this attack. The prevailing norms of parish life troubled many pastors and laymen; yet their cautions spoke against sheer busyness in lay church activity. Actually a complete rethinking of the layman's place was necessary. The formulation of parish life, begun in earnest about the time of World War I, had been carried nearly as far as it could be. But, as is usually the case, that is far clearer by hindsight than at the time.

V

In a number of ways the eras after the two world wars were similar for the synod and its laity. Fund-raising drives and bureaucratic expansion show a parallel sequence. There was a great burst of construction, though the steeply pitched A-frame replaced the Gothic arch. Parish activity expanded considerably in both periods. There were roughly comparable stirrings in associational impulses. If some new organizations, such as the Federation of Lutheran Clubs, Lutheran Bar Association, and Lutheran Collegiate Association, did not especially prosper, this was in part because of other groups already in existence.[57]

But there are significant differences between the two periods, and one of the most important is that a depression did not follow the forties and fifties. Instead, forces that had been gathering much strength below the surface could emerge in the congenial atmosphere of prosperity.

11

Both Feet in the World

I

In retrospect, what occurred in the sixties is remarkable mostly in that it was delayed so long. Surely one could not have expected the synod to have gone on infinitely without progressive forces which were produced by Americanization at some point thrusting their way through Missourian conservatism. In the early sixties that point arrived. Phenomena that had long received little notice finally meshed. The pace of change accelerated spectacularly. In the ensuing ferment Lutherans reexamined the laity and its place in church and world. This review probably could not have taken place without the evolution of the forties and fifties, but once it occurred it irrevocably divided the sixties from the period immediately after the war.

The shape of things to come was concealed during most of the forties and fifties by the deterioration in official synodical journalism. Lutheran spokesmen by then faced the unhappy alternatives of endorsing new attitudes and facing the obloquy of outraged diehards or insisting upon traditional opinions and observing the indifference of the laity. Most chose to say nothing. Rewards for the discipline of creative thought were precious few, the ignominy and irresponsibility of silence hardly perceived. Instead of erecting new bulwarks to replace overrun positions, churchmen fled the field entirely. The *Lutheran Witness* led the rout, for by the fifties it was a bland publication, doggedly conventional, largely incidental to the life and work of most laymen.

In his concern to avoid the ephemeral in religious journalism, editor Lorenz Blankenbuehler also managed to avoid looking at most of what was going on in the church and the world.

Thus the synod entered the final stage of capitulation to what Martin Marty describes as "controlled secularity." American institutional religion, he says, "acquiesced in the assignment to address itself to the personal, familial and leisured sectors of life while the public dimensions—political, social, economic, cultural—were to become autonomous or to pass under the control of other kinds of tutelage."[1] In some ways synonymous with Americanization, the capitulation had been underway for a long time in the synod. For all their wrong-headedness and dogmatism, nineteenth-century pastors had continually reminded the laity in very specific terms that one's religious commitments should inform daily decisions. In the course of assimilation, however, most of the clergy and practically all of the laity, unwilling to continue the clergy-lay styles of the nineteenth century, failed to develop an approach to formulating Christian answers to contemporary dilemmas more suited to a maturing laity and a less omniscient clergy. Perhaps what Theodore Graebner once referred to as Missouri's "burden of infallibility" played a role here. The emphasis on pure doctrine and on a Bible inerrant in all matters molded a cast of mind in which "truth" once articulated could no longer be debated. To admit in public that past pronouncements were mistaken pointed to the possibility that present statements might be. The only way out of the dilemma was silence.[2]

Most churchmen seem to have been quite unaware of what was going on, that, in Marty's phrase, the church was being boxed in. The exceptions, as noted in chapter seven, were men involved with the Associated Lutheran Charities and with the *Cresset*. The *Cresset*'s maturation quickened in 1951 when Valparaiso University assumed sponsorship of the magazine and John Strietelmeier, a Valparaiso graduate and faculty member there, became managing editor. With Strietelmeier writing the editorials, the journal gained a consistency of outlook and judgment it had earlier lacked. Urbane, reasoned, phrased in fine-honed prose, Strietelmeier's comment on the current scene made *Cresset* editorials the best opinion journalism to appear in the synod.

Aside from its editorials, the most intriguing sign in the *Cresset* of a more educated and sophisticated element in the church was "Letter from Xanadu," one of the few Missourian excursions into satire in this era. The column was purportedly written by a middle-aged, small-town businessman in Nebraska who commented upon life in his local parish and occasionally in the church generally from the viewpoint of a dauntless ecclesiastical Babbitt. A sometimes shaky pillar of his congregation, the man in Xanadu was proud he had retained the religion of his childhood without change, was ready to make any sacrifice for his church as long as it was not too great, and was open to all contemporary thought as long as it did not affect the status quo. He was, in other words, a layman who had come of age in the church during the twenties and had learned all the lessons of that era, but understood few of them.

The *Cresset* spoke to and for a constituency mainly in higher education. The pioneering concerns of this same constituency were also expressed in Valparaiso University and the Lutheran Academy for Scholarship. The university's sponsorship of the *Cresset* was but one instance of the shelter offered by the school to a variety of agencies bridging church and world, consistent with President O. P. Kretzmann's publicly stated regret over traditional protectionist appeals to students.[3] The school was not really in a position to move forcefully toward more positive goals until the fifties, when spiraling enrollments and also summer conferences on a wide variety of topics enlarged its impact.

II

Such enterprises bespeak the continued, if quiet, rise in educational levels among laity as well as clergy. Intellectually as well as socially these people were in the world, a tumultuous place indeed by the late fifties and early sixties. In secular life a newly sensitized social conscience, and in the church the ecumenical movement, the Vatican II *aggiornamento,* and radical Protestant

proposals for renewal aroused in the synod a sympathetic response that comparable developments in earlier decades had not.

The most obvious break in existing patterns came after 1960
when Martin W. Mueller and a staff including lay professional
journalists expanded and remodeled the *Lutheran Witness*. The
results should be reviewed as indicative of a more general acceptance of changed views toward the world, as an example of what
the church paper offered the laity, and as background for subsequent reaction. Topics opened for serious and thoughtful consideration in the remodeled *Witness* (race, urban renewal, poverty, extreme anti-communism, hunger, war) could be predicted by
the sequence of topics in the secular press, and deliberately so.
The *Witness* began regular reviews of books in fields other than
religion and, finally like the *Cresset* in the thirties, devoted space
to motion pictures. From pastoral romanticism and middle-class
rectitude, photographic illustrations turned to the hurly-burly,
even seaminess, of urban life; contemporary religious art replaced a good share of prettified depictions.

In all of this the *Witness* presented a double thrust. First and
most obviously, it kept insisting that the church had to speak
specifically and vigorously on secular concerns. "There is an
established opinion abroad in the land," admitted a *Witness* article, "that once an issue becomes involved in politics, the church
should keep its mouth shut." This, however, is incorrect, said the
writer. "Silence doesn't mean neutrality; it means endorsing the
status quo." Furthermore, "issues become involved in politics
only when they become important to people. If the church discusses issues only when they are academic and shuts up when
they are 'controversial,' it commits . . . the sin of being irrelevant."[4]

But a second aspect of the *Witness*'s view of the world was
equally important. A church that expected to speak to the world
also had to listen to it. The *Witness* was ready to do so in its book
and film reviews and in other areas as well. For example, when it
concentrated on business ethics, the *Witness* featured articles not
by clergy but by laymen in the business world.[5] Such openness to
the world both reflected and furthered an unaccustomed modesty

in the expression of the *Witness*'s views. Editorials stressed the difficulty of arriving at ethical judgments at the same time they insisted upon the necessity of doing so.[6] A long-popular question and answer feature, entitled "What's the Answer?," was changed to "Ask the Witness," and the editor added a footnote reminding readers "that there are numerous issues in our contemporary world to which the Word of God is inescapably related but to which simple yes and no answers cannot always be given."[7] The plea of one article's title caught the essence of the new approach: "Quit Hardening the Categories, for God's Sake."[8]

One official organ does not a synod make—or remake. But the radically altered *Witness* was only one (albeit the most important for the laity) of a growing number of Missouri spokesmen sounding this theme. In addition to the *Cresset,* the Lutheran Academy for Scholarship, which sponsored in 1951 its first topical conference (on the question, "what contributions can the Lutheran church make to the culture of the twentieth century?"), devoted its augmented resources to fairly open-minded colloquia on a variety of topics ranging from medical ethics to business practices to visual arts.[9] These sessions showed how far the synod had come since the 1947 LLL seminar in which a layman presented the questions and a theology professor neatly disposed of them.[10] This was in sum not a meeting of professional and layman, but rather of two specialists pooling their knowledge and insights. New editors at Concordia Publishing House also worked with a more affirmative attitude toward the world when they began the CPH "Christian Encounter" series, short paperback books that sought to provide a Christian perspective on topics such as hunger, pop music, urbanization, and obscenity. Still a step further, one pastor suggested that instead of working desperately to get Lutheran material into the homes of the laity, educators should use secular literature already on Lutheran coffee tables.[11] The synod's Board of Parish Education adopted such an approach in adult study guides by the late sixties. Finally, one of the most obvious signs of changed attitudes toward the world was the willingness of synodical conventions to pass resolutions on controversial social issues. In 1962 the delegates authorized a synodical Commission on Social Action to draft guidelines and position papers.[12]

The broadening of a favorable response in the synod to the world was one aspect of changes in the sixties. Less dramatic but equally significant was that some theologians finally began to construct what had previously been lacking, a theological rationale for dealing with the world and its concerns in a positive manner. Martin L. Kretzmann articulated a major initiative in a synodically commissioned report on structuring the church for missions, presented to the 1965 convention. "We must understand again from Scripture that the world is God's creation and is under His providential care," wrote Kretzmann. "Man has been placed in the world as the agent of God to carry out God's purposes in the continuing work of creation and preservation." God "has not confined Himself to the limits of the church," and Christ ministered to man's "body, soul, and mind at one and the same time." The church therefore can do no less; it must deal with the whole society and the whole man. Society and government are "already the scene of His activity. We must look for and joyfully recognize the activities which men carry out as His agents and cooperate with them." Such activities as social welfare, medical work, education, "and all efforts to help man realize his potentialities to serve God and man as full human beings . . . are as much concern of the church . . . as the salvation of man's soul."[13]

III

Aside from the obvious but important point that this is what Lutheran laymen were now exposed to in their church life, the different posture toward the world was instrumental in, first, increasing receptivity within the synod to Christian developments outside Lutheranism concerning the laity. Second, an altered attitude toward the world helped to shape ideas about the layman's role in both church and world. Finally, a willingness to listen to the world was part of change in the synod that drew intense hostility from certain laymen and clergy, to be taken up in the next chapter.

A restudy of the laity was part of the ecumenical movement already in the late 1930's. By 1954 the World Council of Churches included an active department devoted to the laity. A bibliography on the laity compiled in 1961 listed 1,400 items.[14] The most influential work in guiding new developments was Henrik Kraemer's remarkable little book, *A Theology of the Laity,* published in 1958. Compellingly simple, Kraemer's basic syllogism was that the church exists for the world. The laity is the church. Therefore its ministry is the world the church is to serve.[15] *How* the church, the laity, was to serve was strongly influenced by the turn in national concern to the plight of the disinherited. Activist clergy searching for greater leverage in the various campaigns for equity turned inevitably to the laity.

Thus outside the synod the questions, What is the laity to do and Where are they to do it?, prompted new replies. Change in the synod was not entirely derivative, however. In the years following World War II, R. R. Caemmerer continued reflection first articulated before the Associated Lutheran Charities in the 1930s.[16] In 1949 he brought out a small book, *The Church in the World,* in which he deplored the subordination of laymen to professionals in evangelistic work. Caemmerer lamented a shrinking of church work to parish activities. He preferred to liken the church to "the filling station or the restaurant where people go to get fuel for the main task, and the main task is done not in the filling station or restaurant, but out in the homes and factories, in the moments of daily living," for, said Caemmerer, "that is where the real battle goes on."[17]

In the unreceptive climate of the fifties Caemmerer's critique was too advanced, too gentle, and too abstract to arouse readers. When he returned to the subject in the sixties, however, further reading in the growing literature on the laity and additional study of pertinent Biblical passages had sharpened his analysis. And of course during the interval the prevailing winds in the synod had shifted. Probably most influential in Scriptural exegesis was a rereading of Ephesians 4:11-13 (in the Revised Standard Version,

"And his gifts were that some should be apostles, some prophets, some evangelists, some pastors and teachers, for the equipment of the saints, for the work of ministry, for building up the body of Christ. . . .") This, Caemmerer wrote, has long been misread to mean that the clergy was to do the ministry of the church. But, he exhorted, "take out the commas! He gave pastors and teachers for perfecting the saints for the work of the ministry which the saints are to do![18] The layman was not the assistant to the clergy, but vice versa. Pastors were to help laymen to do their, the church's, work. When such a reversal of traditional roles was coupled with the understanding that the church's work was in the world, engaged in a wide range of activities beyond "saving souls" as usually understood, they altered radically the position of the layman.

Of the statements reflecting such a reformulation of lay roles, the Kretzmann report to the 1965 synodical convention presented the most thorough synthesis of the new ideas and exploration of their implications. Kretzmann telegraphed the thrust of his argument in his premises, for he defined the church as the "people of God gathered out of and sent into the world as the body of Christ." Its mission, he wrote, is to the world, not itself, and is carried out by its members in the world. In fact, to accomplish this mission effectually, laymen must be in real partnership with nonmembers, not with a guilty conscience, but assured that God's purposes are served also in the worlds of art and culture, politics, and social service. For Kretzmann, once the layman's daily activities were understood to be his ministry, the distinction between religious and secular activities was untenable. Thus, wrote Kretzmann, the term "church" applies to the "Christian layman as he goes about his activity in the world." The church cannot "be looked upon as a place in which people can retreat from an unfriendly world, but rather as that Body which is continually moving into the world. . . ."[19]

This, then, was a further variation on two of the themes—the role of the layman in the church and in the world—with which we began, and which have coursed throughout this study. At the turn of the century the layman, still very close to his immigrant heritage, had a role, both actual and theoretical, that was quite modest and essentially passive. As the laity moved slowly into American society, prosperous laymen illustrated their economic success by assuming a prominent position in church business and finance. The younger men and the women expressed themselves especially in Sunday school teaching and charitable activities. Lay receptivity to recreational activities was coupled with a view that emphasized the church as believers set apart without equal stress on the need to be in the world. Block by block congregations therefore built up a defensive wall of parish organizations and activities that provided for the laity from baptism to burial.

Meanwhile as the synod interpreted its mission call at home to mean all Americans instead of German immigrants, pastors found that the laity could assist in evangelistic campaigns. And as congregational life became more complex, pastors found that the laity could assist in routine chores. This increased lay participation, however, still revealed a strongly paternalistic strain; pastors were using the laity to help them do their work. Moreover church work was tacitly defined as work somewhere in the parish hall.

When, however, Lutherans gave the mandate to be in the world weight equal to the fear of worldliness, then the laymen in their daily lives became the chief ministers of the church. In sum, the layman's role matured from that of the flock guarded by the clerical shepherd to the position of junior partner in God's work, and from this to the embodiment of the church in the world and central agent of the church's mission.

IV

Obviously such a reformulation had unsettling implications for parish life. When the *Witness* told its readers, "You don't have to do church work to serve the Lord," appeals for lay volunteers for parish jobs had to be rephrased.[20] In fact some began to say that many laymen should not be working on routine parish duties at all, but should be putting their particular talents to work in the community at large.[21] If taken seriously, this meant a reevaluation of the rationale and program of the multitudinous lay groups in the congregation and greatly increased the imperative for strong adult education offerings. As one man put it, "less time needs to be spent in the parish on finding something for the layman to do and more time on preparing him for the task he already has."[22] There was, however, no automatic lessening of the traditional lay inertia and resistance to study. What one churchman called the "confirmation complex" was still entrenched; decades in which laymen had gained the impression that Christianity was encapsuled in truths to be assented to rather than principles to be explored had left their mark.[23]

The reappraisal of lay activities in the local parish was only part of broader reassessments common to many denominations. Unfriendly critics handled the typical American suburban parish quite roughly in the sixties.[24] If Missourian observers were not quite so savage, their criticism of congregational life was still the most searching in the history of the synod. Attacks came especially from three sources. University-trained sociologists in the synod suggested that the typical suburban parish had fallen into a "residential trap."[25] Foreign missionaries were upset by the complacency in American congregations and less wedded to the norms of traditional parish organization and life. Finally, those with insistent social concerns were outraged that Christian congregations lagged so badly behind other agencies in expressing love for mankind and spoke out bitterly about the expenditure of large sums for impressive buildings rather than for more basic human needs outside the parish. Naturally the inanities of congregational busyness drew derision from such critics. Congregational autonomy, too, came under fire for contributing to the idea that a congregation might leave a slum neighborhood to follow the migration of its white middle-class constituency, and for obstructing useful coupling of congregations to pool or transfer resources.[26] Removed from the immigrant crisis that had fostered it, many spokesmen seemed less certain that the congregational unit was as normative as it had appeared in the nineteenth century.[27]

Churchmen at the synod's headquarters acquired at least the

new vocabulary. The synodical official who in 1956 had spoken of the "use of the laity" had by 1964 changed his orientation sufficiently to condemn the expectation that the church is "something to *belong* to rather than *something we are*. . . ."[28] "Form follows function" became common coin by the mid-sixties. Comparatively, there was substantially more flexibility and openness to new approaches than ever before. Officials allocated resources to team ministries, special projects for storefront churches, highrise apartment complexes or universities, and multiple social services performed especially by churches in urban ghetto areas. In some cases there was a stress on geographical connotations of the parish; in others, special constituencies were focused upon. There was also a marked change in parish styles the *Witness* brought to the attention of its readers. The editors were likelier to give coverage to a downtown, racially mixed congregation with antique facilities and subsidized budget than to a prosperous suburban congregation. The paper introduced a feature on individual laymen and women, first entitled "Lutherans You Must Meet," later "Lay Ministries," that reported on many people who were not always distinguished by strenuous activity in their congregations.

In the great majority of Lutheran congregations, regardless of their sympathies, neither clergy nor laity had any personal contact with the most innovative experiments in progress in the synod. The new emphases did, though, permit pastor and people so minded to drop the frantic drive for intra-congregational activism without a guilty conscience. And with a minimum of publicity, many did so. But one advantage of the older ideals that likely helped perpetuate them in many a sacristy was that criteria for success were highly visible and objective. A rising parish budget, elaborate church plant, good parking facilities, crowded schedule of congregational groups for all ages, enthusiastic participation of everyone in some parish function, burgeoning membership: these were the time-honored characteristics of a robust congregation. They provided a means for measuring progress over time and for comparing congregations—and pastors. Things were not so easy for those urging a church that gathered for worship and education and moved into the world for ministry. For this the old yardsticks were inapplicable, but new ones were simply not available. However satisfying emotionally, it was not entirely justified to approve congregations by the *absence* of traditional paraphernalia. The practical impossibility of quantifying lay ministries in the world was a major hurdle for those oriented to the statistical approach in annual reports and in establishing self-esteem. But the increasing apathy of the mass of the laity to time-honored structures was a powerful incentive.

V

In the sixties the synod's two main adult lay organizations were a part of dominant trends in the church. As the decade began, the Lutheran Laymen's League was in an enviable position. It was finally clear of the financial burdens imposed by the project experimentation of a decade earlier; the staff had just moved into a new headquarters building; and it had as president Harry G. Barr, an Arkansas businessman with considerable breadth of vision who had already played an important part in remodeling the Lutheran Hour at home and abroad. Barr began inviting to address the LLL board men like Caemmerer and others who were leaders in a reappraisal of lay roles. About the same time an enlarged LLL staff, more technically competent, theologically sophisticated, and given to thoughtful analysis than ever before in the league's history, began taking time to consider lay roles apart from immediate organizational needs. The *Lutheran Layman* and other occasional publications attempted to emphasize the laity's role as the church in the world.[29] The LLL joined with the Lutheran Academy for Scholarship to sponsor a conference on the layman and current religious development, but shied away from commitment to costly project spectaculars.

The league was, in other words, in the midst of a carefully considered search for a new role. There are a number of basic purposes a lay organization in the church may serve. One, especially visible in youth groups, is to allow the church to minister more efficiently to the particular needs of a distinct part of its constituency. Another purpose, in some respects close to the first, is to bind the laity more tightly to the church, that is, to provide a substitute for a secular organization that would otherwise attract the laity. A third possibility is to accomplish certain tasks in or of the parish or the denomination that without specific attention might be defaulted on or at least be performed badly. Yet another purpose is to utilize the resources of the lay membership to represent the church to the world and also the world to the church, serving in effect as a bridge between the two. Since its founding, the Lutheran Laymen's League had been oriented especially to the second and third of these alternatives. The fourth received scant attention until the rethinking of the sixties. Hence, instead of new and larger, expensive projects, the league staff seemed to be moving toward concerted efforts to make the individual layman conscious of his Christian status in society. Though not yet to the point of seeing its membership as representing the world to the church, the LLL was moving toward a view of the laity as a bridge from church to world.

How fast the league would move, though, was not entirely in the hands of the staff and president. The league Board of Governors was one potential brake. Over the years it became tradition that only men who had worked their way up through the league's zone and district structure and preferably served as a district president would be nominated, to say nothing of elected, to the national board. Such a system had an obviously conservative bias, for men too busy or uninclined to suffer league niceties at a lower level could hardly be co-opted on the national board for their breadth of vision, contacts, or experience. Study of the nearly 200 men nominated from 1955 to 1970 as national officers or board members does not reveal a group unusual in attainments. It seems likely that approximately half had no higher education. Of those whose occupation was reported and could be categorized usefully (nearly 80 percent of the total), about one-fifth were owners or operators of small businesses. Slightly less than another fifth were salesmen or insurance agents. Financial (accountants and bank officers), managerial, and professional (lawyers, physicians, dentists, teachers) categories each accounted for about 10 percent. Considering the synod's constituency, farming seems underrepresented with only about 3 percent. The remainder were classified as in government service. Most of the men running for the first time were in their forties and fifties.[30] The system worked against reappraisal and innovation in the league's governing body. Its constriction of the slate of candidates also helped produce on occasion a level of political maneuver that approached a Jaycees convention, the main difference being the piety with which existence of campaigning and deals was disavowed.

There were other facts, too, that might have given pause to league officers. By the early sixties a growing lassitude in local clubs was apparent; usually it was easy to find enthusiasm only in rural areas and small towns. Recruitment of the younger generation seemed more difficult. These were disquieting signs in view of demographic shifts. Very likely the league membership was as large as it was because the LLL demanded so little of its members. As long as dues were nominal, the league did not embarrass them, and the Lutheran Hour was the main project (visible, prestigious, non-controversial, and directed to traditional church goals), large numbers of laity were willing to join when approached by the local membership representative. But therein lay the dilemma. To move creatively in new directions might well alienate the mass of marginally committed laymen that endowed the LLL with financial strength and prestige. Given the high competence of the league staff, an adroit solution to the problem was probably possible, but was not to be developed before the league succumbed to reaction.

VI

Like the LLL, the Lutheran Women's Missionary League grew rapidly in the postwar years. By 1949 the LWML had more than 100,000 members and 2,500 affiliated congregational societies; it nearly doubled these figures by the early sixties. Despite such growth, LWML structure and staff remained surprisingly slight. At the end of the sixties, while the LLL found about eighty people necessary for its own needs and those of radio programming, the LWML staffed its headquarters with three secretaries, and part-time volunteers.[31]

The LWML constitution specified two purposes: "to develop and to maintain a greater mission consciousness among the women of Synod" and "to gather funds for mission projects, sponsored by Synod, especially such for which no adequate provision has been made in the budget." The league stayed close to these purposes in both its district and national activities. A small quarterly disseminated news of the organization and materials for local study of mission topics. In the fifties the LWML began sponsoring two-day institutes for women to deepen interest and develop leadership. Always the financial aspect was close to the surface. By the early fifties the national LWML was making grants to various mission projects both foreign and domestic at a rate of $75,000 a year, a rate doubled by the late sixties. In addition, district benefices averaged about two and a half times the national total.[32]

The life of the congregational affiliate of the LWML, indeed the typical women's society, is somewhat easier than the local LLL club to discuss, thanks to a major survey conducted under LWML auspices by David Schuller in 1958. Responses were received from 2,500 congregations (about half the synod's membership), but included nearly 4,000 women's societies; larger urban congregations in particular had two or three groups. The majority of these women's societies met monthly. Most common activities, stated in order of frequency, included fellowship (mainly after-meeting refreshments, parties, and family nights), membership campaigns, study of missionary topics, collections for world relief, financial collections for missions, and care of the altar. Participation in these ranged in order from 80 percent of the societies to 56 percent. About half the societies reported they engaged in programs to visit especially the sick and aged. About a quarter had community and civic projects. However, according to the responding pastors' estimates, the average society spent about 75 percent of its time on parish concerns.

Schuller discovered that in nearly 600 congregations women

were active in the Lutheran Laymen's League clubs. Only 65 percent of the women's societies reported were affiliated with the LWML. When member-societies were compared with non-members, differences in educational and fellowship activities turned out to be very slight. Ironically, non-members were as engaged in neighborhood evangelism and much more involved in institutional missions. There turned out to be no correlation between study of the much-urged mission topics and actual engagement in mission work.[33]

Such results counseled drastic alteration in the league's program, yet the LWML moved only with much hesitation. Even a suggestion to change the name of the chief collection method from "mite boxes" was beaten off. The league repeatedly turned down proposals for a full-time executive secretary.[34] A league *Handbook* was finally produced in 1965, but its theological pronouncements were eminently conservative and its orientation parochial. "Every woman's society," it instructed, "ought to recruit a *maximum* number of women and challenge them to discover the joy of rendering loving service. . . . Most of them find that unless they belong to a women's guild they don't do much church work. . . . Even business and career women can schedule their time so as to devote some of it to church work."[35]

Except for the mid-sixties, the Lutheran Laymen's League never engaged itself in or supported serious study of the position of the laity in the church; nor did it involve itself in something affecting members' lives (such as business ethics, for example). It rarely functioned as advocate of the laity. Similarly the Lutheran Women's Missionary League avoided any really difficult or controversial questions and rarely acted as women's advocate in the church. When the LWML *Quarterly* finally did touch on the subject of working women with at least tentative affirmation, it did so with a naivete that was in itself answer to the questions about LWML problems in recruitment of younger women.[36] The league had very little to say even to the woman in the traditional female sphere. Contraception, abortion, divorce, feminism—such matters hardly existed for the LWML, wedded as it was to mission topics and fund raising. The contrast was striking when in one

1969 issue the *Lutheran Witness Reporter* included stories from both the national LWML convention and also that of the women's group in the American Lutheran Church. While the ALC women heard "major presentations" on war, racism, and poverty, the main thrust of the LWML report was the choice of the eight mission projects named as recipients of grants.[37] The point is not that missionary projects were ill-advised, but that the LWML was Missouri's official women's auxiliary, the only women's group in the church on a district or synodical level, and it was unable to free itself from the effects of the apprehensions of the 1930s in order to serve women of the sixties more fully.

Most notably, the LWML carefully refrained from any activity in the controversy over women's suffrage in the church. As early as 1938 a delegate at the synod's triennial convention objected to an essay statement dismissing women's suffrage. Authorities buried the matter in the classic fashion by quoting Franz Pieper's *Dogmatics* and referring to a committee that never reported.[38] The subject could not be killed off, however, and at the 1953 convention delegates agreed to a thorough exegetical study. The study committee, which included no women, reported in 1956. It did not state that Scripture unequivocally denied women the vote, but did reaffirm that the Bible forbade women to teach and direct men. Since it felt that matters taken up in the congregational meeting involved this, the committee advised against woman suffrage and urged all congregations to fall in line with historically sanctioned practice, a conclusion in which the convention concurred.

Small hints that the matter was not closed remained, however. A stubborn minority refused to accept the committee's findings; the convention authorized a standing committee to continue study and "provide guidance," i.e., propagandize for the traditional position. Third, the 1956 report leaned very heavily on historical and practical arguments: "our church has prospered under this system" and "our women generally have not been resentful about their exclusion from this voting membership."[39] In the synod a prudential argument generally is a sign of impending change. Churchmen gave themselves away when they revealed the felt need for more support than Scripture seemed to give. Further, they were in an exposed position indeed as attendance at voters' assemblies continued to dwindle in most congregations and when the letters column of the *Witness* made it quite clear that there *were* women outraged by their exclusion and capable of expressing their dissent in cogent terms.[40]

Whether it knew it or not, the standing committee was deployed in a retreat skirmish. The subject made a nearly consistent triennial appearance.[41] Individual congregations ignored the synod's ruling or worked out a compromise by which the whole congregation met to hear an annual report and elect a small board of directors which then conducted the business of the congregation. Concordia Publishing House refused to print a manuscript by a Missourian clergyman, Russell C. Prohl, which challenged the customary exegesis of pertinent New Testament passages; but when another publisher brought it out, the synod's committee advertised it by condemning its findings.[42]

Despite disclaimers, a main pillar of anti-suffrage thought was not intellectual, but emotional, not Holy Writ, but the traditional view on the place and role of women.[43] As these evolved, usually from one generation to the next, the synod's time-hallowed stance was doomed.[44] The 1969 convention finally ratified the change when a study commission decided that voting and holding office other than the ministry was not usurping authority over men. As assenting congregations dropped the ban, women were permitted to sign constitutions and vote. They also quickly appeared as delegates at district conventions.

Thus at last the matter was settled. Except, that is, for the ordination of women. First the Lutheran Church in America, then the American Lutheran Church approved ordination, but attitudes in Missouri were far behind this. Despite awareness of the twentieth-century retreats, many of the synod's clergy still seemed to be as certain as their nineteenth-century counterparts that they could discern the details of an immutable Order of Creation and differentiate this from the Order of Redemption. The laity however were considerably more liberal on this question than the clergy.[45] Thus the stage was set for the next round in the struggle.

12

Humpty-Dumpty and All the King's Men

I

It cannot be only chronological proximity that makes coherence in the 1960s appear so illusive. Years when pot meant a kitchen utensil, pill meant a tablet, black was the absence of color, pigs were four-legged mammals, and weathermen were meteorologists, seem hardly to belong in the same era as the late 1960s. A fracture jags through the decade and the voices on this side of that line grew immeasureably louder, harsher, and more strident, as revolution and reaction overtook liberal reform. The lexicon of social distance and disjunction dominates the observers' vocabulary: alienation, gaps, polarization.

The church offered little refuge from the conflict.[1] After the heady expansion of the fifties, growth rates slowed, then reversed. Church attendance sagged and by 1967 opinion polls showed a clear majority of Americans believed religion was losing its influence on American life, a striking reversal in opinion since 1957.[2] Even the critics changed style during the decade, from the jeremiads of suburban captivity, comfortable pews, and solemn assemblies, to sober, tabular reckoning of the debilitation of the American church. In hardly any denomination could officials with their wits about them feel at ease. Roman Catholics contended over the limits of hierarchical authority. Presbyterians argued bitterly over a new creedal statement. Lutherans were no exception. The Missouri Synod finally came apart. To put the synod back together as it had once been was impossible. This,

187

then, is the last of the three periods into which the years after World War II may be divided.

II

"To speak of party spirit and divisions in the Missouri Synod, of a liberal and a conservative party among us, would be absurd," wrote Frederick Pfotenhauer during the Liberal-Fundamentalist battles in American Protestantism of the twenties.[3] *Not* to speak of division would have been as absurd by the forties, for a split, primarily over efforts toward union with other Lutheran bodies, was painfully apparent. Divisions widened and hardened in the indecisive struggle that dragged through the forties and fifties. But by the sixties, the old question, why church merger? had become, why not? Kinetic potential rested with advocates of union. In the early stages of this prolonged contest, as we have seen, those who sought union were anxious for allies and attempted, with some success, to draw in lay leaders to strengthen their minority position, accusing conservatives of trying to keep theological judgment out of the hands of the laity. As the tide gradually turned, leaders on the other side began seeking to rally laymen behind them, accusing progressives of trying to keep theological judgment out of the hands of the laity.

The issue of church union alone had limited appeal for the great majority of the laity, but by the sixties it was enmeshed in the whole complex of changes reviewed in the last chapter, the sum of which could create at least unease, to say nothing of extreme hostility, among both clergy and laity. The affirmation of the world and of corporate church involvement in social concerns, the results of a shift in theological concentration from dogmatics to exegetics, aggressive journalism—these were undeniably new thrusts in the Missouri Synod.

The response was as diverse as the synod and its laity had become by the sixties, but there is no gainsaying much was negative. The least common denominator in such resistance was fear of change. As disheartening as synodical exorcists found the persistance of such fear, it should have come as no surprise. Christian metaphor is replete with symbols of rock-like stability and certainty in the face of all inconstancy and adversity. God alone is eternal; only God is steadfast: the promise speaks to a human need so basic that almost inevitably God's immutability is ascribed by the unwary to ecclesiastical structures and theological formulations. Like many others over time, Missouri was tempted here beyond its strength, and for decades Biblical exegesis, hymnody, homiletical gloss, pastoral counseling, and catechetics all pointed to the same lesson: change in the church is an impossible contradiction. For many, then, change in the church was most incomprehensible, most threatening. Could this be any less so when everything else in society was in flux? One result of this line of thinking was reinforcement for a rigorous theological domino theory. To threaten one part of the system was to call all belief into question.

The full potential of this style of thought was not very apparent early in the sixties. In fact after the 1962 synodical convention, Martin Mueller, *Witness* editor and a perceptive observer, optimistically characterized its import in an editorial, "Turning Point." The convention, he wrote, had broken with the past in three areas; it rejected the legalistic tactics of the malcontents on the far right, it listened to advice on achieving a more promising basis for Lutheran union, and it recognized social implications in the Gospel. What Mueller found so encouraging, however, others found alarming and their reaction ultimately made 1962 far less decisive than it appeared at the time.

One index to negative thinking is the *Witness* letter-to-the-editor column, itself a recent and telling development.[4] According to the editor, about two-thirds of the letters were negative, ranging from the incoherently furious to harder questioning. A much larger body of evidence for extremely negative response consists of a number of papers published without synodical sanction, or, for that matter, official recognition. The most important was begun by Herman Otten, who was among those disturbed by the very confirmation of change in 1962 that the *Witness* took note of. Otten first became embroiled in controversy when he objected strenuously to some of the theology he heard taught as a student at Concordia Seminary in the fifties. Denied faculty certification and admission to the synodical clergy roster, he was called nevertheless by a congregation in New Haven, Missouri.[5] Discouraged by the apparent failure of the conservatives at the 1962 synodical convention, Otten decided to begin issuing a newsletter. Since 1940 the *Confessional Lutheran* had spoken for the far right, but its impact was unimpressive. *Through to Victory*, edited by Paul Neipp, a California pastor, began in 1960 but was fixed on communism. Certainly Missouri had a place for a conservative paper written for laity as well as clergy, or as Otten later put it, for "an independent publication designed to supply rank and file Christians with information needed to face the present crisis in Christendom."[6] Otten's *Lutheran News* assumed that role beginning in the winter of 1962–1963. The paper graduated in time to weekly publication. Soon convinced that what he called the liberal-evangelical split crossed denominational lines, Otten changed his title to the *Christian News* in 1968 and broadened his coverage. Though circulation did not achieve his goal of 25,000, by the end of the sixties the *News* had 19,000 subscriptions, with 5,000 complimentary copies mailed.[7]

Otten did not cause the conservative resurgence of the 1960s, nor was he its chief tactician. He was not even the first to raise the alarm. But he was the main publicist of the movement. His paper, intended for laity as well as clergy, was an essential instrument for arousing the disgruntled to action, for putting them in touch with one another, and for maintaining morale. The *News* is therefore an important window on the outlook and susceptibilities of an influential group of clergy and laity.

In associations and content the *Christian News* revolved in the orbit of the American Radical Right. The *News* was aggrieved that Lutherans sang "We Shall Overcome" ("a favorite of Communists everywhere") and that Picasso was not identified as a communist when "Guernica" was used in a *Witness* illustration.[8] *Christian News* pages were available for an astonishing attack on the new mathematics in education (for promoting relativistic thinking), and sallies against paper currency (for moving toward socialism), and social security and fair-housing legislation (for capitulation to covetousness).[9] Otten himself attacked Martin Luther King for liberal theology, and the civil rights movement for its communistic taint.[10]

Editor and contributors vehemently opposed involvement in social action by the church. The most judiciously formulated case argued that the church's business is not to act collectively, but to instruct and inspire the laity. "The layman will often err because he is not infallible, because solutions are seldom simple, and because they must be found while coping with many minds. The church as such cannot afford to err. . . . The layman, and he alone, should run the risk."[11] Such distinction between church and laity was a curious one for Lutherans and the whole formulation raised as many questions as it answered, but it need not be taken seriously because other statements made a shambles of this position. Otten was really objecting not to calls for synodical resolutions, but to the very attempts to "instruct and inspire the laity" for action—though in behalf of the poor, disabled, and disadvantaged close at hand. The instruction and inspiration Otten and his contributors offered was of an entirely different sort. Otten added editorial endorsement to the opinion that "the Church is not at all 'meddling in politics,' but is merely doing her divinely assigned duty when she . . . condemns Communism as a moral evil and warns her children against it."[12] One contributor insisted that condemnation of American action in Viet Nam would "sabotage our mission of spreading the Gospel," ignoring the possibility that absence of pronouncement sabotaged the mission. The church, he wrote, could be involved only in non-controversial matters and he suggested auto safety—presumably as long as one talked of individual drivers and not of General Motors Corporation.[13]

The major concern of the *News,* however, was not social but theological. As the editor explained, "the higher critical assault upon the Scriptures is far more destructive of the Christian faith than the 'new morality,' 'the social gospel' and other anti-scriptural notions which seem to disturb laymen more readily because they are easier to detect."[14] In long columns of close type that assumed great dedication of lay readership, the *News* dissected the errors in liberal theology it found subverting Lutheranism. Working from a literalistic position on the inerrancy of Scripture, Otten's approach was summarized in one headline which asked, "Does God's Bible Lie?"[15]

The *News'* style fit its associations and content. Promises to expose the *real* story covered up by the establishment and rushing to judgment with Manichaean criteria were its mode. Most oppressive was a complete absence of intellectual playfulness—not frivolity, but the willingness to mentally walk around an idea, to contemplate it on its own terms. For Otten, theology was queen only of the *applied* sciences; for him the path of pure science was a primrose one. What was lacking was not intelligence, but certain qualities of mind. But Otten prided himself on this very failing. The *News* was not simply unintellectual, but anti-intellectual. Otten's belittling references to liberal theological gobbledygook, to "Lutheran Intelligentsia" (the quotation marks are his), and to "endless pedantry [and] worthless speculations" in theological publications, catered to the layman's suspicion of the professional, in this case the professional theologian.[16] On the one hand laymen had long been told they had every right and the responsibility to judge doctrine, yet the overwhelming majority were woefully unlettered theologically. On the other hand, contemporary theology was very much in flux, with rapid changes in insight and vocabulary. These were challenging enough in themselves to the professional, let alone attempting to explain them for the layman, especially for a layman half convinced that theology should not be complicated. Under the best of circumstances there might have been problems. Anti-intellectualism ensured them. Explanation and productive debate were impossible when heresy headhunters demolished mutual respect and trust.

Thus, while synodical officials pleaded for deference to men who made Biblical study their profession, the *News* carried counsel for a different approach. "Super Intellectuals," one letter insisted, were the cause of the synod's problems. Activist preachers, another complained, "horned in with rhetoric and made the layman look stupid, not to mention afraid to speak on matters concerning doctrine and church policy.''[17] Such anti-intellectualism shaded into extreme resentment and mistrust of those in positions of authority. There was an enormous amount of conviction—suspicion is too weak a word—that something was being put over on the layman, summarized most succinctly in one layman's rhetorical question, "Are laymen now to be dumb sheep for shearing purposes only?"[18] Otten indulged, indeed aroused, such fears, for as far as he was concerned something *was* being foisted off on Lutherans. Apostasy and hypocrisy, wrote the editor, "are the dominant features of modern church life." Those who regret attacks on this "as 'negativism' either do not understand the gravity of the crisis or are themselves in league with the enemy."[19]

In the crisis, the *News* consistently presented itself as the friend and champion of the beleaguered layman. "We became heroes to the voiceless ones crushed by seeing their church being slowly overtaken by errorists. . . ."[20] But curiously enough Otten rarely considered explicitly the proper place of the laity in the church. His idea of a lay renaissance was of laymen rising together to silence the voice of heresy and, the apostates cast out, to engage in missionary activity. With an essentially negative and hostile view of the world—"the righteous man today . . . is in somewhat the same situation as was Lot when he lived in Sodom"—and with a fear of contemporary theological insights that did not originate in ultra-conservative Protestantism, the *News* avoided both the vocabulary and the vision of postwar thought on the laity.[21]

The *News* was the main but not the only voice of the stand-patters in the synod. For example in 1967 there appeared a small booklet, *A Layman's Concern for His Church.* Though it contained little not already in the *Christian News,* both its authorship and its distribution were noteworthy. The booklet was an expanded version of an address given before an LLL meeting by Marcus Braun, a Kansas City layman. By 1969 Braun had circulated 60,000 copies.[22] They were only a fraction of the mimeographed diatribe aswirl in synodical backwaters.

This literature could not have produced what happened without change both inside and outside the synod and without laity and pastors sensitive to appeals such as anti-communism, anti-intellectualism, suspicion of the establishment, and hostility to deviation from conventional mores. But it is also hard to imagine how subsequent events would have occurred without the *Christian News* and similar pieces. Reaction within the *News'* audience ranged from come-outers on the extreme right who felt Otten endorsed evil by staying with the synod; to those to the left of the *News* who rejected its mentality but subscribed to read in its photographic reproduction items they might otherwise miss; to those whom Otten could not convince but could disturb; to those who might disapprove of Otten's rhetoric but applauded his motives and ends; to hard-core adherents. Out of the last three groups came the constituency for a surprising number of small organizations about the country, formed to coordinate both lay and clergy discontent with the trends in the church. The oldest, slightly antedating the *News,* was State of the Church; it included both clergy and laity and was most active on the national scene, though some of its leading lights eventually withdrew from the synod rather than endure association with heterodoxy. Other more local or regional groups often included in their names the title "Concerned Lutherans." To speak with precision about numbers either of separate groups or of membership is difficult. This was not, in any case, a mass movement in the synod, though debates scheduled by some groups drew large audiences. Almost all, however, had impact well out of proportion to their membership.

III

At the other end of the spectrum from the *Christian News* and its constituency was a left wing, though the term applies only within a Lutheran context.[23] Usually this group was characterized by an unwillingness to accept the fundamentalist view of Scriptural inerrancy, by strong sacramental and liturgical emphases, high commitment to ecumenicity, insistence upon institutional involvement in social concerns (but also a strain of anti-institutionalism), impressive intellectual qualifications, and occasionally a penchant for outrageous satire. It was not nearly so large, so vocal, or so well organized as the far right, nor was it a precise counterpart in its relationship to the secular left; again, in a non-Lutheran context, the synodical left was generally much more restrained.

Within this group a clergyman like Richard John Neuhaus, anti-war militant, Chicago Democratic convention protestor, political activist, writer and editor, comes quickly to one's attention, but one is hard pressed to name an equivalent layman.[24] For a variety of reasons laity on the radical left were less visible, less identifiable as Missourian, than either radical clergy or those in the reactionary camp. Laymen who agreed with progressive clergy on social concerns, expanded intellectual horizons, and church union also were likeliest to have perspectives and contacts broad enough that ecclesiastical politics was a game not worth the candle. Immigrant centripetal force was spent, and other satisfying agencies to express needs and concerns were available. Of course for those on the far right there were also congenial secular agencies open, but the layman appalled by the changes wrought in the sixties was likely to see in the church the last bastion against social (and perhaps personality) disintegration and to engage himself accordingly. Dedicated to theological homogeneity, he was more likely to observe denominational boundaries than his counterpart on the left, and was thus easier to identify. Once again, attitudes toward the world were determinative.

This comparatively low commitment on the left to existing institutions, when combined with a potentially small audience and fortuitous factors, helps explain why those most in advance of the synod had no publication of their own.[25] The journal, *Una Sancta,* with its roots in the Lutheran liturgical movement, was the closest possibility, but despite major surgery in 1969 did not fill the need fully. Most promising was the attempt in 1968 to launch a radical journal, *Lutheran Free Press.*[26] Its failure after a few issues denied the left the functions the *Christian News* performed for the right. Among these was publicizing potential leaders (with their synodical affiliation) and providing a forum before a basically sympathetic audience. The increasingly cautious *Lutheran Witness,* which rarely failed to mention a beauty queen from a Lutheran home, was rather less likely to print the picture of a young man in the vestments of the counter culture who was confirmed in Zion Church back in Wausau, Wisconsin and just named committee chairman in, say, the New Mobe. A Lutheran Action Committee, composed mainly of young people, was formed in 1967 and issued a manifesto dealing with war, poverty, and racism.[27] Campus militance surfaced at least at some of the educational institutions affiliated with the synod. Selective conscientious objection rose considerably, to judge from impressionistic reports. Lutheran underground church activity began in a few large cities. But without some kind of organ, all this was ill-reported and its impact proportionately reduced.

The search for relevancy so typical of many churchmen especially through the mid-1960s was most visible among Lutherans on the left, as one would expect. To dismiss as irrelevant was the most damning indictment, and, perhaps, to be dismissed as irrelevant the most gnawing fear. Unfortunately the synod had no tradition of a loyal opposition. The left was thus poorly served to serve. The middle preferred to ignore it and the right was too shabby intellectually and too joylessly clumsy to prick the least airworthy trial balloons with telling wit and grace. The rightist antagonism to corporate church social involvement especially was so logically disreputable that those who urged strenuous institutional action were not really forced to give a great deal of rigorous thought to the difficult matters in mechanics of decision-making and procedures of involvement so that the results safeguarded as far as possible the conscience of the minority and maintained the best of Lutheran insights.

Among the clergy furthest ahead of the synod, John Elliott was the most obviously aware of the work done by Congar and Kraemer and gave the most explicit attention to lay roles via study of I Peter. This dismissed on exegetical grounds the long-cherished and oft-quoted phrases on "royal priesthood," but provided positive models in the image of a celebrating community bound together in obedience and in service to and in the world.[28] Less formal attitudes toward the laity were sometimes colored by the professional theologian's resentment about controls and attacks by non-professionals, and perhaps by a sacramental emphasis that was probably not latent sacerdotalism but could create considerable self-consciousness about clerical prerogatives.[29] Most influential, however, was the left's view of church and world. If the right saw the church as a tight ark sailing against adverse winds, conveying its passengers over the inhospitable deep while they peered through the storm for the opposite shore, those on the left viewed the church as more like a raft—you know it will never sink but your feet are always wet—whose planking and rigging they could throw overboard to the floundering, confident that the sea would bear all the pieces in the proper direction. For them the parameters of Christian life were not so nicely defined, except of course to exclude the status quo. A *Una Sancta* series in 1967 on styles of Christian life was predictably both ecumenical in authorship and non-definitive, urging chiefly diversity and exploration.

IV

A polarity of such dimensions between the synodical right and left inevitably meant confrontation and contest to capture power. In these the right usually proved itself much more adept. An excellent example in microcosm is the Lutheran Laymen's League. In the early sixties, as already noted, the league was working toward a more mature concept of the laity and of the league's own role. Progressives controlled the league sufficiently to invite professors attacked from the right to speak before LLL meetings. Revolution was in the offing, however. At the 1965 convention Walter Schur, a candidate for president whose sympathies and outlook were close to the retiring Harry Barr's, was skillfully defeated by Robert Hirsch, an attorney and state legislator from Tripp, South Dakota. Under Hirsch the league swung abruptly to the right. At a Board of Governors meeting soon after his election he leveled a general barrage at league orientation, including speakers invited, *Layman* reporting, and convention programming.[30] The speech was never made public and so did not create a widespread sensation at the time, but it was no more startling than what followed. Over the next two years there was a general turnover in virtually all league staff positions except those already occupied by men who shared the conservative view. At least one man was forced to resign, a few were attracted by more challenging positions elsewhere; most left because of the marked change in atmosphere. Although replacements were not all highly conservative, each departure shifted the center of gravity further to the right. Paul Friedrich, already close to retirement as executive director, was succeeded by a clergyman, the personification of the old order in the league, E. R. Bertermann, former aide to Walter Maier.

League publications suffered a marked decline, not only because of changes in staff, but also because of censorship. In one classic case of the transitional period, John Elliott's study of I Peter was released for general circulation as a Bible-study guide, then abruptly dropped amid outraged cries from the right over Elliott's carefully couched statement that Petrine authorship should remain an open question. Except for columns of tacit opposition to Lutheran fellowship negotiations, the *Layman* reverted to the status of house organ. Its view of the laity, the church, and the world was typified in the scurrying back to the parish womb by one columnist: "in fact, if a Christian really wants to do something vital in the Lord's Kingdom the most likely place to begin, outside of the home, is in the church. In a little while a person can find himself so completely immersed in the affairs of a Sunday school, Bible class, altar guild, evangelism group, choir, or what have you, that planning and thinking about the affairs of these groups becomes a primary activity in life. And this is good."[31]

In program, too, the league veered. Circumstances had reversed since the early fifties when the synod itself had money to experiment with television and the LLL did not. Now the television series "This is the Life" was an unacceptable drain on an already strained synodical budget. In 1967 league officials, who had earlier turned down a proposal to support a professor of business ethics at Valparaiso University, agreed to assume by stages the financial burden of keeping the television program on the air. To meet the resulting large fiscal demands required a considerable effort by league officials, publicists, and members.

The league had become the broadcasting arm of the church after all and the role of the layman seemed to be to support the league in order to support radio and television projects. Or to put things most charitably, the role of the layman was to contribute funds for public media evangelistic efforts. By 1970 the league attempted to broaden this somewhat by preparing materials for training individual laymen and women in techniques of personal evangelism. This, however, was hardly a primary emphasis and withal the layman's role under Christian conscience in the world did not come off just a poor second; it hardly came off at all.

The attitude among rank and file members to events at headquarters is difficult to gauge. Likely many had no suspicion of the convention in-fighting to swing elections, had only the foggiest notion of changes in emphases, and wondered at some of the letters to the editor in the *Layman* protesting the turn to the right. Aside from such letters there was little to inform the unwary. But what if they had been informed? The question only raises others (e.g., informed by whom? *Christian News? Una Sancta?*), and variables rise on every side. Whatever defections of individual members took place were more than made up by exertions in behalf of television sponsorship. The membership drive in 1970 reached a new high (153,000), and the league broke ground for an addition to its headquarters. There was a different kind of attrition, however, that got little public attention. The initial decline in enthusiasm for the parish LLL club first noted in the early sixties picked up considerable momentum. Between 1965 and 1970 the league lost a quarter of its club affiliations.[32] Apparently even a conservative league was not immune to the effects of the decade.

V

The successful insurgency in the league took place amid a cataclysmic struggle within the synod. The issues came to be focused in the question of fellowship with the American Lutheran Church (that is, unrestricted recognition of each other's clerical and lay membership), then in the theological position of the faculty at the synod's seminary in St. Louis. As a result, the late sixties and early seventies saw battles of a ferocity unparalleled in the synod during the twentieth century. The *Cresset* spoke for many when, on reading that Lyndon Johnson had accepted election as elder in his church, it wondered whether he had sufficient experience to cope with church politics.[33] Certainly political skills of a high order were required. Synodical officers with progressive instincts found themselves in an untenable and yet inescapable position. In their protestations to reassure the laity that nothing heretical or non-Lutheran was being taught in the synod, they sometimes went too far and sounded as if they were denying any substantive change at all. As a result they could be pictured as either dupes or conspirators by the extreme right and typical bureaucrats by the left. More unhappily yet, in response to the floods of redundant memorials and resolutions presented to the synodical conventions by the radical right, synodical officers elected to enforce rigidly the letter of the constitution and limit the right of presenting resolutions to members of the synod, that is, pastors, teachers, and congregations. This denied individual laymen a voice previously available, if only by tradition. Practically, the move was not very important; except for the far right, few laymen had ever exercised the option. Symbolically, however, in denying the dissidents one weapon, it gave them another. And the change was retrogressive in an age of growing awareness of the laity.

Both sides attempted to plan strategy and rally support prior to the synodical convention in 1969, the right wing with by far the most success. In part this was because of a strong initial distaste outside of the radical right for the tactics of that group; quoting Norman Mailer, Richard Neuhaus warned that engaging the right would be "a war in a wallow with gobbets of dung."[34] As early as 1967 the *Christian News* was openly calling for the defeat of President Oliver Harms, whose term ended in 1969. In the months before the convention, the *News* helped appropriate the name "evangelical" for the conservatives and publicize a slate of approved candidates, a tactic used sub rosa by the right at the preceding convention, but nevertheless a dazzlingly open display of hard-nosed politics in the synod. Heading the slate was Jacob A. O. Preus, Springfield seminary president, heir of a Norwegian immigrant Lutheran come-outer tradition, an opponent of fellowship, and consumate politician.

At the convention itself, veteran tacticians of the Presbyterian battles in the twenties would have felt at home. Well organized and ruthless in the cause of the Lord, the "evangelicals" seized the initiative. In the opening sessions, Preus indeed defeated Harms. But then, confounding observers, the convention went on to approve fellowship with the American Lutheran Church. The key, however, turned out not to be the fellowship vote, but the president-elect. Once elected, Preus disassociated himself from the *Christian News* and promised to bring the synod together again, rhetoric reminiscent of the contemporary White House in both sentiment and effect. Preus's opponents were hardly reassured, for signs and portends of disaster multiplied. Most implications of the fellowship decision were left unexplored, and by 1973 Preus and his supporters had a sufficiently consolidated position to launch a concerted attack on the St. Louis seminary and on the foreign mission administrative staff of the synod. The Preus forces had so defined the struggle that there would be no room in the synod for the loser. For both sides Armageddon was at hand.

VI

Posed somewhere between right and left in the synod was the majority of the laity. To locate them, sociological surveys, available for the sixties in unfamiliar abundance, encourage a process of triangulation. But if for earlier decades a dearth of data is frustrating, for the sixties the embarrassment is contradictory data and conflicting interpretation. Studies by Glock and Stark, Hadden, and Kersten broke important ground in demonstrating that Lutherans were too far from the averages in most inquiries to lump Protestants together as a single response category.[35] These sociologists also popularized a rather pessimistic view of the laity. Their surveys indicated a distressingly small impact of religious commitment on generous social values. Christianity seemed in practice to make little difference in relations with the human as opposed to the divine. In fact, orthodox Christianity was said to contribute to anti-semitism. The social upheavals of the sixties, they reported, elicited a generally positive response from the clergy and a generally negative reaction from the laity, polarizing the two to an alarming degree. The result was an impending crisis, or rather crises: to the outrage of conservative laity, liberal clergy redefined the church as an institution to challenge rather than to comfort; leaders in the church felt theological orthodoxy was untenable but there was no substitute in sight; religious authority was under fire from every side. In reaction, predicted Hadden, some laymen would leave the church entirely, some would withdraw all financial support, and some would stage reactionary revolts at church conventions.

These data and interpretations were forcefully challenged, however, by a massive study of American Lutherans conducted by the Youth Research Center of Minneapolis. Their conclusions were much more hopeful and positive. They confirmed the widespread existence of prejudice among Lutherans, but linked it not to orthodox Lutheranism, but to rigidity of personality and, in the perspective of Lutheran theology, to a system of misbelief—an orientation to Law rather than Gospel. Though they uncovered differences between clergy and laity, among Lutheran groups, and about specific issues, Strommen, Brekke, Underwager, and Johnson claimed the most basic polarity was between, on the one hand, those who valued a transcendent dimension of life, knew a personal, caring God, were relatively certain of their faith, were biblically oriented, and took a positive attitude toward life and death and, on the other hand, those who could not tolerate change, had a need for religious absolutism, were prejudiced and threatened by people different from themselves, were self-seeking in their relation to religion, and believed in salvation by works.[36]

It would be imprudent to say that the argument is closed. If Glock, Stark, Hadden, and Kersten tended to go at the matter in a way critical of the church and impatient with its history, Strommen, Brekke, Underwager, and Johnson approached it more sympathetic to the church and respectful of its past. But whether or not the Research Center team was correct, the technical and theological level of their investigation was of such sophistication that it is difficult to return to earlier studies with a substantial degree of patience and credulity.[37] Important differences and even tension there certainly were between Missourian clergy and laity in 1970, but there are many warnings against exaggerating this dichotomy. Kersten's figures demonstrate that on most indices synodical pastors were closer in attitudes to their laity than were the clergy of the ALC and the LCA. It would be innocent of historical perspective to picture the events of the late sixties as an unprecedented uprising of the laity.[38] To imagine the synod sundered by clergy representing social activism and laity upholding the status quo would be a gross misperception.

Complicating the whole business is that in reality there were two separate questions involved: should Christians, as an expression of their faith, work toward social justice in the world? And if so, how? Some, such as the *Christian News,* certainly based their rejection of corporate church social action on reactionary social attitudes, but that does not mean that everyone who hesitated before institutional action was therefore antagonistic to social justice. At mid-decade, in the Detroit area, nearly half of Missouri Synod laymen felt it "very important" for a Lutheran to work for social justice, but only a third agreed that both individuals and the church as a unit should deal with the question of race relations. *A Study of Generations,* too, found commitment to social concerns that did not automatically accede to institutional participation.[39]

Finally, in dealing with opinion and attitude surveys, invaluable as they are, one must remember that people can and do change their minds. Contexts also change. The visibility (and hence, perhaps offense) of clerical collars decreased in the civil rights movement as Black Power gained prominence, and in the anti-war movement as dissent became more widespread. An initial negative response of some dimension was hardly surprising when proposals as unfamiliar as social action were broached. But we have little survey data to prove that attitudes remained static. In fact, by 1970 figures in *A Study of Generations* showed that as many as three-fifths of American Lutherans in their early twenties thought the church far too little involved in social issues. Overall, half of all Lutherans favored church involvement in social action.[40] Here of course one must choose an emphasis: is the glass with some water in it half full or half empty? Since Lutherans were by 1970 exposed to strong, affirmative expressions on social action for less than a decade, the percentage willing to agree to it seems the more remarkable.

To pit clergy against laity then is too simple a model for analyzing the present. But the fact remains that by the late sixties Missouri Lutheranism was in sore travail. As the *Concordia Theological Monthly* observed in 1969, disagreements remained on three issues: "the doctrine of the Word; the nature of the mission of the people of God; and the quest for fellowship."[41] Survey data indicate that, had fellowship been left up to the laity as a whole, some form of amalgamation with other Lutherans would probably have occurred in short order.[42] On the question of social concerns, as we have seen, individual expression gained assent by a large majority, and corporate action in principle was well supported, though clergy were more sympathetic than most groups of laity. Attitudes toward the Biblical witness were more traditional. All surveys agree that synodical laity were more conservative theologically than their counterparts in the ALC or LCA. *A Study of Generations* discovered no significant differences between Missourian clergy and laity on a liberal-fundamentalist scale. But laymen were somewhat more likely to have a strong need for religious absolutism. Data from the various surveys demonstrate a clear majority of the laity assigned a very high degree of trustworthiness to the Bible in all of its aspects.[43]

But were the majority of the laity as conservative as the conventions of the late 1960s and early 1970s would indicate? This is difficult to say. These matters were not put to a general lay referendum; convention decisions were made by representatives who, to judge from a sample of the 1969 delegates, were distinctly older and more conservative than the average.[44] Of course, many more laymen, though still a small percentage of the total, participated in pressure-groups on both sides to influence the decision-making process. But even assessing relative levels of support for the various camps is difficult. Laity on the far right came to the point of true believer first, convinced that the church was selling out to liberalism. Theirs was the easier task, for they could insist on the literal sense of Scripture and, when challenged, retreat to appeals to simple, saving religion and to invective. At least some progressive clergy found it harder in the sixties than in the union struggles of the forties to raise enthusiasm and funds among the laity. Yet the support (institutionalized in ELIM, Evangelical Lutherans in Mission) given the beleaguered seminary faculty and the mission staff in 1973 and thereafter was a striking contrast to the quiescence of the moderate laymen in the late 1960s. It may indicate that a substantial body of the laity was not nearly so far right as many on the right (and the left) thought. This group of the laity may have disdained participation in what they considered an unseemly, fanatics' quarrel until the unthinkable occurred, and what they viewed as a fundamentalist take-over threatened to associate them with a socially and intellectually disreputable denomination.

Whatever the truth about lay involvement—and confirmation will have to await the opening for research of correspondence files still quite active by the early seventies—many of the laymen were at a decided disadvantage in following theological debate. As O. P. Kretzmann wrote after a convention floor fight, "among the voters on both sides I noticed some laymen whose bewilderment was as clear as Mary's at the wedding feast at Cana. In fact, right in the middle of the heavy theological discussion one of them got behind Microphone Thirteen and asked plaintively: 'What is this here hermeneutics? Won't somebody please tell me?' ''[45] Likely here rests a part of the explanation for the 55–45 edge by which the Preus forces usually prevailed in 1973. "Sincere and devoted people," observed one reporter about the convention delegates, "desperately wanted to 'save the Bible for our children' and 'preserve the Gospel.' ''[46] There were enough laymen who, once their fears were aroused and their faith in the moderates destroyed, felt they had no choice but to support those who claimed the legitimacy of the institution, those who insisted they were waging war for the truth of the fathers.[47] After all, the standard emergency rule is to obey the captain and stay with the boat even when it is swamped.

VII

Among the casualties as the internecine struggle intensified in scope and bitterness during the late sixties was the rigorous and creative thinking about the laity characteristic of earlier in the decade. New concerns preempted time and energy to a remarkable extent. Explicit consideration in synodical publications of lay roles declined spectacularly. Few writers contradicted or disavowed earlier advanced statements about the laity. The swirl of debate simply moved away from the whole issue. Coming to a more informed view of lay roles seemed much less important when the proper understanding of the Biblical authority was at stake, and when power and careers rested on the outcome.

Does this mean that promising developments died a-borning? Perhaps so. But though probably never to be taken up in precisely the same way again, the thrust of the mid-sixties was too powerful to be completely aborted. When Kersten in his questionnaire defined membership in the church "as primarily and basically a group of people to be served or ministered unto by the pastor," more than 80 percent of all synodical clergy in Detroit over the age of sixty agreed. But only 41 percent of the pastors in their fifties assented, and a mere 12 percent of those under thirty did so.[48] Such an age differential among those most involved in an explicit definition of the church does not guarantee change, of course, but should make it more likely.

Furthermore, though discussion of formal definitions (or the absence of discourse) is obviously one factor in the equation, it is not the only variable. Change in the laity does not always wait for theological ratification. Surveys of the late sixties confirmed that the Lutheran constituency was very much in the white middle class. The degree of urbanization was surprising, for less than one-tenth were farmers. Three-quarters had incomes above $9,000; overall, one-third (and among those aged nineteen to twenty-three two-thirds) had some college education. Two-fifths favored the Republicans; one-quarter, the Democrats. Interestingly enough, nearly two-thirds of the respondents rejected labeling Lutherans as different from other Christians, whether the label had positive or negative connotations.[49] When presented with a hypothetical community or subdivision entirely for Lutherans, not quite three-quarters of Missouri Synod Lutherans in Detroit refused to consider living there.[50] For most synodical Lutherans, religion, or certainly the local parish, did not structure their social lives. For more than 40 percent, none of their closest friends were members of their congregation.[51]

Of course, diversity among synodical congregations precludes overconfident generalizations. When in 1969–1970 the *Witness Reporter* ran a series of long feature articles on individual parishes, the range was broad indeed: a congregation of 1,200 members in an Illinois farming community where 92 percent of the town was Missouri Synod Lutheran; a congregation with more than 3,000 members in southern California, not far from Disneyland in distance or in facilities and program; a congregation of some 300, with a large Tudor-Gothic showplace built in the twenties by exuberant Americanized laity, now a lonely fixture in a black ghetto, trying to serve and engage a new constituency.[52]

Yet, despite such differences, certain changes seem common. By 1970 the decline in the Lutheran birth rate had brought the number of baptisms comparable to the figures of a much smaller synod in the 1950s. This, combined with the reduction in adult accessions, produced the lowest gain in baptized membership since 1919, the troubled era of World War I and rapid, forced Americanization.[53] Most observers felt that the core of parish

work-horses was smaller than in a long time.[54] Synodical journalists noted that while once it was axiomatic that one-third of the
congregation carried the remainder financially, the active portion
seemed to be shrinking to perhaps one-quarter.[55] After reaching a
peak in 1967, circulation of the *Lutheran Witness* and *Lutheran
Witness Reporter* fell 20 percent in the next four years.[56] The
astonishing drop in men's club affiliations with the LLL said a
great deal. So, too, did the equanimity with which most greeted
the decline. Attempting to explain it, one league official said that
"at one point LLL clubs were all but abandoned because their
large role in providing recreation for the congregation had suddenly become a stigma."[57] As the president of the congregation in
Great Bend, Kansas, told the *Witness* reporter, "It's difficult to
know what people are looking for outside of worship services.
Most of the programs outside of the worship services seem to be
holding less and less interest."[58]

Motivation for lay participation or acquiescence in parish
changes are indeed not readily fathomed. When surveyed in the
mid-sixties, a high percentage of Detroit Lutherans seemed unaware or unconvinced of the implications of newer emphases
about the laity.[59] About 43 percent agreed that it was highly important for a Lutheran to be active in church activities and organizations. The 57 percent who disagreed may have caught a
larger vision, or they may have simply wanted to be left alone; the
data are not clear. The decline of parish activism in itself no more
guaranteed a lively challenge to relate faith and world than the
frenetic schedules of the 1950s.

But to speak of the death of the parish was, in the Missouri
Synod of 1970 at least, journalistic hyperbole, unless one shortsightedly insisted upon using the norms of mid-century. The immigrant church did not generate the parish activities developed
especially after World War I, in part because the German-
Lutheran enclave itself provided community. Americanization,
however, helped foster the growth of a hyperactive parish as laity
and clergy sought to maintain the congregation as primary group,
a religious community rather than a religious audience. About the
time that a significant percentage of the laity was sufficiently

secularized, urbanized, and diffused through the society to make this kind of effort daunting if not futile, influential voices questioned the whole effort. That such questioning was overdue may be indicated by the unreadiness of most Lutherans, even amid such changes, to admit religious declension, at least in their own lives. Three out of four in 1970 considered themselves as or more religious than their parents.[60]

Curiously enough, in de-emphasizing, for example, institutional trappings and internal organization, the advanced parish at the end of the sixties was not very far from some of the characteristics of the congregations with which we began this book. And after one has listened through the anguish over the introduction of English services and the apprehensions over the aggressive busyness of volunteer lay groups, controversy over guitar liturgy and talk of the impending demise of the parish may elicit a wry smile of recognition. Yet, manifestly, this was not a fruitless return to the same position in a closed cycle. In expectations and in boundaries, physical as well as psychological, the parishes and the laity of 1900 and 1970 were far apart, and to get from one to the other there is no choice but to traverse the course between.

Guide to Abbreviations

AL	*American Lutheran*
ALC	Associated Lutheran Charities
AV	*Advance*
BG	Board of Governors
BD	Board of Directors
BL	Lutheran Laymen's League *Bulletin*
CHI	Concordia Historical Institute, St. Louis, Mo.
CHIQ	*Concordia Historical Institute Quarterly*
CN	*Christian News*
CNV	Convention
CTM	*Concordia Theological Monthly*
DL	*Der Lutheraner*
EIN	*Eingaben*
ExB	Executive Board
ExC	Executive Committee
LCMS	The Lutheran Church—Missouri Synod
LF	*Lutheran Forum*
LL	*Lutheran Layman*
LN	*Lutheran News*
LW	*Lutheran Witness*
LWR	*Lutheran Witness Reporter*
OpC	Operating Committee
PRO	*Proceedings*
RAM	*Reports and Memorials*
SYB	*Statistical Yearbook*
TG MSS	Theodore Graebner Papers
TM	*Theological Monthly*
TQ	*Theological Quarterly*
TY	*Today*
VER	*Verhandlungen*
WKB	*Workbook*

Unless otherwise stated, all minutes cited are those of the Lutheran Laymen's League.

Notes

Part One

1. Daniel Callahan, *The Mind of the Catholic Layman* (New York, 1963). pp. 77-78.

I should here acknowledge my debt to two books from which I learned much, even though, in order to lessen the cranking and creaking of the scholarly apparatus, I have not cited parallels and patterns from them as frequently as I might have. Equally stimulating in their respective areas are Callahan's study of what was long an immigrant laity, and Milton H. Gordon's thoughtful exploration of *Assimilation in American Life* (New York, 1964).

Chapter 1: Laymen in a Clergy's World

1. Quoted with unsigned endorsement, *LW* 18 (1900): 134.
2. Quoted by Ludwig Fuerbringer, *DL* 65 (1909): 231.
3. Theodore Graebner, *LW* 36 (1917): 165.
4. In addition to the standard histories, I found helpful here: *The Voluntary Church: American Religious Life, 1740–1865, Seen Through the Eyes of European Visitors,* ed. Milton Powell (New York, 1967); Borden W. Painter, Jr., "The Anglican Vestry in Colonial America" (Ph.D. dissertation, Yale University, 1965); and Jerald C. Brauer, *The Role of Laity in the Life of the Congregation: A Report to the Lutheran World Federation Commission on Stewardship and Congregational Life* (n.p., 1963).
5. In the absence of a badly needed full-scale history of the synod, the introductions, source readings, and bibliography in *Moving Frontiers: Readings in the History of The Luthern Church—Missouri Synod,* ed. Carl S. Meyer (St. Louis: Concordia Publishing House, 1964), are a valuable presentation of the synod's past. Here and throughout, books published by Concordia Publishing House are so noted to indicate their official standing in the synod.
6. Carl S. Mundinger, *Government in the Missouri Synod: The Genesis of Decentralized Government in the Missouri Synod* (St. Louis: Concordia Publishing House, 1947), p. 104 n.
7. *Ibid.,* p. 99.
8. Walter O. Forster, *Zion on the Mississippi: The Settlement of the Saxon Lutherans in Missouri, 1839–1841* (St. Louis: Concordia Publish-

ing House, 1953), p. 521; D. H. Steffens, "The Doctrine of the Church and the Ministry," *Ebenezer: Reviews of the Work of the Missouri Synod during Three Quarters of a Century,* ed. W.H.T. Dau (St. Louis: Concordia Publishing House, 1922), p. 145.

9. Walther's ideas were expressed in the so-called Altenburg Theses, which summarize the position he took in public debate against Marbach in April 1841. These are reprinted in Forster, pp. 523-25. Walther elaborated his ideas more fully in *Die Stimme unserer Kirche in der Frage von Kirche und Amt* (translated by W.H.T. Dau in *Walther and the Church,* ed. Theodore Engelder [St. Louis: Concordia Publishing House, 1938], pp. 47-86), and in *Die rechte Gestalt einer vom Staate unabhaengigen Evangelisch-Lutherischen Ortsgemeinde* (translated by John Theodore Mueller, *The Form of a Christian Congregation* [St. Louis: Concordia Publishing House, 1963]). There is no adequate biography of Walther.

10. Mundinger, pp. 109-62, 213.

11. *Ibid.,* p. 172.

12. In this discussion I have relied on Conrad Bergendoff, *The Doctrine of the Church in American Lutheranism* (Philadelphia, 1956), pp. 19-36, and on Karl Wyneken, who has in progress a close study of laymen and clergy in the nineteenth century Missouri Synod. I am much indebted to him for guidance amid the marshes of mid-century ecclesiology. He is not to be blamed, of course, for any oversimplification on my part. The quotation is from a letter from Wyneken; see his "Selected Aspects of C.F.W. Walther's Doctrine of the Ministry" and "Later Developments in the Missouri Synod Doctrine of the Ministry, 1870–1900," bound in *Studies in Church and Ministry* (Concordia Seminary, St. Louis, mimeographed, various dates in the 1960s), III, and Walter R. Bouman, "Church and Ministry in the 20th Century," *ibid.,* IV.

13. The last was not technically in force until a constitutional revision in 1854. Bergendoff, p. 192. The 1854 constitution is translated in *Moving Frontiers,* pp. 149-61.

14. In addition, German Lutherans were relatively untroubled by the problem (brought from Scandinavia) of lay preachers that agitated their Norwegian immigrant colleagues. For an extended account of this Norwegian immigrant controversy, and Walther's role in it, see John M. Rohne, *Norwegian American Lutheranism up to 1872* (New York, 1926), p. 174 ff.

15. The language transition is most thoroughly explored in Einar Haugen, *The Norwegian Language in America: A Study in Bilingual Behavior,* 2 vols. (Philadelphia, 1953). My thinking on a continuum of church styles has been stimulated by reflection upon, and sometimes

disagreement with, Charles M. Glatfelter, "The Colonial Pennsylvania German Lutheran and Reformed Clergyman" (Ph.D. dissertation, The Johns Hopkins University, 1952).

16. The work of Timothy Smith suggests caution in generalization about immigration and ecclesiastical passivity. Yet Smith's findings for immigrants from Central Europe are not readily confirmed when applied to Lutherans from Germany proper. Timothy L. Smith, "Lay Initiative in the Religious Life of American Immigrants, 1880–1950," *Anonymous Americans: Explorations in Nineteenth Century Social History,* ed. Tamara Hareven (Englewood Cliffs, 1971), pp. 214-49.

17. The German-American community produced no chronicler of the stature of the Norwegian, Ole E. Rølvaag or the Swede, Wilhelm Moberg. But except for the lack of attention to an urban experience, the trilogies by these two men can serve as an enticing introduction to the immigrant experience of a strongly Lutheran group. See Rølvaag: *Giants in the Earth: A Saga of the Prairie,* trans. Lincoln Colcord, Harper Torchbook (New York, 1964); *Peder Victorious,* trans. Nora O. Solum (New York, 1929); *Their Father's God,* trans. Trygve M. Ager (New York, 1931), and Moberg: *The Emigrants* (1951), *Unto a Good Land* (1954), and *The Last Letter Home* (1961), trans. Gustaf Lannestock (New York).

18. J. W. Th., *DL* 59 (1903): 118.

19. *Ansprachen und Gebete* (St. Louis: Concordia Publishing House, 1888), p. 30.

20. For a moving fictional account of such services, see Rølvaag, *Giants,* pp. 354-423. That such fiction is soundly based for German circuit riders as well is indicated by *LW* 58 (1939): 431. For twentieth-century examples, see *DL* 61 (1905): 118; 65 (1909): 374.

21. For the centrality of the role of the pastor, see Martin Sommer's description of a church founding in "Congregational and Home Life in the Missouri Synod," *Ebenezer,* ed. W.H.T. Dau, pp. 518-19.

22. Mundinger, p. 34; Meyer, p. 25.

23. Of the 326 adult males whose occupations are known, 217 were small craftsmen and 48 worked in agriculture. Only nine men were designated as merchants, but 39 could be classed as members of a profession or as government employees. If this last figure is disproportionately high for the German immigration as a whole, it is worth noting that 24 were pastors, ministerial students, or teachers. Of the remaining 15, seven had left the colony by 1844, and these seven included all of the other professionals. Calculated from immigrant lists reprinted in Forster, pp. 540-63.

24. Mack Walker, *Germany and the Emigration, 1816-1885* (Cam-

bridge, 1964), pp. 69, 184-94. O. H. Restin, the synod's missionary stationed in New York city to serve immigrants, reflected in 1912 on the main origins of the past German immigration—and presumably on the people he had tried to send to synodical congregations. He mentioned first the provinces of Hanover, Mecklenburg, Schleswig-Holstein, Pomerania, and East and West Prussia, all classed by Walker as mostly agricultural. *DL* 68 (1912): 54; Walker, p. 184.

25. Figures in the 1890 census showed nearly two-thirds of German-born workers here had jobs in trades and agriculture. They were proportionately over-represented in the small crafts and trades. They were also over-represented among brewers, and saloon and bar keepers. In the professions, the Germans were proportionately under-represented by a large margin, except for musicians, artists, and chemists. E. P. Hutchinson, *Immigrants and Their Children, 1850-1950* (New York, 1956), pp. 121-28. (The 1900 census unfortunately did not differentiate adequately by country of origin for similar figures.) It seems unlikely that artists and musicians would be attracted into Lutheran congregations, and, while the German Lutherans were opposed to Prohibition, Missouri Synod spokesmen attacked the saloon in no uncertain terms. George Stoeckhardt, *DL* 64 (1908): 106-108, 123-25.

26. *DL* 62 (1906): 105; *LW* 23 (1904): 99.

27. As a bare sampling of periodical literature alone on this subject, see *TQ* 4 (1900): 84-107, 203-29; *DL* 60 (1904): 147-49; *LW* 25 (1906): 89-90.

For A. L. Graebner to suggest that the congregation should help provide for members out of work because they refused as good Lutherans to join unions was strong medicine. It would have been utterly ludicrous had there been many congregations across the country composed mainly of laborers working in large factories. *TQ* 4 (1900): 228. Significantly, opposition to this stand came from the urban East. H. B. Hemmeter to Theodore Graebner, Jan. 8, 1926, TG MSS, Box 56.

28. "The Pastors of the Missouri Synod," *Ebenezer,* p. 503.

29. Arthur C. Repp, "Summary," *100 Years of Christian Education,* ed. Arthur C. Repp, Fourth Yearbook, Lutheran Education Association (River Forest, Ill.: Lutheran Education Association, 1947), pp. 219-20.

30. Mundinger, p. 198.

31. Alfred M. Rehwinkel, *Dr. Bessie* (St. Louis: Concordia Publishing House, 1963), p. 146.

32. The evolution of pastoral care and ministerial roles in the Missouri Synod is a much neglected subject that has intriguing possibilities in a

denomination with Missouri's European background and theological commitments. Studies of the clergy with broader perspectives are helpful, but their findings may not be applied mechanically to the synod. See, e.g., William A. Clebsch and Charles R. Jaekle, *Pastoral Care in Historical Perspective*, Torchbook ed. (New York, 1967); *The Ministry in Historical Perspectives,* ed. H. Richard Niebuhr and Daniel D. Williams (New York, 1956).

33. There is a plethora of literature on attitudes in American denominations toward various social questions, but a dearth when it comes to general advice on what constituted day-by-day Christian living. A useful study with the latter focus is William Davison Blanks, "Ideal and Practice: A Study of the Conception of the Christian Life Prevailing in the Presbyterian Churches of the South During the Nineteenth Century" (Th.D. dissertation, Union Theological Seminary, Richmond, 1960). Blanks' work indicates that Missourian positions were often not unique except in their perpetuation.

34. The documentation here is intended only to provide convenient references to authoritative statements. For life insurance, see A. L. Graebner, *TQ* 3 (1899): 442-43; 6 (1902): 242-50. Also James Albers, "The History of Attitudes Within the Missouri Synod Toward Life Insurance" (Th.D. dissertation, Concordia Theological Seminary, St. Louis, 1972).

On theater, see A. L. Graebner, *DL* 56 (1900): 17-20; *idem,* "Is the Classical Drama Immoral?," *Literary Digest* 20 (March 3, 1900): 268. As late as 1909, Concordia Publishing House was still advertising Walther's *Tanz und Theaterbesuch*, a tract against dancing and theater-going. *Lehre und Wehre*, 55 (Feb. 1909), back cover. Dallmann's opinion may be found in *LW* 13 (1894):78.

35. *LW* 16 (1897): 115. See also W.P.S., *Concordia Magazine* I (1896): 97-98. Once again, the condemnation was not limited to dime novels, but included, for instance, the work of Henry James. Romoser, *LW* 19 (1901): 122. On art, see C. A. Weiss, *LW* 25 (1906): 146.

36. A. L. Graebner, *TQ* 4 (1900): 319-47; 7 (1903): 86-94. Alan Graebner, "Attitudes in the Lutheran Church—Missouri Synod Toward Sexual Morality: 1900–1960" (M.A. thesis, Columbia University, 1961).

37. A.L. Graebner, *DL* 64 (1908): 93-95.

38. A. L. Graebner, *TQ* 7 (1903): 32; 2 (1898): 350-52.

39. See theses 39-43 in C.F.W. Walther, *Pastoral-theologie,* 5th ed. (St. Louis: Concordia Publishing House, 1906). In 1907, George Mezger wrote a series of no less than fourteen installments for *Der Lutheraner*

covering all phases of discipline. *DL* 63 (1907): 98-100 *passim*. For gathering evidence, see A. L. Graebner, *TQ* 6 (1902): 216-31.

40. W. M., *Huelfsbuechlein fuer unsere Gemeinde-vorsteher* (St. Louis: Concordia Publishing House, 1901). I could not locate a copy of this 28-page booklet, but it is reviewed in *DL* 57 (1901): 363, and almost certainly it was this book that was translated in *LW* 22 (1903): 202-203, and 23 (1904): 3-4 *passim*. See also *DL* 67 (1911): 118-19.

41. A. Pfotenhauer, *DL* 46 (1890): 111-12.

42. *SYB*, 1937, p. 156. This was partly a matter of convenience when many congregations and preaching places were short-lived. Nevertheless, the point remains that the synod settled on the convenience it did because of the position of the pastor in the congregation.

43. *"Einer aus den Predigern und zwei aus der Hoererschaft." Allgemeine Aufsichtsbehoerde, DL* 65 (1909): 244. See the same usage in *DL* 48 (1892): 152; *DL* 68 (1912): 296; *VER*, LCMS, 1902, p. 19; *ibid.*, 1914, p. 26.

44. *DL* 56 (1900): 344.

45. *DL* 61 (1905): 262; 68 (1912): 411.

46. See, for example, J.H.C. Fritz, *LW* 24 (1905): 12; John R. Graebner, *LW* 34 (1914): 69. It should be explicit here that I am discussing emphases within a total commitment. No one in the synod was denying the priesthood of all believers—nor was anyone pursuing the full meaning of this concept.

47. Ruth Fritz Meyer, *Women on a Mission* (St. Louis: Concordia Publishing House, 1967), pp. 45-62.

48. P. E. Kretzmann, *CTM* 1 (1930): 352.

49. Synodical publications greeted with dismay ordinations of women abroad and in some other American denominations and reacted similarly to news of woman suffrage granted within church circles. Bente, *DL* 50 (1894): 76; Fuerbringer, *DL* 52 (1896): 145; Pieper, *DL* 55 (1899): 35; George Luecke, *LW* 16 (1898): 125.

50. For opinion here, see George Stoeckhardt, *DL* 51 (1895): 103; Pieper, *DL* 55 (1899): 35; Fuerbringer, *DL* 53 (1897): 65; *idem, DL* 64 (1898): 85.

51. George Luecke, *LW* 16 (1898): 150. On the topic of woman's innate capability, synodical writers were not all of one mind. Some emphasized her physical weakness and more sensitive temperament. A. L. Graebner, *DL* 50 (1894): 71-72. Others, however, granted at least some theoretical intellectual equality, but insisted that common sense required someone be vested with authority; in God's order this was the male. W.H.T. Dau, *LW* 16 (1898): 132-33.

52. W.P.S., 1 (1896): 33.

53. A. L. Graebner, *DL* 50 (1894): 71-72, 96; see also Friedrich Bente, *ibid.*, 76.

54. *LW* 16 (1898): 192.

55. *DL* 51 (1895): 40; *LW* 17 (1898): 55. Activities such as Elizabeth Cady Stanton's Bible commentary and feminine efforts for prohibition could hardly win faith in female theological and political acumen. Ludwig Fuerbringer, *DL* 54 (1898): 198; C. Dreyer, *DL* 54 (1898): 159.

56. *Woman Suffrage*, p. 2; see also *Concordia Magazine* 1 (1896): 33.

57. Timothy L. Smith, *Revivalism and Social Reform: American Protestantism on the Eve of the Civil War*, Harper Torchbook ed. (New York, 1965), pp. 80-83; Clifford S. Griffin, *Their Brothers' Keepers: Moral Stewardship in the United States, 1800–1865* (New Brunswick, N.J., 1960), pp. 23-60; Charles Howard Hopkins, *History of the Y.M.C.A. in North America* (New York, 1951), pp. 15-179.

58. Lewis Howard Grimes, "Making Lay Leadership Effective: A Historical Study of Major Issues in the Use of Laymen by The Methodist Church Especially for Its Educational Program" (Ph.D. dissertation, Columbia University, 1949), pp. 11-50.

59. Winfred E. Garrison and Alfred T. DeGroot, *The Disciples of Christ: A History* (St. Louis, 1948), p. 426.

60. Individual denominations began their own "brotherhoods" or launched their own campaigns, such as the Men and Millions Movement of the Disciples of Christ in 1913. *Ibid.*, p. 427. I have relied here on Leo Vaughn Barker, *Lay Leadership in Protestant Churches* (New York, 1934), H. Paul Douglass, *One Thousand City Churches: Phases of Adaptation to Urban Environment* (New York, 1926), and Howard Grimes, "The United States, 1800–1962," *The Layman in Christian History,* ed. Stephen Charles Neill and Hans-Reudi Weber (Philadelphia, 1963), pp. 240-60.

61. *A New Call to Serve: Lutheran Laymen's Movement for Stewardship* (New York: Lutheran Laymen's Movement for Stewardship of the Lutheran Church in America, n.d. [1962]), pp. 3-6.

62. In 1893 the Walther League was founded to bring together and foster young people's societies. It was followed after the turn of the century by parallel, competing associations in the East, in Texas, and in English-speaking circles.

63. A. L. Graebner, *DL* 51 (1895): 155; *idem, DL* 52 (1896): 16, 82.

64. The Long Island Pastoral Conference issued a stern public refusal to an invitation from the Men and Mission Movement: disregard of denominational boundaries was indicative of an intolerably lax attitude

toward false doctrine. The report was signed by J.H.C. Fritz, Chr. Merkel, Arthur Brunn, W. Arndt, and J. C. Baur, names later to become well known in the synod. *LW* 31 (1912): 51-52.

65. C. Howard Hopkins, *The Rise of the Social Gospel in American Protestantism, 1865–1915* (New Haven, 1940), pp. 296-98; Robert Bremner, *From the Depths: The Discovery of Poverty in the United States* (New York, 1964), p. 157; Franz Pieper, "The Laymen's Movement in the Light of God's Word," *What Is Christianity? and Other Essays,* trans. John Theodore Mueller (St. Louis: Concordia Publishing House, 1933), p. 100. See also A. L. Graebner, *DL* 48 (1892): 69-70; Friedrich Bente, *DL* 51 (1895): 162.

66. Pieper, *DL* 66 (1910): 6, 107.

67. Franz Pieper, *DL* 52 (1896): 34.

68. C. A. Weiss, *LW* 23 (1904): 185; J.H.C. Fritz, *LW* 36 (1917): 349-50.

69. George Luecke, *LW* 25 (1906): 128-29.

70. *Cf.* William A. Clebsch, *From Sacred to Profane America: The Role of Religion in American History* (New York, 1968), pp. 70-79.

71. C. A. Weiss, *LW* 31 (1912): 33.

72. *DL* 66 (1910): 107.

73. C. A. Weiss, *LW* 27 (1908): 2; George Luecke, *LW* 28 (1909): 222; Fuerbringer, *DL* 66 (1910): 186; W.H.T. Dau, *DL* 68 (1912): 56.

74. L., *DL* 66 (1910): 2-4, 18-19, 34-35.

75. *"Die von Gott geordnete Laienbewegung,"* delivered at the 1913 convention of the Southern Illinois District. Translated as "The Laymen's Movement in the Light of God's Word," see note 65 above.

76. *DL* 67 (1911): 272; *VER, LCMS* 1911, p. 172.

Chapter 2: New Cast in Search of Roles

1. See, e.g., Alan Graebner, "World War I and Lutheran Union: Documents from the Army and Navy Board, 1917 and 1918," *CHIQ* 41 (May 1968): 51-64.

2. U.S. Bureau of the Census, *Historical Statistics of the United States, Colonial Times to 1957* (Washington, D.C., 1960), pp. 56-57. Immigration picked up slightly just before the war, but did not approach former peaks. True, there was a substantial influx of German-speaking people from Russia, but these people usually remained on the periphery of the synod in the Dakotas, Montana, and western Canada. *DL* 68 (1911): 395.

3. A. L. Graebner, *TQ* 3 (1899): 205.

4. *DL* 62 (1906): 105-106. One can cite no statistics here, but already in the 1890s concern was expressed about Lutheran girls then moving to the city in search of wider horizons. A. L. Graebner suggested that Christian widows might operate placement bureaus to find jobs for country girls as maids instead of seeing them go to work in factories, the male sphere. Graebner, *DL* 50 (1894): 71-72; 51 (1895): 138; *Concordia Magazine* 1 (1896): 36. In Chicago a *Rettungsliga* was organized to preserve Lutheran girls from the white slave traffic. *DL* 65 (1909): 131-32, 135; *LW* 28 (1909): 266-67. Increasing efforts were made during the prewar years to establish hospices, or boarding homes, for young people, especially in large cities. Much more was also said about providing spiritual care for Lutherans at universities, particularly in the Midwest. *DL* 58 (1903): 317; 62 (1906): 21; 66 (1910): 286.

5. The paraphrases are from H. H. Succop, *DL* 56 (1900): 274, and *VER*, LCMS 1908, pp. 47-48.

6. August C. Stellhorn, *Schools of the Lutheran Church—Missouri Synod* (St. Louis: Concordia Publishing House, 1963), pp. 304-305; W. H. Luecke, "Concordia Collegiate Institute, Bronxville, New York, 1881-1955," *CHIQ* 28 (Fall 1955): 116-17.

7. *VER*, LCMS 1902, p. 64; 1908, pp. 47-48.

8. *Fiftieth Anniversary, 1908–1958: Jehovah Lutheran Congregation, Chicago* (n.p., n.d.).

9. See Paul Kleppner, *The Cross of Culture: A Social Analysis of Midwestern Politics, 1850–1900* (New York, 1970); Frederick C. Luebke, *Immigrants and Politics: The Germans of Nebraska, 1880–1900* (Lincoln, 1969); Douglas C. Stange, "Al Smith and the Republican Party at Prayer: The Lutheran Vote—1928," *Review of Politics* (July 1970), 347-64; Richard Jensen, *The Winning of the Midwest: Social and Political Conflict, 1888–1896* (Chicago, 1971).

10. As late as 1914, synodical officials saw nothing incongruous in subtitling a "mission" report with the phrase, "proclaiming the Word among brothers in the faith" *("Verkuendigung des Worts unter Glaubensgenossen"). VER*, LCMS 1914, p. 72.

11. It was true that a few atypical laymen like A. G. Brauer and J. F. Schuricht might support something like a city institutional mission in St. Louis, but this was rare. See Ludwig Ernest Fuerbringer, *Persons and Events* (St. Louis: Concordia Publishing House, 1947), pp. 104-05, 113-18.

12. F. Dean Lueking, *Mission in the Making: The Missionary Enter-*

prise Among Missouri Synod Lutherans, 1846–1963, (St. Louis: Concordia Publishing House, 1964), pp. 25, 242. For involvement of women's groups, see *ibid.,* p. 110; *DL* 69 (1913): 295, 309-310.

13. Even an incomplete tabulation showed that in this period twelve Lutheran hospitals were founded, compared to two before 1895. Six of eight homes for the aged were begun after 1891; eight of nine home-finding societies were established after 1899. F. W. Herzberger, "The Charitable Activities of the Missouri Synod," *Ebenezer,* ed. W.H.T. Dau (St. Louis: Concordia Publishing House, 1922), pp. 452-56. Some of this "charitable" endeavor was doubtless motivated by exclusionist, protectionist sentiment. See the *"Warnung vor Secten-Hospitaelern"* in *DL* 51 (1895): 71. F. Dean Lueking covers a broad range of charitable activity in *A Century of Caring: The Welfare Ministry Among Missouri Synod Lutherans, 1868-1968* (St. Louis: Board of Social Ministry, Lutheran Church—Missouri Synod, 1968).

14. A Concordia League, for example, was instrumental in founding the first Lutheran high school in Chicago in 1909. *LW* 53 (1934): 82. An auxiliary organized in 1916 to help a Lutheran orphanage in Chicago was later cited as one of the earliest auxiliaries in the synod. *LW* 60 (1941): 354.

15. Laymen were occasionally prominent in the founding of such schools, as for example, John P. Baden in the case of St. John's, Winfield, Kansas, or the group of men in the case of Concordia Teachers College, Seward, Nebraska. But, once again these were the exception rather than the rule. *LW* 18 (1900): 157; Martin P. Simon, "College in the Cornfield: A History of Concordia Teachers College, Seward, Nebraska" (Ed.D. dissertation, University of Oregon, 1953), p. 28 ff.

16. Luecke, 109-112, 115.

17. *DL* 67 (1911): 171. Interestingly enough, the Chicago group was supported at the decisive 1911 triennial convention by a strong resolution from New York. *EIN,* LCMS 1911, pp. 40-41. See also Alfred J. Freitag, *College With A Cause: A History of Concordia Teachers College* (River Forest, Ill.: Concordia Teachers College, 1964), pp. 80-81.

18. *DL* 68 (1912): 328; *LW* 31 (1912): 158; *DL* 69 (1913): 362; *LW* 31 (1912): 77; *LW* 33 (1914): 121.

19. *DL* 68 (1912): 3-4.

20. Interview, Oscar P. Brauer, Sept. 16, 1966; see A. H. Ahlbrand to A. G. Brauer, Feb. 18, 1915, May 15, 1915; Henry Horst to Brauer, Dec. 16, 1914, Dec. 10, 1915, TG MSS, Box 78.

21. Carl F. Eissfeldt, *LL* 5 (1934): 18-19; W. G. Polack, "The Found-

ing of the Lutheran Laymen's League and the First Years of Its Activity.'' *CHIQ* 6 (April 1933): 3-4.

22. Edmund Seuel, quoted *ibid.*, 5.

23. *Ibid.*, 7.

24. There is no comparable figure for the laity at large, but to judge from a careful study of the necrology section of the *SYB* during the late twenties and early thirties, at least half of the synodical clergy were born in Germany.

25. Albert H. Ahlbrand, "My Activity in Synod and District Church Matters" (typewritten memoir, June 24, 1945). This is in the possession of Miss Marletta Wesche, St. Louis, Mo., to whom I am indebted for calling it to my attention and for permission to quote from it.

26. John Boehne from Evansville, Indiana had been a U.S. congressman; Benjamin Bosse was mayor of Evansville. H. A. Luedke was a delegate to a national Republican convention, and William Schlake had been a Chicago alderman.

27. These generalizations are based on information found in most cases in biographical sketches given to John Theodore Mueller, "The Story of the Lutheran Laymen's League" (typewritten manuscript, 1948), pp. 7-62; see also W. G. Polack, *Cresset* 8 (June 1945): 20-26.

28. *AL* 11 (1928): 404-409; Fuerbringer, *Persons and Events,* pp. 106-13. The quotation is reported by Karl Kretzmann, *AL* 11 (1928): 406.

29. Fuerbringer, pp. 113-18.

30. Theodore H. Lamprecht, *LW* 44 (1925): 165.

31. Timothy L. Smith, *Revivalism and Social Reform: American Protestantism on the Eve of the Civil War,* Harper Torchbook ed. (New York, 1965), pp. 80-81.

32. An enlarged role for laymen because of more complex business affairs was not unique to the Missouri Synod. In 1866 and 1872 lay representation was introduced in the Methodist churches for the same reason. Richard M. Cameron, *Methodism and Society in Historical Perspective* (New York, 1961), pp. 267-68.

33. Circular letter, Oct. 2, 1917, filed at CHI with LLL records.

34. See, for example, Lamprecht's circular letter, Oct. 2, 1917; *LW* 37 (1918): 35.

35. Theodore Graebner, *LW* 37 (1918): 35.

36. The constitution is reprinted in *LW* 39 (1920): 236.

37. On the synod's previous system, see *LW* 44 (1925): 345; *LW* 28 (1909): 285-86, 603-604; 30 (1911): 141; 36 (1917): 32, 122, 210; 44 (1925): 345. On broader developments, see Scott M. Cutlip, *Fund Rais-*

ing in the United States: Its Role in America's Philanthropy (New Brunswick, 1965), pp. 93-99; J.A.E. Salstrand, *The Story of Stewardship in the United States of America* (Grand Rapids, 1956), pp. 59-61; *LW* 37 (1918): 12; see also *LW* 39 (1920): 43, 101. In addition, Missourian leaders knew in 1915 of the decision by laymen of the Augustana Synod (Swedish) to raise $500,000 for their own synodical pension fund. *After Seventy-Five Years, 1860–1935* (Rock Island, Ill., 1935), p. 177.

38. *LW* 37 (1918): 189, 380-81; Minutes, BD, Oct. 8-9, 1918, Report of Executive Secretary.

39. Cutlip, pp. 110-52; William Warren Sweet, *The Story of Religion in America* (New York, 1950), p. 404; Clifton E. Olmstead, *History of Religion in the United States* (Englewood Cliffs, N.J., 1960), pp. 513-14; "Report of the Lutheran Church Board for Army and Navy . . . to February 1st, 1919," filed at CHI under LLL, 1923.

40. Minutes, General Conference, Dec. 15, 1918. The decision to ask for bonds was based upon the observation of some businessmen that once the war ended, rural German-Americans especially were liquidating the war bonds they had sometimes been partially coerced into buying. H. H. Zimmerman to Graebner, June 17, 1925, Graebner MSS, Box 78; LLL Minutes, BD, Oct. 9, 1918. For methods used during the war to "encourage" citizens to buy bonds, see Charles Steward, "Prussianizing Wisconsin," *Atlantic Monthly*, 124 (Jan. 1919): 99-105.

The aversion to bonds was not necessarily based on immigrant alienation from the American government. According to Theodore Eckhart, many Lutheran farmers had little experience with intangible assets and little faith in their investment. Interview, July 16, 1963.

41. *LW* 38 (1919): 151; 39 (1920): 144, 166.

42. Minutes (first draft), Officers, May 23, 1919, p. 8. The only opposition came from a few who still maintained that life insurance was gambling and so identified the pension fund. LLL Transcript, June 14-15, 1920, p. 78; Dorothea Stipp to Theo. Graebner, Oct. 14, 1919; Graebner to Lamprecht, Oct. 11, 1919, TG MSS, Box 78.

43. More than 200,000 separate contributions were received from a communicant membership of 633,000. *LW* 39 (1920): 223. The league also added contributors' names to the *Witness* subscription list. With this help, voluntary subscriptions to the emerging English periodical rose nearly 50 percent in less than three years. Circulation climbed briefly from 19,000 to at least 75,000. It dropped precipitously after the drive, as one would expect, but not below 29,000. *LW* 37 (1918): 111; 39 (1920): 41; *DL* 77 (1921): 168.

44. *LW* 37 (1918): 412; Minutes (first draft), Officers, May 23, 1919, p. 11; *LW* 39 (1920): 394; 40 (1921): 14.

45. *LW* 39 (1920): 167, 133.

46. *DL* 75 (1919): 6.

47. Pritzlaff in 1917, for example, knew previously only Brauer and Luedke out of the original twelve in the LLL. *LL* 13 (1942): 35.

48. In the formulation of Milton Gordon, "with a person of the same social class but of a different ethnic group, one shares behavioral similarities but not a sense of peoplehood. With those of the same ethnic group but of a different social class, one shares the sense of peoplehood but not behavioral similarities. The only group which meets both of these criteria are people of the same ethnic group *and* same social class." *Assimilation,* p. 53.

49. *Walther League Messenger* 28 (1920): 267-68.

50. LLL Transcript, June 14-15, 1920, pp. 87, 91. Speakers, identified only by last name, were Hillman and Reller.

Chapter 3: Auditions and Casting

1. *AL* 10 (1927): 260-61; 25 (1942): 3.

2. Theodore Graebner to Theodore H. Lamprecht, March 28, 1925, TG MSS, Box 78. A sketch of the association's history is in George A. W. Vogel and Walter S. Wendt, *Seventy-five Years of God's Grace: A History of the Lutheran Church—Missouri Synod in Iowa, 1879-1954* (n.p.: Iowa District East and Iowa District West, 1954), pp. 66-70; see also Theodore A. Aaberg, *A City Set on a Hill: A History of the Evangelical Lutheran Synod (Norwegian Synod), 1918-1968* (Mankato, Minn: Board of Publications, Evangelical Lutheran Synod, 1968), pp. 102-103.

3. May 27, 1915, TG MSS, Box 78.

4. Quoted by Zorn, LLL Transcript, Nov. 7, 1919, p. 14. In these transcripts only the last name of the speaker was identified.

5. Ahlbrand to Brauer, May 27, 1919, TG MSS, Box 78.

6. Theo. Graebner, *LW* 36 (1917): 212.

7. Leschin [Leschen?], LLL Transcript, Nov. 6, 1919, p. 19.

8. Letter fragment, W. H. Buchholz to "My dear editor," n.d. [1917-24], TG MSS, Box 61.

9. Minutes (first draft), Officers, May 23, 1919, p. 10.

10. *Ibid.*, p. 2; Minutes, ExC, Feb. 11, 1921; Secretary's Report, July 10, 1919, p. 15; interview, Oscar P. Brauer, Sept. 16, 1966.

11. For Boehne's sentiments, see Minutes (first draft), BD, May 24,

1922, p. 9. The quotation is from *ibid.,* Oct. 27, 1926, p. 5.

12. Carl Manthey-Zorn, *Wachet! Ein Handbuch fuer Reihenfolgen von zeitgemaessen Betrachtungen* (Milwaukee: Northwestern Publishing House, 1921). See review in *LW* 40 (1921): 126. To be fair, it should be said that this description is, of necessity, based mainly on extensive correspondence between Graebner and C. M. Zorn, Jr., a Cleveland businessman. See TG MSS, Box 78. No other analysis has as yet come to light. For news reports, see *LW* 39 (1920): 41-42.

13. See Alan Graebner, "The Acculturation of an Immigrant Lutheran Church: The Lutheran Church–Missouri Synod, 1917–1929 (Ph.D. dissertation, Columbia University, 1965), pp. 15-55.

14. In fact, early publicity speculated that the national LLL constitution would be revised to include Fort Wayne objectives. *Der Sekretaer* [W. D. Holterman], *Lutheraner! Wachet Auf!* (n.p.: American Luther League, n.d. [Spring, 1919], TG MSS, Box 78.

15. C. M. Zorn, Jr., to Theo. Graebner, July 30, 1919, TG MSS, Box 78.

16. Schlake, LLL Transcript, Nov. 7, 1919, p. 7.

17. Scheimann, *ibid.,* p. 9, p. 11.

18. Lamprecht circular letter, Oct. 2, 1917, filed at CHI under LLL.

19. *Lutheraner! Wachet Auf!* Reported a Ft. Wayne pastor, "There is no doubt in my mind that the membership is made up largely of pro-German (language) workers." John Graebner to Theo. Graebner, Oct. 5, 1922, TG MSS, Box 133. Compare The Secretary [W.D. Holterman], *Lutherans! Wake Up!* (n.p.: American Luther League, n.d. [Fall, 1919], filed at CHI under Oregon school fight materials, with *Lutheraner! Wachet Auf!*

20. Schulze, LLL Transcript, Nov. 7, 1919, p. 9.

21. ALL circular letter, Dec. 1919, TG MSS, Box 133.

22. Pfotenhauer to Graebner, Jan. 3, 1920; Graebner to Pfotenhauer, Jan. 11, 1920, TG MSS, Box 133.

23. Martin F. Kretzmann to John C. Baur, Feb. 18, 1920, TG MSS Box 133.

24. *Lutherans! Wake Up!; Constitution of the American Luther League . . . 1920* (single printed sheet), TG MSS, Box 133.

25. The best summary of the more mature ALL is in Baur to Graebner, Sept. 27, 1922, TG MSS, Box 133. For league activities, see *LL* 3 (1922): 133-34; 2 (1921): 31.

26. For coverage of these campaigns, see Erwin F. Vonderlage, "Saving the Private Schools: A Study of Pressure Group Influence on State

Referenda in Michigan and Oregon" (M.S. thesis, Washington University, 1958). This is partly reprinted in "The Michigan Storm Center in the School Question," *CHIQ* 35 (April 1962): 37-44; and "The American Luther League," *CHIQ* 36 (July 1963): 34-42.

27. *LL* 2 (1921): 35-36, 90; Minutes, Synodical School Board, July 1921, CHI; *LL* 3 (1922): 133.

28. National conventions were held in towns such as Elgin and Dundee, Ill., Fort Wayne, Ind., and Fort Dodge, Kan. Advertisements and addresses in the *Layman* as well as general atmosphere give a strong impression of a rural and small town constituency.

29. *LL* 3 (1922): 8; 2 (1921): 60; 3 (1922): 46; 3 (1923): 189; 5 (1924): 240.

30. *LL* 2 (1921): 7; 4 (1923): 117-19, 205; 2 (1921): 53; 3 (1922): 108-109; 4 (1923): 14.

31. *LL* 7 (1926): 99.

32. *LL* 6 (1925): 168.

33. *LL* 7 (1926): 99.

34. Interview, John C. Baur, June 11, 1964.

35. Baur, Herman A. Duemling, William C. Dickmeyer, W. D. Holterman, H. D. Mensing—all once prominent in the ALL—soon sat on the Valparaiso Board of Directors. John Strietelmeier, *Valparaiso's First Century: A Centennial History of Valparaiso University* (Valparaiso, Ind.: Valparaiso University, 1959), pp. 182-83.

36. Minutes, BG, Exhibit D, Dec. 18, 1930, p. 11; *LL* 4 (1933): 22.

37. Minutes, LCMS BD, May 22, 1929, 290522s.

38. Membership table in Minutes, BD, Oct. 27, 1926.

39. Minutes, ExC, Sept. 25, 1922, p. 4. The idea was stronger in 1924: "in our membership campaign we must at all times have a real live issue to present." Minutes, Organization and Membership Committee, April 5, 1924, p. 3.

40. *LW* 42 (1923): 41.

41. Minutes, ExC, May 19, 1926; June 6, 1926.

42. Minutes, Campaign Committee and ExC, May 19, 1926.

43. For general background on radio I have relied on Erik Barnouw's entertaining and informative *A Tower in Babel: A History of Broadcasting in the United States to 1933* (New York, 1966).

44. For a more detailed outline of the early years of KFUO, see Alan Graebner, "KFUO's Beginnings," *CHIQ* 37 (Oct. 1964): 81-94.

45. Minutes, ExC, Feb. 5, 1926; Campaign Committee and ExC, May 19, 1926, p. 3; *PRO,* LLL, 1926, p. 15.

46. A. H. Ahlbrand and Henry W. Horst, for example, served on the synodical Board of Directors during this decade.

47. League officials were aware of the need for younger men. George Harms, then serving as temporary LLL president, declined to run in 1926, insisting on the need for young blood. Lamprecht, *AL* 3 (1920): 69-70; Ahlbrand to Brauer, June 12, 1923, Ahlbrand MSS, in the possession of Miss Marletta Wesche, St. Louis, Mo.; John Theodore Mueller, "The Story of the Lutheran Laymen's League" (typewritten manuscript, 1948), p. 147.

48. *LW* 48 (1929): 241.

49. Minutes, BD, May 14-15, 1920; *PRO*, LLL, 1923, p. 25; A. A. Grossmann to Lamprecht, March 19, 1923, LLL, CHI; Minutes, ExC, April 11-12, 1924, p. 6; Feb. 25, 1927; Minutes, Organization and Membership Committee, March 19, 1927; Theo. Graebner to Lamprecht, March 28, 1925, TG MSS, Box 78.

50. In 1948, Martin Daib, a man with wide knowledge of local clubs, termed the men's club at Holyoke, Mass., then celebrating its fiftieth anniversary, without a doubt the oldest men's club in the synod. *LL* 19 (1948): 64.

51. When J.H.C. Fritz wrote about social activity in the churches in 1917, he did not even mention rural congregations. *LW* 36 (1917): 349-50. Very few reports of local men's club appeared in the German *Lutheraner,* while the *Witness* carried relatively frequent notices, mainly from English District congregations. There is no guarding, of course, against disproportionate sampling due to selective reporting or editing.

During the early twenties, more than half of all American churches in towns were likely to have clubs compared to only 10 percent or less in village or rural churches (using 5,000 population as the dividing line). Harlan Paul Douglass, *One Thousand City Churches: Phases of Adaptation to Urban Environment* (New York, 1926), p. 81.

52. *LW* 43 (1924): 268; ALL circular letter, Dec. 1919, TG MSS, Box 133; *LW* 31 (1912): 198; Jack Ungemach to Theo. Graebner, Jan. 15, 1913, TG MSS, Box 78.

53. There were organizations in Buffalo, Cleveland, Akron, Sheboygan, Baltimore, and a few other places. *LW* 30 (1911): 5, 54; 31 (1912): 92, 101; 32 (1913): 190; 33 (1914): 21; 34 (1915): 141; 35 (1916): 358; 36 (1917): 184; 40 (1921): 385; 43 (1924): 268; 44 (1925): 423; 45 (1926): 132; 47 (1928): 99. But comparative absence of men's clubs seems confirmed by careful scrutiny of minor notes and reports of local activity printed in the *Witness* back pages. For comments on male attention in

the synod, see A. L. Graebner, *TQ* 4 (1900): 243; John H. C. Fritz, *LW* 25 (1906): 205-206; *idem, LW* 32 (1913): 35-36; Francis Pieper, *DL* 69 (1913): 6; Martin Sommer, *LW* 42 (1923): 70-71; *WLM* 37 (1929): 457.

54. Apparently amid disagreement about the wisdom of reorganization, matters took an unhappy turn at a meeting in March 1929. Without a quorum present, the reorganization was recommended to the league. For Executive Secretary Cramer, who opposed reorganization anyway, this was the last straw and he resigned. Even though a later meeting ratified the earlier reorganization decision, Cramer's resignation stood and the league was without an executive secretary. Minutes, ExC, April 26, 1929; Minutes, CNV, June 17, 1929.

55. Theo. Graebner, *LW* 49 (1930): 37.

56. Paul Lindemann, Walter A. Maier, and A.R. Kretzmann were all called (unsuccessfully). Minutes, BG, July 19, 1929, p. 36; Oct. 18, 1929, p. 62; Sept. 19, 1930, p. 147.

Chapter 4: Auditing the Father's Business

1. *LL* 4 (1933): 33.

2. Quoted in *Moving Frontiers: Readings in the History of The Lutheran Church—Missouri Synod,* ed. Carl S. Meyer (St. Louis: Concordia Publishing House, 1964), p. 243.

3. In the voluntary assessment system, each member was levied a designated amount, or a sliding scale based on wealth was fixed. H. Studtmann, *"Vom Geben der Christen fuer Christi Reich," VER,* Texas District, LCMS, 1913, pp. 43-44. For pew renting see A. L. Graebner, *DL* 53 (1897): 4; *AL* 2 (1919): 54. Confusion on voting membership is reported in Studtmann, pp. 25-26; *DL* 63 (1907): 308-309.

4. *LW* 39 (1920): 311-12. President J. W. Behnken remembered driving his father, a rural pastor, around on visits to collect for synodical purposes. *This I Recall* (St. Louis: Concordia Publishing House, 1964), p. 76. City pastors may have dispensed with the buggy and the barn's shadow, but some still made the rounds to collect for church purposes, including their own salary. *LW* 21 (1902): 197.

5. Hugh George Anderson, *Lutheranism in the Southeastern States, 1860–1886: A Social History* (The Hague, 1969), pp. 161-66.

6. John H. C. Fritz, *Church Finances: A Handbook for the Pastor and the Layman* (St. Louis: Concordia Publishing House, 1922), p. 8; *DL* 56 (1900): 407.

7. *DL* 49 (1893): 4; *LW* 16 (1897): 20; *DL* 57 (1901): 340.

8. A penny was long considered the appropriate coin for the *Klingelbeutel*. Ernst Eckhardt, *SYB*, 1937, p. 154. With its rigid bottom, the basket was at least easier to make change out of than the deep recesses of the *Klingelbeutel*. Sometimes the plate was not passed in the pews, however, but simply held at the church door. *LW* 37 (1918): 62. The *Witness* description is by Graebner, *LW* 39 (1920): 311.

9. Edward Pardieck, *DL* 69 (1913): 107. See also Behnken, p. 114, for a similar observation from modern Germany.

10. *DL* 70 (1914): 324. This was not unique; see *DL* 59 (1903): 331.

11. The quotation is from Franz Pieper, *DL* 58 (1902): 227. For statistics, see Ernst Eckhardt, *DL* 70 (1914): 159.

12. *AL* 6 (1923): 66.

13. J.A.E. Salstrand, *The Story of Stewardship in the United States of America* (Grand Rapids, Mich., 1956), p. 50. William H. Leach, "Financing the Local Church," *Religion in American Society,* vol. 332 (Nov. 1960), *The Annals of the American Academy of Political and Social Science,* 76.

14. *LW* 16 (1897): 101; *LW* 22 (1903): 3; *DL* 63 (1907): 421-22; *DL* 64 (1908): 403; 65 (1909): 26.

15. It was pointed out that envelopes encouraged everyone to give, even if he could not give much; envelopes applied no legalistic pressure, but were reminders for regular contributions; even if a donor was not present when a special collection was taken up, he could drop in his offering later. See, for example, Studtmann, p. 41. By 1913, envelope orders from the publishing house had climbed from 8,000 to 2,000,000. *DL* 70 (1914): 7. The rise rather than the absolute number is significant here, for it is impossible to say how many communicants this serviced. George Buettner, "Concordia Publishing House As I Knew It (1888–1955)," *CHIQ* 47 (Summer 1974): 63.

16. *LW* 48 (1929): 338; *VER,* LCMS, 1866, p. 78; *LW* 35 (1916): 194-96; 36 (1917): 51, 53, 87.

17. By the early twenties about half of all American country churches generally used envelopes and canvasses. H. N. Morse and Edmund deS. Brunner, *The Town and Country Church in the United States* (New York, 1923), p. 141. A survey by the synodical fiscal office in 1930 suggested, however, that only one-third of the congregations used envelopes for synodical purposes. Minutes, Synodical Finance Committee at Large, Jan. 15, 1930, p. 4, Lawrence B. Meyer MSS, Box 16. Fritz spent much time on envelopes in his *Pastoral Theology* of 1932 (St. Louis: Concordia Publishing House), pp. 270-77, but by the thirties, the subject was getting much less attention in the synodical press.

18. When Chicago pastors launched a campaign in 1905 to pay off the debt by ten-dollar contributions, Editor Fuerbringer hailed the plan and followed it in *Der Lutheraner* for a number of issues, helping to build interest and suspense. *DL* 61 (1905): 132-34, 148-50, 166-67, 178-80, 229-30. The following year in a building fund drive, the usually conservative *Lutheraner* printed a campaign issue that even included pictures. 62 (1906): 33-44.

19. At the 1914 convention, hard as it is to believe, consideration of a well thought out and much supported program was tabled for lack of time to discuss it. *VER*, LCMS 1914, pp. 148-53.

20. LLL Transcript, Nov. 8, 1919, pp. 59-60; *VER*, LCMS, 1920, p. 207; Theodore Eckhart to District Presidents, May 24, 1921, TG MSS, Box 65. As later, district treasurers were known to cover district deficits with funds donated for the synodical treasuries. *DL* 76 (1920): 134; Edmund Seuel to BD, LCMS, Sept. 26, 1922, bound with Minutes, BD, LCMS.

21. *DL* 70 (1914): 126-27; *DL* 69 (1913): 220.

22. *AL* 3 (1920): 68. Perhaps Lamprecht was a trifle defensive, but he stated things nicely in 1922 when he said that to aid synod in financial matters "is not a mean purpose—a cold-blooded business proposition." It is necessary "because slipshod business methods hinder the Gospel; because the work of the Lord among men cannot go on when money is not forthcoming; because debts in the household of Synod blight its work." *AL* 5 (1922): 46.

23. For mechanics, see *LW* 37 (1918): 265. After three years of effort, a "Jubilee Fund" to celebrate the four hundredth anniversary of the Reformation barely reached $300,000 in 1918. *DL* 74 (1918): 72.

24. Interview, July 16, 1963.

25. Jan. 29, 1919, TG MSS, Box 78.

26. It was probably no coincidence that the first million-dollar appropriation by the synod was passed at the 1920 convention the morning after the LLL had formally turned over the endowment fund. *LW* 39 (1920): 212. See Ludwig Fuerbringer, *DL* 76 (1920): 97.

27. *DL* 75 (1919): 217.

28. When studying federated charities fund raising of this period, Lubove was struck by similar phenomena: the crucial impact of World War I and emphasis on efficiency. See his helpful chapter in Roy Lubove, *The Professional Altruist: The Emergence of Social Work As A Career, 1880–1930,* Atheneum ed. (New York, 1969), pp. 183-219. See also William T. Doherty, "The Impact of Business Upon Protestantism, 1900–1929," *Business History Review* 28 (June 1954): 141-53. In addition

to the synodical examples cited on following pages, two extended illustrations of business models in ecclesiastical affairs are in Eugene
Wengert to Graebner, Jan. 2, 1920, TG MSS, Box 69, and an untitled
mimeographed MS by Louis H. Waltke, which, according to a covering
letter (Lawrence B. Meyer to Graebner, April 20, 1936) was sent to all
district presidents. TG MSS, Box 66. Wengert, for example, called for
a financial secretary; "his work should be similar to that of a credit and
advertising manager of a larger business establishment." Waltke reminded his readers that manufacturers had shifted from reliance on
wholesalers to direct advertising. "My answer would be that we adopt
business methods by reaching the consumer; in this case the communicant member."

29. Graebner is cited in Minutes, Meeting of Representative Laymen,
St. Louis, May 20-21, 1936, TG MSS, Box 66. Paul Lindemann, *AL* 1
(May 1918): 2. The article was entitled, "Delivering the Goods." For
more of the same, see Virsilva, *AL* 3 (1920): 15; G. E. Hageman, *AL* 6
(1923): 57.

30. See autobiographical letter to Lawrence Meyer, June 13, 1929, TG
MSS, Box 80.

31. Feb. 18, 1915, TG MSS, Box 78.

32. LLL Transcript, Nov. 8, 1919, p. 82. Ahlbrand to Meyer, June 13,
1929, TG MSS, Box 80.

33. Ahlbrand, LLL Transcript, p. 48; Minutes, BD, Jan. 20-21, 1919,
p. 5.

34. Ahlbrand, LLL Transcript, pp. 56, 62.

35. Even then the synodical board modified the exclusively lay orien-
tation by insisting that clergy as well as laymen attend the proposed
meetings. Minutes, BD, LCMS, May 25, 1921, 210525H; Alan Graebner,
"The Acculturation of an Immigrant Lutheran Church: The Lutheran
Church—Missouri Synod, 1917–1929" (Ph.D. dissertation, Columbia
University, 1965), p. 327.

36. Ahlbrand to Richard Jesse, Dec. 8, 1918, TG MSS, Box 65.

37. LLL Transcript, p. 43.

38. Minutes, BD, May 24, 1922, p. 5. The hostility is obvious in a
comparison of first draft and official minutes for a joint LLL and district
presidents meeting, May 23-24, 1922.

39. Minutes, BD, March 1, 1923.

40. *VER*, LCMS, 1923, pp. 209-216. The quotation is from p. 213.

41. The auditors continued to agitate for standardized accounting and
sound business procedures. In successive conventions, they achieved a

measure of success. By 1929, almost all boards in the synod were making regular reports, and the triennial convention finally approved the office of comptroller. *VER*, LCMS, 1926, pp. 294-97; *PRO*, LCMS, 1929, pp. 164-69.

42. *LW* 66 (1947): 300.

43. *LW* 45 (1926): 25.

44. *DL* 82 (1926): 176.

45. For his early stewardship statements, see *LW* 21 (1902): 182-83; 24 (1905): 29; 28 (1909): 277-78. His approach was three-fold, summed up in "Gospel, Information, System." The Gospel "furnishes the motive power, the information arouses the interest, the system supplies the opportunity." *Finances*, p. 7.

46. Minutes, Ways and Means Committee, Aug. 14, 1923, CHI.

47. Wrote Theo. Graebner in another campaign, "we have resolved to shroud ourselves in invisibility and to organize a Laymen's Committee. . . ." To Theodore Lamprecht, Oct. 3, 1925, TG MSS, Box 78.

48. Interview, John C. Baur, May 21, 1963. Pledges were used by the Lutheran Education Societies at Bronxville and River Forest; they were introduced on a large scale by the government and Red Cross during the war. Increasing installment buying during the twenties made the pledge still more familiar, and thus attractive. *LW* 36 (1917): 368; *DL* 73 (1917): 35; Fritz, *Finances*, pp. 40-52; LLL Transcript, June 14-15, 1920, p. 99.

49. *PRO*, LCMS, 1926, pp. 212-14.

50. C. M. Zorn, *DL* 64 (1908), 186.

51. Minutes, BD, LCMS, Dec. 21, 1927, 271221R; March 2, 1928, 280302Z; April 13, 1928, 280413K; June 29, 1928, 280629B; *PRO*, LCMS, 1929, p. 178; *PRO*, LCMS, 1932, p. 208; *LW* 57 (1938): 266.

52. *LL* 13 (1942): 26.

53. *Christian Stewardship and Its Modern Implications* (St. Louis: Concordia Publishing House, n.d.), p. 32.

54. An early version was delivered before the Atlantic District convention in 1933. For *American Lutheran* articles, see *AL* 10 (1927): 219; 11 (1928): 449; 12 (1929): 763-64.

55. P. 3.

56. Unsigned, 26 (1943): 232.

57. Paul Lindemann, 18 (1935): 2402.

58. Unsigned, *AV* 1 (Nov. 1954): 21. See also *AL* 38 (1955): 69-71. Evangelism campaigns also demonstrated borrowing from business sales techniques.

59. Figures are taken from issues of the *SYB*.

60. *LW* 68 (1949): 362. Proposals for a Stewardship Department were made already in 1935. *PRO,* LCMS, 1935, pp. 276-77; *RAM,* LCMS, 1938, p. 261. District secretaries are cited in *LW* 65 (1946): 243; 68 (1949): 414; 70 (1951): 248; 73 (1954): 287, 300, 429; 74 (1955): 234.

61. *LL* 25 (Sept. 1954): 1; *RAM,* LCMS, 1962, p. 330.

62. *RAM,* LCMS, 1965, p. 410.

63. CPH still advertised Karl Kretzschmar's *The Stewardship Life* of 1929 in 1946 and brought out Lindemann's essay in 1950 under the title, *My God and I. LW* 75 (1946): 216; 69 (1950): 62. See also, for example, CPH books by R. C. Rein, *That I May Be His Own* (1954), *Adventures in Stewardship* (1955), and *First Fruits* (1959).

64. On tithing, one side continued to cite Old Testament precedent and anecdotes proving how the Lord blessed the tither financially; the other side, which had a distinct edge among Lutherans, preferred the idea of 'proportionate giving' to a term that might smack of legalism. As a sampling see George Luecke, *LW* 19 (1901): 129; Franz Pieper, *DL* 68 (1912): 395-96; Albert H. Ahlbrand, *LW* 42 (1923): 141; O. W. H. Lindemeyer, *ibid.*: 131-32; Allen H. Fedder, *AL* 24 (1941): 73; Unsigned, *AL* 31 (1948): 3; Anonymous, *LW* 74 (1955): 206.

65. See Fred Rutz, *A Businessman Looks at His Church* (Painesville, Ohio: published by the author, n.d.) and a mimeographed "Supplement," 1968.

66. See Richard Carter, *The Gentle Legions* (Garden City, 1961).

67. 1 (Nov. 1954), 40.

68. See Victor Thiessen, "Who Gives a Damn? A Study of Charitable Contributions" (Ph.D. dissertation, University of Wisconsin, 1968), and Kenneth Lutterman, "Giving to Churches" (Ph.D. dissertation, University of Wisconsin, 1962).

69. *Philanthropy in England, 1480–1660: A Study of the Changing Pattern in English Social Aspirations* (London, 1959), p. 20.

Chapter 5: Laborers in the Vineyard

1. As late as 1916, 68 percent of the Synodical Conference constituency lived in places of less than 25,000, and 20 percent in cities of more than 300,000. U.S. Bureau of the Census, *Religious Bodies: 1916* (Washington, D.C., 1920), I, 121. The 1906 religious census did not sufficiently discriminate among Lutheran groups to cite a comparable earlier figure.

2. F. C. Streufert, " 'In the Service of My Lord' " (mimeographed

memoir, n.d.), p. 25. Care must be exercised in speaking of the residential pattern, since this apparently varied from city to city. Germans in St. Louis, for example, were more spread out residentially than those living in Cincinnati. Even in St. Louis, however, there were whole wards in which a quarter of the residents were German-born. See Sr. Audrey Louise Olson, "St. Louis Germans, 1850–1920: The Nature of An Immigrant Community and Its Relation to the Assimilation Process" (Ph.D. dissertation, University of Kansas, 1970), and Guido Dobbert, "The Disintegration of an Immigrant Community: The Cincinnati Germans, 1880-1920" (Ph.D. dissertation, University of Chicago, 1965).

3. These figures are based upon my own punch card tabulation of all congregations reported in the 1900 *SYB*. Statistics for 1930 are from *SYB*, 1930, p. 151.

4. *TQ* 1 (1897): 332. The document was a translation of the constitution of Old Trinity Church in St. Louis and was widely used. Carl S. Mundinger, *Government in the Missouri Synod: The Genesis of Decentralized Government in the Missouri Synod* (St. Louis: Concordia Publishing House, 1947), p. 133n; *LW* 55 (1936): 31. This was a good example of something necessary at an early stage of a congregation's life being perpetuated thereafter. *LW* 21 (1902): 171-72. It may also represent an effort to end lay meetings behind the pastor's back. *Ibid.,* 180-81.

5. For variant constitutional provisions on elders, see Theodore Graebner, *Handbook for Congregational Officers* (St. Louis: Concordia Publishing House, 1928), pp. 64-82.

6. Herman H. Zagel, *Jack Roostand* (St. Louis: Louis Lange Publishing Company, 1909), p. 103.

7. *SYB,* 1937, p. 156.

8. *Concordia Magazine* 6 (1901): 767; *LW* 45 (1926): 53; 46 (1927): 205; 47 (1928): 355; 48 (1929): 329; 55 (1936): 318.

9. Theo. Graebner, *LW* 36 (1917): 78.

10. C. M. Zorn, *DL* 57 (1901): 51; George Luecke, *LW* 21 (1902): 10; John H. C. Fritz, *LW* 27 (1908): 124, 140-41; L., *DL* 66 (1910): 3 ff.

11. Alan Graebner, "The Acculturation of an Immigrant Lutheran Church: The Lutheran Church—Missouri Synod, 1917–1929" (Ph.D. dissertation, Columbia University, 1965), pp. 183-85; *LW* 35 (1916): 196; 36 (1917): 87; *AL* 7 (1924): 165-66; *LW* 47 (1928): 436; 50 (1931): 294. Both Olson and Dobbert document the scattering of especially upperclass German-born in St. Louis and Cincinnati in the years before 1920, a dating that supports similar, imitative action by less prestigious classes strongly underway after World War I. For a detailed study of Lutheran

outward expansion in Chicago, see Sharvy Greiner Umbeck, "The Social Adaptations of a Selected Group of German Background Protestant Churches in Chicago" (Ph.D. dissertation, University of Chicago, 1940). Umbeck found that the memberships of three old congregations closest to the core of the city dropped from an average of more than 1,800 in 1885 to about 300 by the late thirties. These members as well as those of the next outward tier of congregations lived in a fan-shaped concentration, with the handle of the fan pointing toward the Chicago Loop.

A further indication of the breakup of the immigrant Lutheran enclave, as Professor James Albers has suggested to me, is the decline in attention paid to Old Testament marriage legislation, especially the laws on consanguinity. This received much space as late as the turn of the century. Thereafter, though the synod's position on the degrees of relationship within which marriage was forbidden was not dropped, discussion in publications for laymen was quite rare. The dearth of reference may very well reflect fewer cases in the average pastor's experience. And this, in turn, reflects the broader range of potential spouses as the Lutheran ghetto began to dissolve geographically and to some extent psychologically as well.

12. U.S. Bureau of the Census, *Religious Bodies: 1926* (Washington, D.C., 1930), II, 734; U.S. Bureau of the Census, *Lutherans: Statistics, Denominational History, Doctrine, and Organization,* Bulletin No. 18, Census of Religious Bodies, 1936 (Washington, D.C., 1940), p. 69. Alan Graebner, "Birth Control and The Lutherans: The Missouri Synod as a Case Study," *Journal of Social History* 2 (1969): 303-332. For resort lists, see *LW* 43 (1924): 206-207; *AL* 7 (1924): 102-103; 10 (1927), 143.

13. Author unidentified, quoted by Theo. Graebner, *LW* 46 (1927): 450.

14. *LW* 44 (1925): 113; 47 (1928): 210; 57 (1938): 174. John Strietelmeier, *Valparaiso's First Century: A Centennial History of Valparaiso University* (Valparaiso, Ind.: Valparaiso University, 1959), pp. 77-109. For census results, see *LW* 59 (1940): 361.

15. Theo. Graebner, *LW* 39 (1920): 10. Later, during the Depression, the *Witness* reported that the Lutheran laymen were better insulated by more secure positions. *Idem* 53 (1934): 162.

16. *Idem, LW* 46 (1927): 449. By the thirties, O. A. Geiseman, a prominent pastor in a Chicago suburb, could list more than 50 occupations represented in his congregation, adding for contrast, "the days of our childhood were spent in a rural congregation whose members were without exception farmers, who spoke low-German and received their

knowledge of world affairs from the Abendschule, Rundschau, and Germania." *AL* 20 (1937): 3163.

17. Theo. Graebner, *LW* 52 (1933): 140.

18. J. H. Witte, *LW* 37 (1918): 389. *CTM* 6 (1935): 400. Some English Synod congregations had papers already before the turn of the century. *Concordia Magazine* 6 (1901): 140. On the other hand, as late as 1956, *Advance* magazine carried an instructive article on the subject in which the author commented, "with the advent of multiple services and the demise of the congregational picnic, the parish paper becomes the common meeting ground of people in the modern church." See Delbert Schulz, 3 (Oct. 1956): 5-8.

19. Lewis Atherton, *Main Street on the Middle Border* (Bloomington, Ind., 1954), pp. 245-49.

20. See Genevieve Knupfer, "Portrait of the Underdog," *Class, Status and Power: A Reader in Social Stratification,* ed. Reinhard Bendix and Seymour Martin Lipset (Glencoe, Ill., 1953), pp. 255-63; David L. Sills, *The Volunteers: Means and Ends in a National Organization* (Glencoe, Ill., 1957), pp. 100-101; Stephan Thernstrom, *Poverty and Progress: Social Mobility in a Nineteenth Century City* (Cambridge, 1964), pp. 169-70.

21. Robert S. Lynd and Helen Merrell Lynd, *Middletown: A Study in Modern American Culture* (New York, 1929), p. 399. Similarly Harlan Paul Douglass, *The Suburban Trend* (New York, 1925), p. 207.

22. When John H. C. Fritz itemized the bases for social activity in 1917, he placed first the movement to the cities with their cheap amusements and temptations, and then went on to growing heterogeneity; shifting population and large memberships in city churches, he said, made it difficult not only for the pastor to keep in touch with his members, but also for the members to keep in touch with one another. *LW* 36 (1917): 349-50.

23. Theo. Graebner, *LW* 54 (1935): 450. See also *idem, Pastor and People: Letters to a Young Preacher* (St. Louis: Concordia Publishing House, 1932), p. 130.

24. *AL* 23 (1940): 254.

25. *LL,* 11 (1940): 22; *LW* 64 (1945): 107; the quotation is from *LW* 56 (1937): 140.

26. Fritz, *LW* 49 (1930): 278; Lindemann, *AL* 11 (1928): 548; O. P. Kretzmann, *AL* 14 (1931): 1358-59; Lindemann, *AL* 18 (1935): 2444-45; *idem, AL* 20 (1937): 3162; A. W. Koehler, *ibid.*: 3105.

27. *CTM* 5 (1934): 2.

28. By 1930 church athletic teams were a commonplace and the *Witness* complained about headlines in which "Jehovah beats Redeemer." 49 (1930): 331.

29. Lindemann, *AL* 13 (1930): 1130; 16 (1933): 1895-96; 17 (1934): 2062-63; 18 (1935): 2351-54. Kretzmann, *AL* 18 (1935): 2430. Geiseman, *LL* 5 (1934): 36.

30. Adolph Haentzschel, *LW* 31 (1912): 1-2; H. A. Ott to Theo. Graebner, Aug. 8, 1918; F. R. Webber to Graebner, Oct. 26, 1922, TG MSS, Box 56; John H. Schnackenberg to Graebner, Dec. 2, 1922, TG MSS, Box 61; Graebner to Bertha Meyer, Nov. 29, 1922, TG MSS, Box 123; F. C. Brandhorst, *LW* 43 (1924): 45.

31. See, for example, *A Treatise on Freemasonry* (St. Louis: Concordia Publishing House, 1914); *Winning The Lodge-Man: A Handbook of Secret Societies* (St. Louis: Concordia Publishing House, 1925); *The Secret Empire: A Handbook of Lodges* (St. Louis: Concordia Publishing House, 1927). Jerrald Pfabe, "Theodore Graebner: Apologist for Missouri Synod Lutheranism" (Ph.D. dissertation, St. Louis University, 1972), pp. 128-69.

32. These themes may be found articulated by Fuerbringer and Graebner in the *Lutheraner* and *Witness* respectively. *DL* 63 (1907): 55-56; *LW* 36 (1917): 8; *DL* 67 (1911): 22; *LW* 37 (1918): 124-25; *DL* 56 (1900): 137; *LW* 36 (1917): 199-200; *LW* 42 (1923): 18 ff.

33. See correspondence in TG MSS, Boxes 55 and 56.

34. *LW* 40 (1921): 233, 311, 346; 43 (1924): 430; 44 (1925): 372, 404, 439; Frederick Pfotenhauer to Theo. Graebner, 30 Sept., 1921, TG MSS, Box 56. *PRO,* LCMS, 1926, pp. 146-48.

35. J. R. Graebner to Theo. Graebner, Sept. 3, 1918, TG MSS, Box 56.

36. Quoted in M.W.H. Holls to Theo. Graebner, April 18, 1928, TG MSS, Box 55.

37. *Report to the Conferences by a Committee Appointed . . . To Define the Position of the Church Toward the Communing of Members of Secret Societies* (n.p.: [presumably Concordia Publishing House], 1927); *PRO,* LCMS, 1929, pp. 113-20; 1932, pp. 171-78.

38. To Alex von Schlichten, March 12, 1928, TG MSS, Box 55.

39. *LW* 53 (1934): 57-58; 58 (1939): 305.

40. Robert S. Lynd and Helen Merrell Lynd, *Middletown in Transition: A Study in Cultural Conflict* (New York, 1937), p. 285.

41. *PRO,* LCMS, 1935, p. 216; *LW* 60 (1941): 57. A survey of attitudes on lodges, which does not go much beyond printed sources, is in John

Constable, "Lodge Practice Within the Missouri Synod," *CTM* 39 (1968): 476-96. A lengthier treatment, completed after my own study, but which forced no changes in my conclusions, is George F. Lobien, "A Systematic-Historical Study of the Polity of the Lutheran Church—Missouri Synod with Respect to Fraternal Organizations in the Past Fifty Years" (Th.D. dissertation, Concordia Seminary, St. Louis, 1971).

42. The generalization is based on a careful reading of church dedication reports in the synodical press, reports much more detailed and informal than they are today.

43. C. O. Smith, *LW* 22 (1903): 20-21; C. A. Weiss, *LW* 23 (1904): 185. Fritz, *LW* 36 (1917): 349-50.

44. Unsigned, *LL* 12 (1941): 9. My point here is the approving comment and the extensive facilities more than the date, for this particular parish hall had been built earlier in the century.

45. Theo. Graebner, *Handbook,* pp. 209-210.

46. Pieper, "The Layman's Movement in the Light of God's Word," *What is Christianity? and Other Essays,* trans. John Theodore Mueller (St. Louis: Concordia Publishing House, 1933), p. 157. Dau, *Woman Suffrage in the Church* (St. Louis: Concordia Publishing House Print, n.d. [1916]), p. 7.

47. *TM* 4 (1924): 337. See additional comments by Dau and Pieper, quoted in *Moving Frontiers: Readings in The History of The Lutheran Church—Missouri Synod,* ed. Carl S. Meyer (St. Louis: Concordia Publishing House, 1964), p. 380.

48. Unsigned, *LW* 39 (1910): 100-101. For more of the same, see Arthur T. Bonnet, *LW* 30 (1911): 74-75; Richard Jesse, *LW* 44 (1925): 337.

49. *LW* 38 (1919): 179.

50. To Laurence Acker, n.d. [1920]; to E. H. Renter, Nov. 17, 1920, Graebner MSS, Box 14.

51. *TQ* 24 (1920): 120-21. See also Theodore Graebner, *Pastor and People: Letters to a Young Preacher* (St. Louis: Concordia Publishing House, 1932), pp. 125-27.

52. *LW* 48 (1929): 234-35.

53. Carbon copy of Walter A. Maier to "Dear Brethren," Feb. 13, 1928 [which I take to be transmittal of a faculty opinion]; Theodore Graebner to "Dear Otto," Nov. 24, 1942, TG MSS, Box 14.

54. *AL* 11 (1932): 1656, 1973; *50 Years of God's Grace: Grace Lutheran Church* [Escondido, Calif.] (n.p., 1969).

55. See, for example, Fritz, *LW* 51 (1932): 161-62. The only clear sign of impending dissent I have located through the early thirties came,

predictably, in the English District. In 1921, an essay by Pastor C. C. Morhart of Cleveland, "Woman Suffrage and Its Implied Privilege of Preaching, Teaching, and Holding Office in the Church," was not accepted by the convention, but "because of its particular difficulties was referred back to the essayist." *LW* 40 (1921): 232. The official *Proceedings* do not even mention the subject of the paper, much less reprint it as was usually the custom. *PRO*, English District, LCMS, 1921, p. 85.

56. Theo. Graebner, *Handbook*, pp. 207-208. The custom had already been attacked, however, in 1901. J. G. Haefner, *"Ueber Gemeindeversammlungen,"* *VER*, Kansas District, LCMS, 1901, pp. 44-46.

57. Theo. Graebner, *Handbook*, p. 208.

58. *Ibid.*, p. iv.

59. Reprinted in *Moving Frontiers*, pp. 151, 155.

60. *LW* 47 (1928): 266-67.

61. Representative comment upholding *Christenlehre* may be found in Friedrich Bente, *DL* 51 (1895): 45-46; C. Purzner, *"Warum sollen wir fleissig Christenlehre treiben?,"* *VER*, Western District, LCMS, 1895, pp. 38-55; Ludwig Fuerbringer, *DL* 55 (1899): 2. References to the *"Laien-Bibel"* are in Bente, p. 45 and Purzner, p. 45.

62. *LW* 57 (1938): 166.

63. Theodore Graebner, *Magazin fur ev. luth. Homiletik* 44 (1920): 36.

64. *Idem, AL* 6 (1923): 13.

65. Lindemann, *AL* 9 (1926): 14.

66. *SYB*, 1937, p. 174; for conflicting sentiments on Sunday school, see Martin A. Haendschke, *The Sunday School Story: The History of the Sunday School in The Lutheran Church—Missouri Synod*, Twentieth Yearbook, Lutheran Education Association (River Forest, Ill: Lutheran Education Association, 1963), pp. 7-47.

67. "What are the Underlying Reasons for the Opposition to the Sunday School?" (preliminary draft), in Minutes, LCMS School Board, Bulletin to School Board, Oct. 18, 1924, CHI.

68. Fritz, *LW* 24 (1905): 12; J. R. Graebner, *LW* 34 (1915): 69-70. These reminders were so urgent they arouse suspicion that some aggressive laymen used the Sunday school as an end-run around the pastor. The clearest indication is in G. A. Romoser, *LW* 21 (1902): 162-63.

69. "Underlying Reasons," Minutes, LCMS School Board, Bulletin to School Board, Oct. 20, 1924.

70. The pages of the *Sunday School Teachers Quarterly* were filled with advice to teachers to study and learn. For teacher education, see *LW* 34 (1915): 220; *AL* 3 (1920): 120-21; *LW* 40 (1921): 27; 44 (1925): 59; *AL* 11 (1928): 458-59; *LW* 57 (1938): 57; Haendschke, pp. 61-62.

71. *SYB*, 1937, p. 174.

72. Synergos, *AL* 3 (1920): 108-109. There is a remarkable similarity between this comment and the observation fifty years earlier by a clergyman in the native American southern Lutheran church, then discovering the Sunday school: "[the Sunday school] brings the laity to the front in church work . . . Hitherto to a great extent the work of the Church . . . has rested in the hands of the ministry. Now the door is open. Let the cry go forth from every pulpit in the land, Laymen to the front!" (Quoted, with ellipses, by Hugh George Anderson, *Lutheranism in the Southeastern States, 1860–1886: A Social History* [The Hague, 1969], p. 126.) Missourian unconsciousness of such a parallel is a pertinent reminder of the long-standing ethnic and geographical divisions among Lutherans and of the seemingly inexorable sequence in Americanization in groups separated by time, space, and nativity.

73. H. B. Hemmeter, *LW* 24 (1905): 123.

74. *LW* 19 (1900): 58; 32 (1913): 51; 39 (1920): 295; *AL* 4 (1921): 109; 10 (1927): 121.

75. Theo. Graebner, *LW* 44 (1925): 13.

76. *LW* 49 (1930): 324; 57 (1938): 118-19; 64 (1945): 22.

77. *AL* 20 (1937): 3053.

Chapter 6: Which Vineyard?

1. Paul Lindemann, *AL* 9 (1926): 52; O. A. Geiseman, *AL* 18 (1935): 2337-38.

2. Harlan Paul Douglass, *The Suburban Trend* (New York, 1925), p. 208.

3. Lindemann, *AL* 9 (1926): 51.

4. The rise in the college educated is reported by O. A. Geiseman, *LW* 55 (1936): 367. For a sampling of comments on education, see O. H. Pannkoke, *AL* 14 (1931): 1353; Theo. Graebner, *LW* 53 (1934): 410; Paul Lindemann, *AL* 18 (1935): 2375-76; Martin Walker, *LW* 54 (1935): 230; *PRO*, LCMS, 1935, p. 32.

5. Wrote one layman, "When I seek spiritual advice, I go to a minister; when I seek legal advice, I go to a lawyer; and when I seek medical advice, I go to a doctor. . . ." Wm. H. Kroeger, *LW* 66 (1947): 238.

6. Even in the Depression, when the colleges had empty seats, suggestions that doors be thrown open to laymen drew sharp reprimands at first from the synodical Board of Directors. Theo. Graebner to O. Krueger, Oct. 30, 1935, TG MSS, Box 67.

7. The quotation is from E. A. Mayer, *DL* 62 (1906): 402. Further

evidence is in book advertisements by Concordia Publishing House. The *Witness* of 1906 carried a pre-Christmas advertisement which employed such descriptions as "interesting, evanglical, comforting," "teaches contentment with one's situation in life," "brimful of sweet counsel," and "a good lesson for married people, showing envy to be the rottenness of the times." 25 (1906): 192. See also *LW* 53 (1934): 348.

8. "Proceedings of the Lutheran Collegiate Association Convention," June 23, 1945 (mimeographed).

9. "Christian Citizenship," *PRO,* English District, LCMS, 1937, p. 12. Though Graebner did not admit it, he was speaking of an attitude he had earlier shared.

10. Luther Bonnet Miller, *LW* 46 (1927): 267.

11. Lindemann, *AL* 14 (1931): 1349-50; *AL* 16 (1933): 1816-17.

12. Paul E. Kretzmann, *CTM* 5 (1934): 4.

13. *CTM* 8 (1937): 243, 248.

14. *LW* 52 (1933): 257.

15. See, for example, O. H. Pannkoke, *AL* 14 (1931): 1353; Lindemann, *AL* 18 (1935): 2310.

16. *LW* 52 (1933): 179-80, 181-82; 55 (1936): 383; 56 (1937): 387-88; 57 (1938): 115; 59 (1940): 288.

17. E. L. Roschke, *LL* 5 (1934): 9-11. Lindemann, *AL* 19 (1936): 2697.

18. Lindemann, *AL* 9 (1926): 140. Virsilva, *AL* 2 (1919): 128-30.

19. *AL* 9 (1926): 104.

20. B. J. Jordan, *AL* 17 (1934): 2110.

21. P. J. Gold, "The Layman in Church-Work," *PRO,* Michigan District, LCMS, 1936, p. 26. See also A Layman, *LW* 49 (1930): 244.

22. Oscar Fedder, *AL* 7 (1924): 131-32.

23. G. E. Hageman, *AL* 6 (1923): 58.

24. Fred Lindemann, *AL* 7 (1924): 27. For practical instruction, see *AL* 6 (1923): 78-79; 7 (1924): 113-14; 10 (1927): 238-39; 11 (1928): 475, 501-503; 12 (1929): 672-74, 709-710; 13 (1930): 988-89.

25. *RAM,* 1950, p. 128.

26. *LW* 50 (1931): 55-56; 52 (1933): 232, 257, 259; 53 (1934): 39-40, 77. Parenthetically, if the titles used during the thirties were evidence of Americanization in the appeal to the laity, so too was the growth of acronyms especially after World War II. It is intriguing that the LLL and the ALPB led this trend by a considerable margin.

27. *LW* 58 (1939): 444; 59 (1940): 24, 42-43, 57-58, 63, 154, 373-74; *PRO,* LCMS, 1941, pp. 193-98.

28. Much of the campaign's material may be found in the extensive

Lawrence B. Meyer MSS, CHI. See also *Ad Clerum: Being the Story of an Incident at a Mid-Summer Conference* (St. Louis: Concordia Publishing House, n.d.), L. Meyer MSS.

29. *LW* 63 (1944): 116. Graebner was here establishing the legitimacy of lay support for his own position in the heated polemics of the forties, but few of his predecessors or contemporaries would have publicly disagreed with the essence of his statement. See Thesis X of Walther, *Die Stimme unserer Kirche in der Frage von Kirche und Amt,* trans. W.H.T. Dau in *Walther and the Church,* ed. Theodore Engelder (St. Louis: Concordia Publishing House, 1938), p. 85; William F. Arndt, *LW* 42 (1923): 329; Graebner, *LW* 52 (1933): 152.

30. The charge was quoted and answered by Graebner, *LW* 52 (1933): 7. See also *LW* 26 (1907): 153; George V. Schick, *LW* 60 (1941): 203.

31. John Philipp Koehler, *The History of the Wisconsin Synod,* ed. Leigh Jordahl (St. Cloud, Minn., 1970), pp. 239-41.

32. See, e.g., Charles H. Boyer, *An American Lutheran University: Address delivered at the biennial convention of the Lutheran Brotherhood of America held in Madison, Wisconsin, Oct. 3-5, 1923.*

A brief history of the LBA is given in *Lutheran Men in War and Peace* (n.p.: The American Federation of Lutheran Brotherhoods, 1946). The Lutheran Brotherhood of America should not be confused with the Lutheran Brotherhoods of the General Synod and, after merger in 1917, of the United Lutheran Church in America. The General Synod Lutheran Brotherhood grew out of, and was distinct from, the Laymen's Movement common in the most Americanized Lutheran bodies early in the century. A national group was formed in 1911 and was essentially an affiliation of men's clubs tied to individual local congregations.

Historians of both Danish and Swedish immigrant Lutheran bodies have noted lay incomprehension of and impatience with theological niceties. Enok Mortensen, *The Danish Lutheran Church in America: The History and Heritage of The American Evangelical Lutheran Church* (Philadelphia, 1967), p. 247; G. Everett Arden, *Augustana Heritage: A History of The Augustana Lutheran Church* (Rock Island, Ill., 1963), p. 226.

33. H. B. Hemmeter to Theo. Graebner, March 17, 1924, Graebner MSS, Box 79.

34. See statements quoted in Alan Graebner, "World War I and Lutheran Union: Documents from the Army and Navy Board, 1917 and 1918," *CHIQ* 41 (1968): 56, 62.

35. The oversight was not pointed out to a synodical convention until

1944, when the membership was changed to include three professors of theology, three parish pastors, but only two laymen. *PRO,* LCMS, 1944, p. 250.

36. For varying interpretations of these and subsequent developments, see Thomas Kuster, "The Fellowship Dispute in the Lutheran Church—Missouri Synod: A Rhetorical Study of Ecumenical Change" (Ph.D. dissertation, University of Wisconsin, 1969); Jack Greising, "The Status of Confessional Conservatism: Background and Issues in the Lutheran Church—Missouri Synod" (Ph.D. dissertation, St. Louis University, 1972); Jack Treon Robinson, "The Spirit of Triumphalism in the Lutheran Church—Missouri Synod: The Role of 'A Statement' of 1945 in the Missouri Synod" (Ph.D. dissertation, Vanderbilt University, 1972).

37. *LW* 62 (1943): 382; 63 (1944): 61-62; *AL* 32 (June 1949) front cover. *LW* 62 (1943): 44-45, 72-73; 63 (1944): 124-25; *AL* 26 (1943): 234-35; 27 (1944): 63-65. Unsigned, *AL* 26 (1943): 88; Graebner, *LW* 63 (1944): 67-68, 84.

38. Unsigned, 30 (1947): 99-100.

39. "Hans" of Ridgeway, N.C. to George Meyer, Dec. 10, 1945, George Meyer MSS, Box 3, CHI.

40. *AL* 26 (1943): 188. For further comment on this remark, see Graebner, *LW* 62 (1943): 337; Ewald Schuettner, *ibid.*: 308.

41. *The Lutheran* 30 (Jan. 28, 1948): 39.

42. W. H. Allen, *AL* 27 (May 1944): 20.

43. F. Dean Lueking, *A Century of Caring: The Welfare Ministry Among Missouri Synod Lutherans, 1868-1968.* (St. Louis: Board of Social Ministry, The Lutheran Church—Missouri Synod, 1968), p. 61.

44. *RAM,* LCMS, 1950, pp. 536-39. Dickmeyer did request and receive assistance from friendly clergy in writing the report, but the initiative and tenacity behind it were his own.

45. Letter to Graebner, Dec. 31, 1945, TG MSS, Box 79. On the founding see *LW* 64 (1945): 385-86. Missouri Synod participants were John W. Boehne, Jr., W. C. Dickmeyer, E. J. Gallmeyer, H. H. Hackstedde, Frederick C. Strodel.

46. *LW* 64 (1945): 139; *AL* 28 (1945): 117, 212.

47. Minutes, Lutheran Men in America, 1946-50. Interviews, O. P. Kretzmann, July 5, 1966; W. C. Dickmeyer, Sept. 24, 1966; E. J. Gallmeyer, Sept. 24, 1966.

48. The Federation of Lutheran Clubs was unable to broaden its support from a core of loyal supporters, and was soon in financial trouble. It faced the familiar problem; small membership precluded an aggressive

program, but a weak program attracted few members. See minutes and correspondence in TG MSS, Box 79, and the organization's quarterly, *Federation News,* begun in 1946.

49. Quoted in F. R. Webber to Graebner, Oct. 26, 1922, TG MSS, Box 56.

50. Unsigned, 35 (1952): 4.

Chapter 7: Watchmen on Zion's Walls

1. Philip Gleason, *The Conservative Reformers: German-American Catholics and the Social Order* (Notre Dame, 1968), p. 159. See also Fred W. Meuser, *The Formation of the American Lutheran Church: A Case Study in Lutheran Unity* (Columbus, 1958), pp. 28-38; Frederick C. Luebke, "The Immigrant Condition as a Factor Contributing to the Conservatism of The Lutheran Church," *CHIQ,* 38 (April 1965): 19-28.

2. Anon., *Cresset* 10 (Nov. 1946): 56.

3. See Frederick C. Luebke, "The German-American Alliance in Nebraska, 1910–1917," *Nebraska History,* 49 (Summer 1968), pp. 166-67.

4. *The Christian College: Its Importance for This and the Life to Come* (Chicago: American Lutheran Publication Board, 1894), p. 14.

5. C. A. Weiss, *LW* 23 (1904): 105; H. B. Hemmeter, *LW* 24 (1905): 89-90; Edward Pardieck, *DL* 68 (1912): 316; O. Ungemach, *LW* 32 (1913): 28; Graebner, *DL* 70 (1914): 8; Weiss, *LW* 29 (1910): 178. The quotation is from Weiss, *LW* 19 (1900): 58.

Care must be exercised in evaluating these judgments so that they are not automatically ascribed to Victorian repression. For example, not all silent motion pictures are fitting for re-runs on television children's hours. But synodical spokesmen gave themselves away by their blanket condemnation and by use of doctrinal moralism as an esthetic principle; the beauty and truth, the value, of any performance was determined by its anticipated moral consequences and by the private ethics of the participants.

6. Fritz, *Pastoral Theology* (St. Louis: Concordia Publishing House, 1931), pp. 152-153. Kretzmann, *The Problems of Adolescence and Youth, and Their Treatment in Educational and Pastoral Work* (Burlington, Iowa: Lutheran Literary Board, 1925), p. 64; see also *idem, The Christian Woman as a Social Worker* (n.p., n.d. [1928]), p. 38. Maier's book was put out by Concordia Publishing House in 1935 and went through four printings and three editions by the end of 1939.

7. Alan Graebner, "Attitudes in the Lutheran Church—Missouri Synod Toward Sexual Morality: 1900–1960" (M.A. thesis, Columbia University, 1961); Martin Sommer, *LW* 51 (1932): 192; John H. C. Fritz, *LW* 49 (1930): 71-72; Theo. Graebner, *LW* 51 (1932): 288-89; *idem, LW* 52 (1933): 116-17; *idem, LW* 53 (1934): 174. Much of this was typical of the conservative denominational press of the time. The synod did diverge, however, when it came to Prohibition. Partly this was because of opposition to denominational social action, but that does not explain the Atlantic District convention's resolution of hearty thanks "to the Haffenreffer Brewing Company and the Burkhardt Brewing Company for their generous supply of refreshments." *PRO,* Atlantic District, LCMS, 1931, pp. 67-68. "Only fanatical temperance agitators," wrote Graebner in the *Witness,* "will decry the medicinal value of the famous *liqueurs* . . . the products of two famous French abbeys. We have sometimes been inclined to look upon the production of these marvelous *liqueurs* as a mitigating circumstance when considering the faults of and wrongs of Roman monasticism!" *LW* 49 (1930): 326.

8. On the general topic of Missouri Synod and social questions, see Ralph Moellering, "The Missouri Synod and Social Problems, A Theological and Sociological Analysis of the Reactions to Industrial Tensions, War, and Race Relations from 1917 to 1941" (Ph.D. dissertation, Harvard University, 1964). For an introduction to attitudes toward government, a helpful study is Arthur Simon's "Social and Political Thinking in The Lutheran Church—Missouri Synod from 1920 to 1955" (S.T.M. thesis, Concordia Seminary, St. Louis, 1957). Useful historical background is in the essays of *Christian Social Responsibility, Vol. II: The Lutheran Heritage,* ed. Harold C. Letts (Philadelphia, 1956). The subject is one that in the Missouri Synod deserves the painstaking attention of a scholar conversant with both German and American sources.

9. P. E. Kretzmann, *The Christian Woman As a Social Worker,* p. 81.

10. *DL* 50 (1894): 135.

11. George Luecke, *LW* 30 (1911): 18-19; Paul Bente, *LW* 47 (1928): 219-20; Theo. Graebner, *LW* 53 (1934): 242.

12. *DL* 67 (1911): 150.

13. Paul Woy, *"Die Aufgabe der Kirche in der Welt," PRO,* Atlantic District, LCMS, 1931, p. 25. The quotation was from *Christianizing the Social Order* (New York, 1913), p. 42.

14. *Christianizing the Social Order,* p. 25.

15. Terminology was not very precise here. Lutherans certainly did

not deny that there were Christians outside Lutheranism. But the rhetoric of argument tended implicitly to equate world, non-Christian, and non-Lutheran.

16. J. C. Ambacher, *LW,* 13 (1894): 3. See also George Stoeckhardt, *DL* 46 (1890): 2-3; P. T. Schumm, *LW* 42 (1923): 241-42, 257-58.

17. Theo. Graebner, *LW* 37 (1918): 228. J. C. Ambacher, *LW* 13 (1894): 3.

18. The first, Arcadia, was opened in 1923; by 1927 there were sixteen Lutheran summer camps. *LW* 46 (1927): 53-54.

19. A. L. Graebner, *DL* 49 (1893): 195. For samples of the Nehemiah metaphor, see Theo. Graebner, *LW* 41 (1922): 129; Martin Sommer, *LW* 49 (1930): 70; J. W. Behnken, *LW* 57 (1938): 105.

20. *A Great Church Finds Itself: The Lutheran Church Between The Wars* (Quitman, Ga.: privately printed, 1966), p. 28.

21. In addition to other works already cited, see Phyllis Keller, "German-America and the First World War" (Ph.D. dissertation, University of Pennsylvania, 1969).

22. W. F. Sternitsky, *LW* 40 (1921): 116-17.

23. George Stoeckhardt, *DL* 46 (1890): 2-3.

24. Quoted by Theo. Graebner, *LW* 53 (1934): 196.

25. *LW* 55 (1936): 2.

26. George Stoeckhardt, *DL* 51 (1895): 167-68.

27. Theo. Graebner, *Handbook for Congregational Officers* (St. Louis: Concordia Publishing House, 1928). H. W. Bartels, *LW* 42 (1923): 17-18. Theo. Graebner, *LW* 55 (1936): 421.

28. *LW* 42 (1923): 38; 43 (1924): 284; 44 (1925): 63; Otto Heerwagen, "Church Discipline," *PRO*, Colorado District, LCMS, 1924; August Burgdorf, "Brotherly Admonition," *PRO*, Northern Illinois District, LCMS, 1928; M. Mencke, "Church Discipline," *PRO*, South Wisconsin District, LCMS, 1936; Bernard H. Hemmeter, "The Church and Christian Discipline in the Light of Matthew 18," *PRO*, English District, LCMS, 1940; A. P. Marutz, "The Office of the Keys, with Especial Reference to Church Discipline," *PRO*, Michigan District, LCMS, 1940; John H. C. Fritz, *Pastoral Theology,* pp. 232-56; Edgar J. Otto, "Church Discipline," *The Abiding Word,* ed. Theodore Laetsch (St. Louis: Concordia Publishing House, 1947), II, 538-61.

29. Closer to half the clergy in the fifties were prepared at least to condone discipline, although this is of course by no means assurance that they would take measures when themselves confronted with an actual case. Paul G. Hansen *et al., Engagement and Marriage* (St. Louis: Con-

cordia Publishing House, 1958), p. 172. A sermon in Concordia's annual homiletical compendium entitled, "What Pastor and People Are to Do When People Sin," managed to avoid any reference to discipline at all. E. H. Gade, *Concordia Pulpit* (1956), pp. 110-14. For the 1970 survey, see Merton Strommen, Milo Brekke, Ralph Underwager, Arthur Johnson, *A Study of Generations* (Minneapolis, 1972), pp. 275-76.

30. Richard M. Cameron, *Methodism and Society in Historical Perspective* (New York, 1961), p. 271; W. D. Blanks, "Corrective Church Discipline in the Presbyterian Churches of the Nineteenth Century South," *Journal of Presbyterian History,* 44 (June 1966), 89-105; Emmer E. Engberg, "Augustana and Code Morality," *Centennial Essays: Augustana Lutheran Church, 1860–1960,* ed. Emmer Engberg (Rock Island, Ill., 1960), pp. 122-49. Emil Oberholzer, Jr., "Saints in Sin: A Study of the Disciplinary Action of the Congregational Churches of Massachusetts in the Colonial and Early National Periods" (Ph.D. dissertation, Columbia University, 1954).

31. O. E. Rølvaag, *Peder Victorious: A Tale of the Pioneers Twenty Years Later,* trans. Nora D. Solum and author, Perennial Classic ed. (New York, 1966), pp. 19-44.

32. *DL* 51 (1895): 167.

33. Everette Meier and Herbert T. Mayer, "The Process of Americanization," *Moving Frontiers: Readings in the History of The Lutheran Church—Missouri Synod,* ed. Carl S. Meyer (St. Louis: Concordia Publishing House, 1964), p. 366.

34. Paul Lindemann, *AL* 8 (1925): 13; F. R. Webber, *AL* 17 (1934): 2187.

35. Virtus Gloe, *PRO,* ALC, 1936, pp. 66-67.

36. Glabe, *ibid.,* 1933, p. 45. Witte, *ibid.,* 1935, p. 34. Gloe, *ibid.,* 1935, p. 21, and 1936, p. 67.

37. Witte, *ibid.,* 1933, p. 36.

38. For exceptions, see Adolph Haentzschel, *ibid.,* 1938, pp. 54-55; Paul E. Kretzmann, *ibid.,* 1938, p. 29.

39. Caemmerer, *ibid.,* 1946, p. 56. Kretzmann, *ibid.,* 1938, p. 30.

40. Friedrich, *ibid.,* 1937, p. 72. Caemmerer, *ibid.,* 1946, p. 51.

41. Although it would be unjustified to push the parallels too far, within American Roman Catholicism during the thirties there was also a development of a connection between social concerns and greater emphasis on the laity, particularly in the Catholic worker movement. David J. O'Brien, *American Catholics and Social Reform: The New Deal Years* (New York, 1968), pp. 182-211.

42. *LW* 65 (1946): 388; 66 (1947): 325. The name, so often to be confused with Mohammedan symbolism, was suggested by Theodore Graebner, *Concordia Magazine* 6 (1901): 445; *LW* 42 (1923): 204; *LW* 46 (1927): 147.

43. For Kretzmann on homiletics, see *CTM* 7 (1937): 572. There is a striking difference between Kretzmann's statement on education (reprinted in *Moving Frontiers,* p. 395) and the appeal of his predecessor made in 1931. O. C. Kreinheder, *LW* 50 (1931): 262-63.

44. *Cresset* 1 (Nov. 1937): 10. For a similar judgment, see Robert S. Lynd and Helen Merrell Lynd, *Middletown in Transition: A Study in Cultural Conflict* (New York, 1937), p. 318.

45. *Cresset* 1 (Nov. 1937): 12.

46. 12 (Feb. 1949): 72.

47. Alfred Klausler, 1 (Sept. 1938): 24.

48. Victor E. Swenson, 4 (Nov. 1940): 68-69.

49. Kretzmann, 4 (Nov. 1940): 69; anon., 4 (Feb. 1941): 64.

50. 3 (May 1940): 17-18; 5 (June 1941): 67.

51. Lloyd Warner, 1 (Feb. 1938): 65; Martin Schmitt, 1 (April 1938): 67; quoted in Agenda, March 25, 1938 meeting of the Cresset editors, TG MSS, Box 26.

52. 2 (Jan. 1939): 60. 2 (July 1939): 51.

53. Kretzmann, 2 (Sept. 1939): 10-11. See also 5 (Feb. 1942): 15.

54. H. F. Wind, 6 (March 1943), inside back cover.

55. *The Lutheran Academy for Scholarship: History, Services, The Future, Membership, Constitution* (n.p.: The Lutheran Academy for Scholarship, n.d. [1957]); interview, Martin H. Scharlemann, Nov. 21, 1966.

56. *Lutheran Scholar* 6 (1949): 44-45.

57. John Sauerman to O. A. Geiseman, March 7, Sept. 25, 1945, Geiseman MSS, Box 14; interview, O. P. Kretzmann, July 5, 1966.

58. *Lutheran Scholar* 3 (1946): 52-54. Minutes, *Cresset* staff meeting, Sept. 26, 1947, TG MSS, Box 26.

Chapter 8: Oppressed by Depression

1. *BL* 1 (1930): 105. Paul Lindemann was even more frank. The old LLL, he wrote in 1929, "was primarily a salvaging organization. It was the rescuing crew which went out to save the Synodical ship from the results of its own weakness." *AL* 12 (1929): 693.

2. *BL* 1 (1930): 38.

3. Minutes, BG, Sept. 19, 1930, p. 148. On leadership, see H. C. Dilges, *BL* 1 (1930): 56.

4. Paul Walther to Theodore Graebner, May 23, 1930, TG MSS, Box 80.

5. Unsigned, *BL* 1 (1930): 34. A speakers bureau was promised, but did not materialize. *Ibid.*, 39.

6. Anonymous [Theodore Graebner] (St. Louis: Concordia Publishing House, 1930), pp. 107-116.

7. *BL* 1 (1930): 115. *LW* 49 (1930): 41.

8. Minutes, CNV, May 31, 1930, p. 40. So few club delegates attended annual conventions in the early thirties that the by-laws were suspended to give ballots to all members present. Minutes, CNV, June 17, 1929, p. 17; May 30, 1930, p. 3.

9. Louis Buchheimer, Jr., Minutes, BG, April 25, 1930, p. 107.

10. Erik Barnouw, *A Tower in Babel: A History of Broadcasting in the United States,* 1 (New York, 1966). By 1930, at least a dozen cities around the country had weekly Missouri Synod broadcasts. *BL* 1 (1930): 97; *LW* 49 (1930): 271.

11. The multiplicity of paternity is an important point, given Walter A. Maier's subsequent incarnation in national Lutheran broadcasting. KFUO manager H. H. Hohenstein, A. A. Grossmann, assistant manager at CPH, *Witness* editor Theodore Graebner, layman Henry Dahlen, Lawrence B. Meyer of the synodical publicity office, and Walter A. Maier and J.H.C. Fritz from the St. Louis seminary were all centrally involved at the formative stage. See Minutes, KFUO Committee, filed at KFUO offices; Minutes, BG, 1929–30, *passim;* A. A. Grossmann to Graebner, April 5, 1930, TG MSS, Box 80; Graebner to J.A.C. Beyer, Oct. 28, 1930, TG MSS, Box 79. National Broadcasting Company to H. H. Hohenstein, May 20, 1929, TG MSS, Box 79; *BL* 1 (1929): 28. Compare claims of *LW* 58 (1939): 236, and those of *LW* 61 (1942): 187. See also *BL* 2 (1930): 65.

12. Minutes, BG, Nov. 9, 1930, p. 183; Nov. 10, 1930, pp. 185-86; ExC, Nov. 19, 1930, pp. 188-89; BG, Dec. 18, 1930, pp. 199-200; Paul Maier, *A Man Spoke, A World Listened: The Story of Walter A. Maier* (New York, 1963), p. 124.

Although he remained well in the background, the real manager of an underwriting effort to keep the program afloat was O. H. Pannkoke, a highly experienced, if a controversial, fund raiser. O. H. Pannkoke, *A Great Church Finds Itself: The Lutheran Church Between the Wars* (Quitman, Ga.: privately printed, 1966), pp. 154-57. LLL minutes indicate Pannkoke's account is substantially correct. Minutes, National Lutheran Hour Committee, Feb. 27, 1931, TG MSS, Box 79; ExC, Feb. 13, 1931, p. 238; *BL* 2 (1931): 109-119.

In order to win over opposition, the campaign apparatus included a pyramid of committees composed mostly of well-known pastors and seminary professors. At the major meeting to rescue the LLL in its commitment to the Lutheran Hour, there were sixteen laymen, but eighty-one clergy. List in *BL* 2 (1931): 111-12.

For an informal report on the June 11 session, see Theo. Graebner to Henry Grueber, June 5, 1931, TG MSS, Box 80.

13. The Board of Governors seriously considered varying the speakers, but finally decided to stay with Maier. Minutes, BG, Oct. 23, 1930, p. 166. The board was not to deliberate formally on the matter again until after Maier's death.

14. Unsigned, *BL* 2 (1931): 131. Martin Walker to Graebner, March 19, 1931; J. Franklin Yount to Graebner, March 25, 1931, TG MSS, Box 79. See also the remarks by J.H.C. Fritz, reported in *LW* 49 (1930): 343.

15. Minutes, BG, Exhibit C, Jan. 23, 1931, p. 232.

16. Minutes, CNV, May 30, 1930, p. 14; BG, Oct. 23, 1930, p. 167; CNV, May 22, 1931, p. 305; BG, Oct. 20, 1932, p. 460; ExC, Jan. 5, 1933, p. 473.

17. *BL* 1 (1929): 18.

18. Letter to Graebner, June 22, 1930, TG MSS, Box 80.

19. The matter is taken up in Minutes, BG, Jan. 23, 1931, pp. 223-24, 227-31; *BL* 2 (1931): 95. The quote is from p. 223 of the minutes.

20. These included the Orphans Home Ladies' Society; Lutheran Hospital Ladies' Aid Society; Lutheran Ladies' Mission Aid Society; St. Louis Colored Missions Ladies' Auxiliary; Lutheran Foreign Missions Ladies' Aid Society; Altenheim Ladies' Auxiliary; Lutheran Children's Friend Society Women's Auxiliary; and the Board of the Lutheran Convalescent Home. Cursory inspection of officers reveals a highly interlocked directorate, as might be expected. See issues of the *Lutheran Charities Review*.

21. The quotation is found in *History of Central District Lutheran Women's Missionary Endeavor, 1928–1942, and Lutheran Women's Missionary League, 1943–64*. (n.p., 1966), p. 8. Unless otherwise noted, for women's activities I have relied upon Ruth Fritz Meyer's *Women on a Mission: The role of women in the church . . . including a history of the Lutheran Women's Missionary League during its first twenty-five years* (St. Louis: Concordia Publishing House Print, 1967), pp. 63-90. Since the

book is well documented, I have not here supplemented Mrs. Meyer's citations by my own references to LLL or synodical sources. It should be made explicit, however, that the conclusions stated here are not necessarily Mrs. Meyer's.

22. There is apparently no record of the method used to select the women; in all likelihood it depended upon personal ties, hearsay, and chance.

23. Theo. Graebner to L. Meyer, Dec. 7, 1929, TG 80.

24. Paul E. Kretzmann, 1 (1930): 360; cf., however, Kretzmann, *CTM* 4 (1933): 95.

25. See Gladys Gilkey Calkins, *Follow Those Women: Church Women in the Ecumenical Movement, A History of the Development of United Work Among Women of the Protestant Churches in the United States* (New York, 1961).

26. As late as 1938, Pfotenhauer, by then retired as president, was still warning against church societies as dangerous to the loyalties properly owed the congregation itself. "Foreword," in William Dallmann *et al.*, *Walther and the Church* (St. Louis: Concordia Publishing House, 1938), p. iv.

27. A. C. Kroeger, *CTM* 2 (1931): 85-95; Martin Sommer, *LW* 50 (1931): 121; J.H.C. Fritz, *LW* 51 (1932): 161.

28. P. E. Kretzmann, *CTM* 4 (1933): 644. M. H. Coyner, "The Christian Home," *PRO*, Central Illinois District, LCMS, 1936, p. 35.

29. A. W. Meyer, *LW* 48 (1929): 291; P. E. Kretzmann, *The Christian Woman As a Social Worker* (n.p., n.d. [1928]), p. 39; W. A. Maier, *For Better, Not for Worse*, 3rd ed. (St. Louis: Concordia Publishing House, 1939), pp. 467-80.

30. The best example here is the fiction of G. L. Wind, whose novel *Natalie* was released by Concordia Publishing House in 1926. It was followed by a quick succession of other novels and by short stories in the *Walther League Messenger*.

31. W. G. Polack, *LW* 49 (1930): 344.

32. *LL* 31 (1950): 38.

33. A statistical analysis was made by punch card of the congregations sponsoring the first two hundred men's clubs to join the LLL (between 1929 and 1939). This demonstrates that as far as the LLL was concerned, the men's club was something distinctly connected with large, urbanized, active congregations. Measured against the synod as a whole (as reported in *SYB*, 1937, pp. 146-47), the LLL congregations were somewhat more likely to have a Sunday school than the synodical aver-

age (about 91 percent against about 83 percent) and much more likely to have a parochial school (65 percent against about 30 percent for the synod as a whole). What is much more impressive is the degree of urbanization among the LLL congregations. About 37 percent were located in cities of more than 100,000 population, about 80 percent in places above 2,500 population. No comparable figure is available for the synod as a whole, but as late as 1947, 58 percent of all congregations were in places of *below* 2,500. *SYB,* 1950, p. 239. Also unusual is the size of the congregations with a men's club in the LLL during the 1930s. In the synod as a whole (according to figures in *SYB,* 1934, p. 150), 57 percent of the congregations had between 1 and 199 baptized members; 28 percent between 200 and 499; 10 percent between 500 and 999; and only 4 percent more than 1,000. For the LLL congregations, the comparable figures are 11 percent; 38 percent; 32 percent; and 17 percent.

I am indebted to Professors Arne Garness and Laurence Falk for suggstions on this analysis and for access to data processing equipment at Concordia College, Moorhead, Minn.

34. Issued initially in mimeographed form early in 1933, the first printed program appeared in November of that year and thereafter on a more or less monthly basis.

35. B. J. Jordan to Graebner, June 5, 1930, TG MSS, Box 80.

36. Interview, July 5, 1966. That Kretzmann was later allowed to remain LLL pastoral advisor after he became executive secretary of the Walther League further confirms the guess.

37. Graebner to Harry J. W. Niehaus, April 23, 1935, TG MSS, Box 66.

38. The 800-member St. Louis group, for example, established an employment bureau during the early 1930s; it collected Christmas gifts for needy children and sponsored educational trips for parochial school students. In 1934 it anticipated the future LLL seminars with a week-long series of evening lecture topics on the Christian and the world around him. *LL* 5 (1934): 4, 27; interview, John A. Fleischli, Sept. 15, 1966. For other areas, see *LL* 4 (1933): 22; 5 (1934): 27-28; 11 (1940): 22.

39. Meyer, *Women on a Mission,* pp. 94-112.

40. For example, the constitution for the new group specified three pastoral advisors, to be elected from a slate chosen by the synod's president, who were to attend all meetings where power was exercised. Church officials were reacting in this case to the LLL's preoccupation with the Lutheran Hour, though this was never explicitly stated. As Theodore Graebner put it in urging the LWL pastoral adviser toward

specificity in the proposed association's purposes to prevent subversion by some enthusiast for a specific project, "we have had more than once in our Synod seen such perversions of enthusiasm, and the prospect of an entire league of women being withdrawn from a deeper spiritual purpose to activities which have the glamor of a national program, is disquieting." To Herbert C. Claus, July 16, 1937, TG MSS, Box 80. A similar concern was expressed in 1942 by the synodical committee charged with aiding the establishment of a national group. Meyer, p. 119.

41. The statistical appendices in Ruth Meyer's history are the most convenient and authoritative summary and provide, moreover, further evidence of the LWML's project-oriented approach.

Chapter 9: Conquest by Radio

1. By 1934, the LLL was supporting five such broadcasts. Minutes, ExC, Feb. 10, 1933, p. 485; CNV, June 16, 1934, p. 623.

2. Minutes, ExC, Sept. 15, 1932, p. 452; June 22, 1933, p. 514; BG, Jan. 31, 1935, p. 671; Paul Maier, *A Man Spoke, A World Listened: The Story of Walter A. Maier* (New York, 1963), pp. 164-68; *LL* 6 (1935): 18; *PRO*, LCMS, 1935, pp. 295-96; Minutes, BG, May 18, 1935, p. 703; CNV, June 18, 1935, pp. 716-19.

3. By 1944 a financial surplus equaling a year's budget had been built up to protect the program. Minutes, BG, June 19, 1944; March 11, 1944; ExB, Dec. 16, 1944, p. 6.

4. Paul Maier has given an exhaustive coverage of the growth of the Lutheran Hour, and no effort is made here to duplicate that story.

5. Quoted in Paul Maier, p. 186.

6. "For people who read little, a sermon is a useful way to guidance in some of their problems," observed one contemporary survey. Bureau of Applied Social Research, Columbia University, *The People Look at Radio: Report on a Survey Conducted by The National Opinion Research Center* (Chapel Hill, N.C., 1946), p. 63. The LLL itself recognized its program was strongest on farms and in small towns. Minutes, ExB, Sept. 9, 1944, p. 8.

7. Minutes, ExB, May 4, 1946, p. 5.

8. Paul Maier, pp. 384-85; Milton L. Rudnick, *Fundamentalism and The Missouri Synod: A Historical Study of Their Interaction and Mutual Influence* (St. Louis: Concordia Publishing House, 1966), pp. 91-102; Ralph Moellering, "The Missouri Synod and Social Problems, A Theological and Sociological Analysis of the Reaction to Industrial Ten-

sions, War, and Race Relations from 1917 to 1944'' (Ph.D. dissertation, Harvard University, 1964), pp. 144, 529.

9. See, however, Minutes, ExC, March 27, 1942; BG, Oct. 2, 1943, p. 2.

10. Minutes, CNV, July 1-3, 1951, p. 40. Small grants were made annually to the Post-Graduate Home Society to finance graduate study by professors at synodical institutions. In the thirties, scholarship awards were made to the graduates of the synod's main schools; in the forties, this was changed to four-year scholarships to Valparaiso University. In 1938–1939 the league experimented with a Church Finance Service Department, a committee of experienced businessmen to offer advice on financial problems to congregations, but only three requests came in the first year and the venture died. Minutes, CNV, June 14, 1938, pp. 1008-1009, 1014-15; CNV, Exhibit VIII, June 10-11, 1939, p. 39.

11. According to Martin Daib, Minutes, BG, April 10, 1937, pp. 882-83.

12. Minutes, ExB, Sept. 9, 1944, p. 1. Eggers was explicit that the Depression and expansion of radio work had retarded the organization of districts. Minutes, BD, Oct. 17, 1942, p. 9.

13. Letter from Theo. Graebner, April 6, 1936, TG MSS, Box 66. Some ministers, however, were adamantly opposed, resisting bitterly any approach that did not come through them or fearing an emphasis on the laity at the expense of the clergy; they repeated the accusation that the laymen were trying to run the synod. "I trust that the source of this list [of laymen] will be kept quiet," cautioned one participating pastor. "Otherwise I'll become persona non grata in worse measure than the Liturgical Movement ever made me." Letter to Graebner, April 30, 1936, TG MSS, Box 66.

14. Theo. Graebner to L. G. Bickel, Jan. 11, 1937, TG MSS, Box 41; see correspondence in TG MSS, Box 66.

15. Statement to Pittsburgh Pastoral Conference, Oct. 5, 1936, TG MSS, Box 66.

16. The league drew back from proposals of the merger with the American Lutheran Publicity Bureau largely because the LLL feared the reputation of the *American Lutheran* for discussion free from the synod's censorial controls. Minutes, BG, Feb. 12, 1938, p. 976; BG, March 4, 1939; ExC, Exhibit A, May 25, 1939; BG, July 9, 1939; interview with O. P. Kretzmann, July 5, 1966. On seminars, see *LL* 18 (1947): 25.

17. The 1941 convention did agree to send a letter to the synodical

negotiating committee, encouraging further talks. *LL* 12 (1941): 28. However, at the 1943 convention, when Gallmeyer spoke for Lutheran union, he was sharply challenged. Instead of debating the issues and engaging itself in study, the league was content to have Gallmeyer strike his remarks from the record. Minutes, CNV, Exhibit 2, July 9-11, 1943, p. 21.

18. Richard A. Jesse to Graebner, March 11, 1948, TG MSS, Box 79.
19. Minutes, CNV, June 16-17, 1941, p. 19.
20. *Ibid.*
21. E.W. Schroeter, *LL* 18 (1947): 25. See also *LL* 14 (1943): 7, 34; 17 (1946): 10, 16-17.
22. Minutes, CNV, June 25-26, 1948, p. 5.
23. *LL* 18 (1947): 11.
24. Lyle L. Schaefer, *Faith to Move Mountains: A History of the Colorado District of The Lutheran Church—Missouri Synod . . . 1872–1968* (Denver: The Colorado District, LCMS, 1969), p. 147.
25. Herbert W. Knopp to Oscar T. Doerr, Nov. 24, 1944, Knopp MSS, CHI.
26. Minutes, BG, Jan. 26-27, 1946, p. 16.
27. The postwar issues of the magazine of practical church work, the *American Lutheran*, were filled with articles on audio-visual education.
28. Minutes, BG, Jan. 11-12, 1947, p. 14; ExB, May 31, 1947, p. 3; *LL* 18 (1947): 63. About $200,000 was collected initially, with campaign expenses running close to 20 percent. Minutes, ExB, Oct. 15-16, 1949, p. 8. Conventions in 1948 and 1949 confirmed the project, but little further progress was made. Minutes, CNV, June 25-26, 1948, pp. 19-20; ExB, Oct. 15-16, 1949, p. 8.
29. Minutes, OpC, Aug. 5, 1948; ExB, July 30, 1949, pp. 1-4; interview, Oscar P. Brauer, Sept. 16, 1966; *Convention Yearbook,* 1950, pp. 28-30; unsigned, *LL* 20 (1949): 74-76; unsigned, *LL* 24 (April 1953): 7.
30. Minutes, ExB, Dec. 9-10, 1950, p. 14.
31. John Pollock, *Billy Graham: An Authorized Biography* (New York, 1966), pp. 79-86.
32. The broadcasting deficit for the 1950–51 season was more than $100,000. Minutes, ExB, May 5-6, 1951, p. 6.
33. Minutes, BG, March 26-27, 1955, p. 8.
34. Minutes, CNV, July 1-3, 1951, p. 39. The LLL was at least consistent; the pastor it approached, A. R. Kretzmann, had been asked to take the job twenty years earlier.
35. Paul M. Harrison, "Church and Laity Among Protestants," *Reli-*

gion in American Society, vol. 332 (Nov. 1960), *The Annals of The American Academy of Political and Social Science*, p. 42.

36. Herbert Knopp, "Report to the Committee on the Lutheran Laymen's League—Valparaiso Memorial Building," n.d., LLL, CHI.

37. Quoted in Krupnick and Associates, Inc., "Sales Betterment Plan for Lutheran Laymen's League" (typewritten ms, 1959), p. 37.

38. The number of zones rose from 26 in 1951 to 282 by 1957. Minutes, CNV, June 30–July 3, 1957, p. 88.

39. Material of such variety, sophistication, and quantity was produced that the LLL staff members had to reassure somewhat overwhelmed LLL leaders that every club was not expected to use all the material. Minutes, CNV, July 16–19, 1961, p. 11.

40. Minutes, Membership Services Comm., Jan. 16, 1959, p. 3.

41. *LL* 25 (May 1954): 1.

42. Minutes, CNV, July 10–13, 1960, p. 55.

43. *LL* 26 (Feb. 1956): 6.

Chapter 10: Using the Laity

1. *AL* 23 (Feb. 1940): 11.

2. Circulation figures are in *SYB*, 1937, p. 183. Average actual church attendance, when sampled in 1938, showed a synod-wide ratio of 3:1 between English and German services, very close to the ratio of the current subscriptions of the *Witness* and *Lutheraner*. *SYB*, 1939, p. 154.

3. See John E. Hofman, "Mother Tongue Retentiveness in Ethnic Parishes," in Joshua Fishman, *Language Loyalty in the United States* (The Hague, 1966), pp. 127-55; Paul T. Dietz, "The Transition from German to English in the Missouri Synod from 1910 to 1947," *CHIQ* 22 (Oct. 1949): 97-127; Alan Graebner, "The Acculturation of an Immigrant Lutheran Church: The Lutheran Church—Missouri Synod, 1917–1929" (Ph.D. dissertation, Columbia University, 1965), pp. 94-161.

4. In 1965 only about 5 percent of all congregations in the U.S. and Canada had any German services. Calculated from *SYB*, 1965.

5. J. W. Behnken to I. C. Heinicke, Dec. 31, 1938, TG MSS, Box 55; *LW* 60 (1941): 21; *LL* 33 (Jan. 1962): 8; *RAM*, LCMS, 1962, p. 198.

6. "The Christian in the World Today," *PRO*, Texas District, LCMS, 1948, p. 20. Approximately half of the adults confirmed into the church in 1945 were already engaged or married to Lutherans. *TY* 1 (Sept. 1946): 22. See also *PRO*, LCMS, 1953, p. 345; Walter A. Juergensen, "The Church in Town and Country, St. Peters," *The Lutheran*

Parish in an Urbanized America, ed. Ross P. Scherer, Fifteenth Yearbook, Lutheran Education Association (River Forest, Ill: Lutheran Education Association, 1958), p. 64.

7. See, e.g., *LW* 80 (1961): 304-305; *PRO,* LCMS, 1953, p. 345; *RAM,* LCMS, 1956, p. 242; *PRO,* LCMS, 1959, pp. 205-216. A typically thorough summary of the interwar Lutheran position is the chapter, "Mixed Marriages," in W. A. Maier's *For Better, Not for Worse* (St. Louis: Concordia Publishing House, 1935).

8. *PRO*, LCMS, 1935, pp. 134-35. *PRO*, LCMS, 1947, p. 537; *LW* 67 (1948): 243; *RAM*, LCMS, 1950, p. 283. For the committee's work see, for example, *Helping Families Through the Church*, ed. Oscar E. Feucht (St. Louis: Concordia Publishing House, 1957); *idem, Ministry to Families: A Handbook for Christian Congregations* (St. Louis: Concordia Publishing House, 1963); *RAM,* LCMS, 1956, p. 240; 1959, pp. 261-62; 1965, p. 197; *LW* 75 (1956): 261.

9. Explicit reference is in W. G. Polack, *LW* 68 (1949): 176; and *RAM,* LCMS, 1941, p. 98.

10. After a high of 115,000 in 1959, circulation dropped to below 45,000 in the late sixties, and the magazine was discontinued at the end of 1970. *RAM,* LCMS, 1959, p. 548; *SYB,* 1969, p. 49.

11. *SYB,* 1950, p. 239; 1968, p. 203. The 1950 report says simply "Synod" was 58 percent rural in 1947; I interpret this as congregations, not communicants.

12. *AV* 11 (Feb. 1964): 14-15.

13. *LW* 80 (1961): 38.

14. *LW* 81 (1962): 221.

15. F. A. Hertwig, *TY* 1 (1946), 5. For rhetoric of the fifties, see *RAM,* LCMS, 1956, p. 280; William Drews, *LW* 75 (1956): 92 ff.

16. *AV* 11 (Feb. 1964): 14-15.

17. For efforts at counteraction see *LW* 79 (1960): 246-47; *LL* 26 (Nov. 1955): 8; *LL* 24 (May 1953): 4.

18. *SYB,* 1947, p. 145; 1965, p. 250.

19. Calculated from *SYB,* 1970, p. 276.

20. *LW* 66 (1947): 149.

21. One must wait until 1970; when the Study of Generations project focused on Lutherans who had previously belonged to another denomination—nearly one-quarter of the membership in 1970—four groups stood out as chief sources: Methodist (5.1 percent of the total sample), Baptist (4.3 percent), Roman Catholic (3.6 percent), and Presbyterian (2.6 percent). No significant differences between these people

and those born Lutheran were found. Unfortunately, of course, there is no comparable data for twenty-five years earlier, when the synod was less Americanized. Merton Strommen, Milo Brekke, Ralph Underwager, and Arthur Johnson, *A Study of Generations* (Minneapolis, 1972), and unpublished data from that study.

22. Rodney Stark and Charles Y. Glock, *American Piety: The Nature of Religious Commitment* (Berkeley, 1968), p. 166.

23. *God's Grace and Blessing* [anniversary history, Good Shepherd Lutheran Church, Inglewood] (n.p., n.d.).

24. *LW* 63 (1944): 9; 72 (1953): 4-5.

25. E. W. Frenk, *AV* 2 (Sept. 1955): 2-3.

26. *AL* 13 (1930): 1012-13, 1036-38; 17 (1934):2082; 26 (1943): 241; interview, Oscar E. Feucht, Nov. 18, 1966; *PRO*, LCMS, 1944, p. 136.

27. *AL* 3 (1920): 32; 5 (1922): 29; 6 (1923): 13-14; 8 (1925): 105-106; 9 (1926): 14; 17 (1934): 2104; 28 (1945): 279-80; 30 (1947): 140-141; 31 (1948): 45-46. *RAM*, LCMS, 1965, p. 282.

28. *Ibid.*, 1956, p. 234. See also *ibid.*, 1953, p. 202; *LW* 73 (1954): 241.

29. *AV* 1 (Nov. 1954): 13; 2 (Sept. 1955): 3. A special program, "Train Two," was established in the late fifties to help prepare lay teachers. *RAM*, LCMS, 1962, p. 195.

30. Quoted in "Digest of the Consultation on Church and Laity" (St. Louis: mimeographed by the Department of Adult Education, Board of Parish Education, 1965), pp. 9-10.

31. Stark and Glock's data further confirm the relatively high level of Missourian commitment and the entirely undistinguished level of religious study and knowledge. See their chapters 3, 4, and 7.

32. *TY* 6 (Jan. 1951): 27.

33. *AV* 3 (Dec. 1956): 3.

34. "Each One Reach One" in 1946. "Preaching-Teaching-Reaching" in 1955, a program that gained participation by 4,700 congregations by 1965. Later, a modification, known as "Families for Christ," was introduced. The American Lutheran Publicity Bureau came up with still another mission campaign outline, the "Sharing Christ Plan."

35. Ralph Richman, *AL* 33 (1950): 246. In fairness, it should be added that in such columns laymen spoke out more bluntly than they usually did in public. See, for example, *idem, AL* 39 (1956): 237-38.

36. O. A. Geiseman, *AL* 31 (1948): 217; Elmer Maschoff, *TY* 3 (Jan. 1948): 1; IMAPREA CHERTOO, *AL* 43 (1960): 101. Richman, *AL* 36 (1953): 306.

37. Statistics are from appropriate editions of the *SYB*. Early tabula-

tions in that annual were based upon baptized membership. However after World War II the statistical office used communicant membership, making comparisons difficult between figures given above and those reported in Chapter 5. The 1930 figure was estimated by using 65 percent as a communicant membership percentage of baptized membership.

Communicant membership	1945	1955	1970
0-99	35%	31%	20%
100-199	26	25	25
200-499	17	31	36

38. H. Marten, *LW* 69 (1950): 194; see also Herman W. Gockel, *TY* 1 (Nov. 1946): 21; W. G. Polack, *AL* 21 (1948): 305-306. After interviews with a group of southern California Lutherans, Jeff Johnson concluded that their expressions revealed the traditional bifurcation. For them the pastor's responsibility included worship, synodical machinery and educational efforts. The congregation's responsibility was for the budget and church property. "An Analysis and Description of Role Expectation for Ministers of the Southern California District of The Lutheran Church—Missouri Synod" (Ph.D. dissertation, University of Southern California, 1961), p. 87.

39. *LW* 67 (1948): 161.

40. *PRO,* LCMS, 1953, pp. 606-607; Richman, *AL* 37 (1954): 37; *AV* 2 (Feb. 1955): 48.

41. *AV* 1 (Oct. 1954): 17-18; insert in *AV* 2 (Dec. 1955).

42. Lyle L. Schaefer, *Faith to Move Mountains: A History of the Colorado District . . . 1862–1968* (Denver: Colorado District, LCMS, 1969), p. 51; R. R. Caemmerer, *LW* 65 (1946): 103-104; H. W. Gockel, *TY* 5 (May 1950): 16; *PRO,* LCMS, 1950, pp. 479-88; *RAM,* LCMS, 1953, pp. 222-24; Robert Just, *AV* 1 (Nov. 1954): 6; *AV* 3 (March 1956): 18-19; *PRO,* LCMS, 1956, p. 276; *RAM,* LCMS, 1956, pp. 257-58; Unsigned, *AL* 39 (1956): 95; *RAM,* LCMS, 1959, pp. 287-303; 1962, p. 22; *WBK,* LCMS, 1965, pp. 238-39.

43. *LL* 31 (April 1960): 6; (June 1960): 5; 32 (April 1961): 4.

44. *LW* 83 (1964): 565. The Peace Corps of course encouraged this development; furthermore, emergent nationalism abroad frowned less on worker-missionaries than on clergy.

45. *AL* 39 (1956): 97.

46. Unsigned, *LW* 69 (1950): 212. Eldor A. Cassens, "The Christian as a Worker in God's Kingdom," *PRO,* Southeastern District, LCMS, 1948, p. 18. Clarence Peters, *TY* 1 (March 1946): 8.

47. Elmer Maschoff, *TY* 3 (Jan. 1948): 1.

48. Cassens, p. 7; probably the summary statement of the period was a book by Carl W. Berner with the instructive title, *Spiritual Power for Your Congregation: A Guide to Lay Activity in the Kingdom* (St. Louis: Concordia Publishing House, 1956).

49. Lamenting absence of lay teachers in churches, one synodical official noted that secular societies *"draw off* these potential teachers for positions of leadership." Oscar E. Feucht, *Building Better Bible Classes* (St. Louis: Concordia Publishing House, 1951), p. 58. Emphasis added.

50. Berner, p. 60.

51. J. E. Herrmann, "The Priesthood of Believers and a Functioning Congregation," *PRO,* North Dakota District, LCMS, 1952, p. 46.

52. Survey form in *TY* 4 (Aug. 1949): 2. The suggested parish committees were membership, finance, auditing, house, music, Christian education, stewardship, evangelism, public relations. *AL* 43 (1960): 340.

53. *AL* 28 (1945): 193; 39 (1956): 233; 43 (1960): 343; *AV* 2 (Jan. 1955): 38. The problem was the climax of a long-term trend. J. H. Theiss, *"Gemeindeversammlungen," PRO,* California and Nevada District, LCMS, 1904, p. 68; *LW* 42 (1923): 278-79; 53 (1934): 320.

54. *RAM,* LCMS, 1956, p. 240; David S. Schuller, *Women's Work in The Lutheran Church—Missouri Synod: A Survey Report* (St. Louis: Lutheran Women's Missionary League, n.d.), p. 25. A few such clubs had been founded in the late thirties and early forties. Minutes, CNV, June 10-11, 1939, p. 20; *LW* 62 (1943): 392.

55. *LL* 30 (Feb. 1959): 12.

56. Though these figures give no opportunity to judge change over time, they are a salutary reminder that to discern trends is not necessarily to describe even a majority of the laity. Stark and Glock, pp. 92, 94.

57. For the bar association, see *LW* 64 (1945): 108. For the LCA, see *ibid.,* 268; interview, R. W. Hahn, Feb. 27, 1970.

Chapter 11: Both Feet in the World

1. *The Modern Schism: Three Paths to the Secular* (New York, 1969), p. 98.

2. "The Burden of Infallibility: A Study in the History of Dogma" (mimeographed, 1948), reprinted *CHIQ* 38 (1965): 87-94. Parenthetically one might add that this same cast of mind helps to explain why archives have flourished in the synod while historical scholarship has not. To

collect the texts of the fathers in one thing; to expose change quite another.

3. *LW* 67 (1948): 44.

4. Clifford Brueggemann, *LW* 83 (1964): 517. Compare this with Paul Bente's statement of 1928 in *LW* 67 (1928): 219-20.

5. On ethics, see *LW* 84 (1965): 379-88.

6. *LW* 81 (1962): 443; 83 (1964): 85; 84 (1965): 124; 86 (1967): 14.

7. *LW* 85 (1966): 86.

8. *LW* 86 (1967): 30.

9. The statement was by Martin Scharlemann, quoted in *Proceedings of The First Institute on The Church and Modern Culture*, ed. John G. Kunstmann (Valparaiso: Lutheran Academy for Scholarship, 1953), p. 19. LAS sessions are reported in *Colloquoy on Law and Theology*, ed. Andrew J. Buehner (St. Louis: LAS, 1960); *Proceedings of the Colloquium on Medical Ethics* (St. Louis: LAS, 1961); *Proceedings of the Second Colloquium on Christian Medical Ethics,* ed. Karl W. Linsenmann (St. Louis: LAS, 1964); *Law and Theology: Essays on the Professional Responsibility of the Christian Lawyer,* ed. Andrew J. Buehner (St. Louis: Concordia Publishing House, 1965); *The Christian in Business: Thoughts on Business and the Social Order* (St. Louis: LAS, 1966); *The Layman and the Church: The Church's Responsibility and Concern for Its Professionally Trained Laity,* ed. Andrew J. Buehner (St. Louis: LAS, 1967); *The Church and the Visual Arts,* ed. Andrew J. Buehner (St. Louis: LAS, 1968); *The New American Revolution: Moral, Student, and Theological,* ed. Andrew J. Buehner (St. Louis: LAS, 1968).

10. See John W. Klotz, "Foreword," *Colloquium on Medical Ethics,* p. iv.

11. Wilfred Bockelman, *AV* 13 (April 1966): 34-35. There is very likely a correlation between the rise of the view of the world described here and the decline of expressions with apocalyptic overtones. Unfortunately, even after a conscientious reading of the sources, it is more difficult to prove the absence of statements than their presence. Nevertheless it should be said that there seem many fewer counterparts in the Age of Deterrence to statements in the thirties and forties emphasizing the degeneration of world conditions as a sign of the imminent Second Coming. For the latter, see but one example in *PRO,* LCMS, 1935, p. 91.

12. *PRO,* LCMS, 1962, pp. 138-39; 1967, p. 150. Whether such actions were sufficiently proportioned to meet the situation eliciting them is another and dubious proposition; the point here is that what a decade earlier was impossible in this denomination now occurred.

13. *RAM*, LCMS, 1965, pp. 118, 140. See also John Elliott, quoted in *LW* 85 (1966): 27.

14. I have drawn here from Hans-Ruedi Weber, "The Rediscovery of the Laity in the Ecumenical Movement," *The Layman in Christian History,* ed. Stephen Charles Neill and Hans-Ruedi Weber (Philadelphia, 1963), pp. 377-94. See also *Laici in Ecclesia: An Ecumenical Bibliography on the Role of the Laity in the Life and Mission of the Church* (Geneva, 1961).

15. (Philadelphia, 1958). Kraemer in turn borrowed from—while rejecting the ecclesiology of—Yves Congar, *Lay People in the Church— A Study for a Theology of the Laity,* trans. Donald Attwater (Westminster, Maryland, 1965).

16. See his column, "We Look at the World," begun in 1942 in the *Witness.* Public statements similar to Caemmerer's were made by an official like Feucht or a professor like John Strietelmeier or a theologian like Jaroslav Pelikan. But these exceptions only prove the rule. Strietelmeier, *LW* 71 (May 27, 1952): 4-5; Pelikan, *LW* 70 (1951): 126-27.

17. (St. Louis: Concordia Publishing House), pp. 81, 96. See also Martin Marty, "The Church in the World," *The Lively Function of the Gospel,* ed. Robert Bertram (St. Louis: Concordia Publishing House, 1966), pp. 133-48.

18. *Feeding and Leading* (St. Louis: Concordia Publishing House, 1962), p. 38.

19. *RAM,* LCMS, 1965, pp. 114-23. The quotations are from pp. 115-16.

20. Unsigned, 83 (1964): 139. The quotation is a good example of the fact that what differed in the sixties were emphases and context rather than abstract definitions. Probably no informed spokesman of the 1930s would have disagreed with the sentence as stated. He would never have drawn the conclusions from it that came in the 1960s, however.

21. *AV* 12 (Jan. 1965): 39; "Digest, Consultation on Church and Laity" (St. Louis: mimeographed by the Department of Adult Education, Board of Parish Education, 1965), p. 6. Earlier movement in this direction is apparent in IMAPREA CHERTOO, *AL* 41 (1958): 151.

22. Roy Blumhorst, "In the Suburbs," *Death and Birth of the Parish,* ed. Martin Marty (St. Louis: Concordia Publishing House, 1964), p. 120.

23. Donald Hoefferkamp, quoted in William M. Ramsey, *Cycles and Renewal: Trends in Protestant Lay Education* (Nashville, 1969), p. 141.

24. See Gibson Winter, *The Suburban Captivity of the Churches: An Analysis of Protestant Responsibility in the Expanding Metropolis* (Gar-

den City, N.Y., 1961); Peter Berger, *The Noise of Solemn Assemblies: Christian Commitment and the Religious Establishment in America* (Garden City, 1961); Harvey Cox, *The Secular City: Secularization and Urbanization in Theological Perspective* (New York, 1965). Radical and insistent proposals also came from Stephen Rose in the various issues of *Renewal* magazine. A critical review of the literature is in Gabriel Fackre, "The Crisis of the Congregation: A Debate," *Voluntary Associations: A Study of Groups in Free Societies,* ed. D. B. Robertson (Richmond, Va., 1966), pp. 275-98.

25. David Schuller, *The Christian Encounters the New Urban Society* (St. Louis: Concordia Publishing House, 1966), pp. 47-48. See also Ross P. Scherer, "The Nature of Urban Civilization and Its Effect on the Church," *The Lutheran Parish in an Urbanized America,* ed. Ross P. Scherer, Fifteen Yearbook, Lutheran Education Association (River Forest: Lutheran Education Association, 1958), p. 17.

26. Richard Sommerfeld repeatedly sounds this theme in *The Church of the 21st Century: Prospects and Proposals* (St. Louis: Concordia Publishing House, 1965); see also Schuller, *Urban Society,* pp. 52-53; Unsigned, *AL* 43 (1960): 36-37.

27. See, e.g., *AV* 12 (Sept. 1965): 8. In such onslaughts against extreme congregational autonomy, the critics coincidentally joined forces with synodical officials. Pressure from the latter source grew in force from its beginnings in the 1920s, when national administrators and laymen were frustrated by the lack of cooperation in fund-raising drives.

28. William Hillmer, *AV* 11 (June 1964): 5-6.

29. See, e.g., Paul Malte, *The Frozen and the Chosen* (n.p.: Lutheran Laymen's League, 1964); Omar Stuenkel, *Both Feet in the World* (n.p.: LLL, 1966).

30. Information was gathered from biographies appearing each spring in the pre-convention issues of the *Layman.* According to these, 46 percent could be clearly identified as having attended at least for a short time a college other than a proprietary business school. About 16 percent reported graduation from high school or attendance at a trade or business school. Approximately 37 percent of the biographies, however, did not mention education. Since only in 1968 was this obviously an editorial decision, I am inclined to believe the absence of mention usually indicated the absence of college experience, a judgment concurred in by others with league experience.

31. Ruth Fritz Meyer, *Women on a Mission: The role of women in the church . . . including a history of the Lutheran Women's Missionary*

League during its first twenty-five years (St. Louis: Concordia Publishing House Print, 1967), p. 246; *SYB,* 1969, pp. 53, 55.

32. See Meyer, pp. 134-239, 255 ff.

33. David Schuller, *Women's Work in The Lutheran Church— Missouri Synod: A Survey Report* (St. Louis: Lutheran Women's Missionary League, 1961).

34. Meyer, pp. 205-206; *PRO,* LWML, 1961, p. 29; 1963, pp. 37-38; 1967, p. 31.

35. P. 11.

36. *Lutheran Woman's Quarterly,* 27 (Spring 1969), *passim.*

37. *LWR* 5 (Aug. 10, 1969): 3, 11.

38. *PRO,* LCMS, 1938, p. 346.

39. *PRO,* LCMS, 1956, p. 568.

40. See, e.g., *LW* 84 (1965): 168.

41. A survey of convention considerations is in *Women Suffrage in the Church: Report of the Commission on Theology and Church Relations* (n.d. [1969]).

42. *Women in the Church: A Restudy of Woman's Place in Building the Kingdom* (Grand Rapids: Eerdman's, 1957); *LW* 77 (1958): 525.

43. See *LW* 76 (1957): 198, 371.

44. Generational changes were not always necessary. The correspondence of Theodore Graebner reveals a mind that over several decades gradually became quite dubious about the synod's position, though unwilling to challenge it publicly. He was by no means unique in this. Graebner to W. Luebkeman, July 17, 1946; to R. P. Sieving, Aug. 21, 1947; to C. M. Beyer, Jan. 18, 1950, TG MSS, Box 14.

45. In the Detroit area, 71 percent of the synodical laity, but only 47 percent of the clergy, were in 1966 ready to agree that women should have an equal voice in church decisions. The separation was even greater on the question of ordination; 47 percent of the laity, but only 8 percent of the clergy, agreed. Lawrence L. Kersten, *The Lutheran Ethic: The Impact of Religion on Laymen and Clergy* (Detroit, 1970), p. 125. A national sample produced a comparable figure for the laity on ordination. Merton Strommen, Milo Brekke, Ralph Underwager, Arthur Johnson, *A Study of Generations* (Minneapolis, 1972), p. 272.

Chapter 12: Humpty-Dumpty and All the King's Men

1. For a survey of some themes in religious developments, see the articles in *The Sixties: Radical Change in American Religion,* ed. James

M. Gustafson, vol. 387 (Jan. 1970), *The Annals of the American Academy of Political and Social Science*. Strangely, not a single article is devoted explicitly to the laity.

2. A convenient assemblage of survey results is in *Gallup Opinion Index: Special Report on Religion, 1967* (Princeton, 1967).

3. *LW* 42 (1923): 238.

4. In the forties, the *Witness* occasionally solicited letters from laymen. In the fifties a letters column was a fairly regular feature, but the contents were almost never controversial. In the sixties practically any editorial stand of the journal generated letters of sharp dissent and enthusiastic endorsement. Charges of slanted reporting grew so common that in 1969 the *Witness* staff in effect did away with the front page of the *Reporter* completely by converting to a tabloid size and devoting the front page to a large picture and a minimum of (noncontroversial) reporting. For a sampling of letters, see *LW* 82 (1963): 342; 83 (1964): 373.

5. Autobiographical statements may be found in *LN* 5 (Sept. 18, 1967): 1 ff.; (Dec. 11, 1967): 5; *CN* 2 (June 2, 1969): 5-6.

6. *CN* 1 (Jan. 1, 1968): 4.

7. According to Grace Otten, *LWR* 6 (March 1, 1970): 2; see also *CN* 1 (Oct. 14, 1968): 2.

8. *CN* 1 (March 11, 1968): 7; (Feb. 5, 1968): 3. Otten's anti-communism is the focus of Arnold Krugler's "For God and Country" (STM thesis, Lutheran School of Theology, Chicago, 1968).

9. T. Robert Ingram, *LN* 5 (June 12, 1967): 14; Rousas Rushdoony, *LN* 5 (June 26, 1967): 15; T. Robert Ingram, *CN* 1 (Feb. 19, 1968): 5; Marcus Braun, 1 (March 25, 1968): 12. For some of Otten's connections with the far right, see Erling Jorstad, *The Politics of Doomsday: Fundamentalists of the Far Right* (Nashville, 1970), pp. 160-63.

10. *LN* 5 (Oct. 16, 1967): 6; *CN* 1 (Feb. 26, 1968): 6; (Dec. 9, 1968): 5. Virulent anti-Catholicism is much more difficult to find in the *News*. Otten saw in challenges to official dogma the same liberal forces undermining Roman Catholicism as he was fighting in Lutheranism.

11. *CN* 2 (Jan. 20, 1969): 5.

12. Quoting Kurt Marquardt, *CN* 2 (Aug. 25, 1969): 7-9. Otten also cited the anti-communism of Walter A. Maier, interestingly enough the editor's greatest hero in the synod's history, though Otten gave little sign that he fully appreciated Maier's role as a transitional figure in the synod's social attitudes.

13. John Neuhaus, *LN* 5 (April 3, 1967): 11.

14. *CN* 1 (Sept. 2, 1968): 5.

15. *CN* 2 (June 2, 1969): 1.

16. *CN* 1 (May 27, 1968): 7; (Dec. 9, 1968): 9; *LN* 5 (June 26, 1967): 13.
17. *CN* 2 (Nov. 7, 1969): 11; (March 31, 1969): 11.
18. Marcus Braun, *CN* 2 (June 23, 1969): 8.
19. The statement was regularly carried on the *News* editorial page.
20. *CN* 2 (Aug. 18, 1969): 4.
21. Peter Krey, *LN* 5 (Dec. 11, 1967): 4.
22. *CN* 2 (June 23, 1969): 8.
23. Survey results presented by Jeffrey Hadden revealed a Missouri Synod clergy in 1965 sufficiently conservative that one could be to the left of it and still be close to the middle relative to Protestantism at large. Hadden found impressive unanimity among synodical clergy on a substantial body of belief. Consensus broke down, however, on the item, "Scriptures are the inspired and inerrant Word of God not only in matters of faith but also in historical, geographical, and other secular matters." Items on the historicity of Adam and Eve, the virgin birth, and resurrection of Jesus Christ, on the actuality of eternal judgment and of the demonic all drew assent from 90 percent or better of the synod's pastors, putting them in a category distinct from the clergy of the other denominations polled (Methodist, Episcopalian, Presbyterian, American Baptist, and American Lutheran). *The Gathering Storm in the Churches* (New York, 1969), pp. 37-53.
24. For expositions of Neuhaus' thought, see his column in the *Lutheran Forum* or *Movement and Revolution* (New York, 1970), written with Peter Berger.
25. The *Study of Generations* found Lutheran youth to be about representative of American youth generally, but makes the point that American youth generally are much more conservative than the focus of some journalists and social scientists would lead one to believe. Merton Strommen, Milo Brekke, Ralph Underwager, and Arthur Johnson, *A Study of Generations* (Minneapolis, 1972), pp. 219-62.
26. To my knowledge the *Free Press* lasted only three issues, between Dec. 13, 1968 and Feb. 21, 1969. The *Cresset* shifted staff with the resignation of John Strietelmeier in 1969, but those who took up the reins were mostly of the college generation that ushered in the sixties. They might be disenchanted, but they were not radicals, at least not yet. Much the same could be said of the *Lutheran Forum,* pan-Lutheran successor to the *American Lutheran.*
27. The *Lutheran News* reprinted at length what appears to be the press release of that group in 5 (Sept. 18, 1967): 1, 16. A RNS release was reproduced in *LN* 5 (Dec. 25, 1967): 2.
28. John H. Elliott, "Death of a Slogan: From Royal Priesthood to

Celebrating Community," *Una Sancta* 35 (1968): 18-31; *Doxology: God's People Called to Celebrate His Glory* (St. Louis: Lutheran Laymen's League, 1966).

29. See, e.g., *LF* 2 (Jan. 1968): 8-9.

30. Minutes, BG, Sept. 18-19, 1965.

31. Jon Suel, *LL* 41 (June 1970): 12.

32. *LL* 41 (July 1970): 12.

33. *Cresset* 30 (Jan. 1967): 6.

34. *LF* 2 (July 1968): 19.

35. Charles Y. Glock and Rodney Stark, *Religion and Society in Tension* (Chicago, 1965); Charles Y. Glock, Benjamin B. Ringer, and Earl Babbie, *To Comfort and to Challenge: A Dilemma of the Contemporary Church* (Berkeley, 1967); Rodney Stark and Charles Y. Glock, *American Piety: The Nature of Religious Commitment* (Berkeley, 1968); Lawrence L. Kersten, *The Lutheran Ethic: The Impact of Religion on Laymen and Clergy* (Detroit, 1970).

36. Strommen *et al., passim.*

37. For example, in a perplexing piece of background research essential to his thesis, Kersten managed to construct a "Lutheran ethic" from Weber, Troeltsch, Tawney, and Fromm without a single reference to such contemporary specialists in Luther scholarship as Forell, Brauer, or Pelikan. Perhaps needless to say, his "Lutheran ethic" is not a very attractive thing and the focus of his interpretation is similarly negative.

38. One must be careful as well not to assume automatically that liberal or even radical clergy will inevitably suffer at the hands of conservative laity. Clyde Griffen reveals a much more optimistic picture in "Rich Laymen and Early Social Christianity," *Church History* 36 (March 1967): 45-65. See also E. V. Toy, Jr., "The National Lay Committee and the National Council of Churches: A Case Study of Protestants in Conflict," *American Quarterly* 21 (Summer 1969): 190-209.

39. Kersten, pp. 122, 139. Strommen *et al.,* p. 290. In studying a parish of the LCA which divided during the 1960s, Heenan discovered the expected literalist-nonliteralist division, but also found the non-literalists had in turn to be differentiated between those who favored church involvement and those who favored individual involvement in social concerns. Edward F. Heenan, S. J., "Congregation in Conflict: A Study of the Emergence of Religious Conflict in a Lutheran Congregation" (Ph.D. dissertation, Case Western Reserve University, 1970).

40. Strommen *et al.,* pp. 157-249. Confirmatory data is provided by a study of Lutheran students at the University of Missouri and at Stephens

College in 1968. Those who felt their denomination under-involved in social and political issues outnumbered those who felt it over-involved by 11 to 1 and 5 to 1, respectively. Kenneth Lee Frerking, "Social and Religious Attitudes Among Lutheran Students" (Ph.D. dissertation, University of Missouri, 1970), pp. 207-208.

    41. 40 (1969): 527.

    42. Kersten, p. 207, found 75 percent of Detroit laity favored merger. The national sample of *A Study of Generations* (p. 288) produced a figure of 62 percent.

    43. The questions asked were not quite comparable. Kersten, p. 34, used the following: "The Bible is God's word and all it says is true" (62 percent lay agreement); "The Bible was written by men inspired by God, and its basic moral and religious teachings are true, but because the writers were men, it contains some human errors" (27 percent lay agreement); "Even though the Bible contains many errors and myths, it still represents God's teachings" (10 percent lay agreement). *A Study of Generation*'s question was "The Bible is the Word of God. God inspired men to report verbally what He said. The Bible in the original texts contained no errors." Of the laity, 38 percent marked "I strongly agree. Persons who disbelieve this are not true to the Christian faith." But 36 percent marked "I agree. But exact agreement on this point is not necessary. There may have been mistranslations and slips in copying the original texts of Scripture." And 20 percent marked "I agree in part. The Bible communicates the Word of God. But God spoke through fallible men. Therefore the Bible contains errors because of the human element, which we may judge by reason." Unpublished data furnished me by Dr. Ralph Underwager.

    44. For one thing, at that convention half the synod (all women) was unrepresented, an important point according to Strommen's discovery of a higher Gospel orientation among women. Fewer than one-tenth of the delegates were under thirty-five and one-third was over fifty-five. Their responses on specific items were usually more conservative than various samples of laity not at a convention. They were distinctly more conservative than the clergy delegates on the statement, "Scriptures are the inspired and inerrant Word of God not only in matters of faith, but also in historical, geographical, and other secular matters (in other words, there are no errors of any kind in the Bible as it was originally written)." Of the lay delegates, 83 percent agreed, but of the parish clergy delegates, 65 percent assented. (When Hadden, p. 41, used the same item—but without the words in parentheses—for a national sample in 1965, he found

agreement from 76 percent of synodical clergy.) See W. Theophil Jan-
zow, "Secularization in an Orthodox Denomination" (Ph.D. dissertation, University of Nebraska, 1970).
    45. *Campus Commentary* (July 1965), p. 2.
    46. Richard Koenig, *Forum Letter* 2 (July 1973): 6.
    47. For laymen in the middle, one important key to attitudes on
theological questions was the local pastor, to judge from the frustrated
complaint of the activist on either side: "the trouble is you can't get to
those people because—[the pastor] keeps giving them a different line and
won't let you in." Probably for those susceptible to the extreme appeals
of the far right, something like the *Christian News,* that could be mailed
directly to the layman, was more important—a threat to pastoral status
that helped discredit the *News* among many clergy.
    48. Kersten, pp. 120-21.
    49. Strommen *et al.,* pp. 40, 34, 46, 108-109.
    50. Kersten's question was, "If somebody would plan and design a
community or subdivision entirely for Lutherans, do you think you
would like to live there." He interprets a positive answer as indication
that the respondent *"wants* to live" [italics mine] in such a community—
which seems to me to load more onto the question than it will bear. See
p. 50.
    51. 15.8 percent had one of their closest friends in the congregation;
15.2 percent, two friends; and 25.7 percent three or more. These figures
are quite comparable to the results for the Lutheran Church in America.
Unpublished data from Strommen *et al.*
    52. *LWR* 5 (Oct. 19, 1969): 6-7; 6 (Jan. 4, 1970): 4-5; (June 7, 1970):
6-7. For further warning against underestimating diversity among synodical parishes, see Ross P. Scherer, "Epilogue," *The Lutheran Parish in
an Urbanized America,* ed. Ross P. Scherer, Fifteenth Yearbook, Lutheran Education Association (River Forest: Lutheran Education
Association, 1958), p. 104.
    53. *LWR* 6 (April 19, 1970): 1-2.
    54. *A Study of Generations* data indicate relatively high personal par-
ticipation in parish activities by about one-quarter of the membership.
Such participation is correlated especially with having two or more close
friends in the congregation. Pp. 177-78, 191.
    55. *LW* 86 (1967): 275.
    56. *LWR* 7 (Dec. 12, 1971): 1.
    57. *LL* 41 (July 1970): 12. Statistics of the U.S. congregations whose
clubs disbanded between July 1968 and July 1970 (about 116) were com-

pared with synodical averages. This can be misleading for there is no assurance that congregations with LLL clubs represent a cross section of the synod. But for what it is worth, the only size congregation seriously under-represented in this sample of disbanding clubs was that with fewer than 100 communicants. This under-representation is balanced by fairly even over-representation among congregations with 200-499, 500-999, and more than 1,000 communicants. No distinct anomalies were apparent in age or location of the congregational sample. In sum, the movement seems widespread throughout the synod.

58. *LWR* 6 (April 5, 1970): 6.

59. Of the older laity, 89 percent (and 75 percent of those under 30) agreed that the "membership of the church is primarily and basically a group of people to be served or ministered unto by the pastor." For comparison's sake, 47 percent thought it highly important for a Lutheran to work for social justice. Kersten, pp. 121-22.

60. Strommen *et al.,* p. 54.

Bibliographic Note

This study rests on sources and judgments in five main categories: periodicals, manuscript collections, minutes and records of organizations, interviews with leading principals and observers, and the work of others who have studied some aspect of the Missouri Synod. Full citations for the last are given in appropriate footnotes. But readers may desire a summary of the other major sources, and scholars may find particulars on availability and location useful.

PERIODICALS

There is an enormous amount of information relating to the laity in the synodical press, but little is designated as such. Most can be mined only through patient reading not only of major articles and news items but of personal columns and routine notices and announcements. Given the plethora of material in print, I was forced to limit myself to the national press. The synod's official English organ, the *Lutheran Witness,* is an indispensable source for the historian. I read it from 1900 to the 1970s; for some periods I returned to it repeatedly as different questions presented themselves. The magazine is most valuable when most opinionated—early in the century, between the world wars, and in the sixties.

I read the official German *Der Lutheraner* for the period in which it was more important than the *Witness* or a serious alternative for large numbers of the laity: from the turn of the century into the mid-twenties. It is useful as a check on the *Witness* and sometimes for stray facts or ideas that did not make *Witness* columns. Generally its reports are no fuller and its opinions (of whatever variety) more restrained than those of the *Witness.*

Among publications for pastors, *Lehre und Wehre* was scanned for the first decade of the century but proved not very helpful. The *Theological Quarterly* (begun 1896) and its successor (after 1920), the *Theological Monthly,* were considerably more illuminating in the realm of social attitudes. Results of sampling in the *Concordia Theological Monthly* (successor to the *Theological Monthly* in 1930) proved disproportionately small for the time invested, and I did not pursue this source further.

The early magazine of practical church work published by the American Lutheran Publicity Bureau, the *American Lutheran,* proved exceptionally helpful, and I studied it carefully from its first issue in 1918 to its last in 1966, when it merged into the *Lutheran Forum,* a pan-Lutheran venture. The *American Lutheran* deserves more attention than it has so far received from Lutheran historians, because for a long time it was the only outlet within the synod which was not under the censorship of the St. Louis seminary faculty. In the thirties the magazine gradually turned from questions of parish techniques to matters of polity and theology. The shift was even more pronounced after the mid-forties, when the synod issued its own practical magazine, *Today,* begun in 1946 and terminated in 1950. Its eventual successor was *Advance,* begun in 1954. After reading several decades of articles on parish administration, I found I could predict the contents of *Advance* with some accuracy and turned to extensive sampling rather than page-for-page reading from 1954 until the early sixties, when a close reading is again necessary.

For a study of the laity, the most interesting of the far right press is the *Lutheran* [later, *Christian*] *News,* begun in 1963. Fairly complete files of the *News,* and also the *Confessional Lutheran* (begun in 1940) and *Through to Victory* (begun in 1960), are available at CHI.

The American Luther League's *Lutheran Layman* is the major source extant for the history of that organization. To my knowledge, the only existing volumes are at CHI; even these are not complete for the years from 1921 to the last issue of the publication in 1926. CHI files of the *Federation News* (published by the Federation of Lutheran Clubs beginning in 1946) are also incomplete; enough issues are available, however, that one can make an informed judgment of the association's size and strength.

Complete files and microfilm copies of the *Bulletin* (1930–1933) and the *Lutheran Layman* (1933—) of the Lutheran Laymen's

League are available at CHI. The same is true of the LLL's *Men's Club Meeting Program* (begun 1933), succeeded by the *Men's Club Program* in 1940 and the *Leader's Guide* in 1943. These were studied for the thirties with special attention, and sampled extensively in subsequent years. I read enough in the more ephemeral, mimeographed League house publications, such as MEMBERanda and ACTIONotes, to decide that a detailed perusal of their contents would not affect the generalizations made here about the league; more or less complete runs are in LLL files. In the case of both the *Lutheran Scholar* of the Lutheran Academy for Scholarship (1944 to the present) and the *Cresset* (1937—), the earlier years were read with the greatest care as the most important for this study.

MANUSCRIPT COLLECTIONS

Chapters 2 through 6 draw heavily on the Theodore Graebner papers at CHI. Editor and seminary professor, Graebner had a strong sense of history and apparently few limits on space. He saved much of the extensive correspondence that flowed in and out of his office. His papers are especially rich in the years between about 1917 and 1940. Also at CHI are many of the files of Lawrence B. Meyer, which include much mimeographed and miscellaneous printed publicity and fund-raising material, available nowhere else.

The papers of John W. Behnken at CHI available to me were disappointing for my purposes. A detailed letter-by-letter search through CHI holdings in the papers of O. A. Geiseman, W. G. Polack, William F. Arndt, and Karl Kretzmann proved prohibitive in ratio of time to results. The files of Frederick Pfotenhauer and John H. C. Fritz were destroyed. Mrs. Walter A. Maier gave me unrestricted access to the papers of her husband, but they are unaccountably thin. Dr. O. P. Kretzmann at Valparaiso University allowed me to read through his files dealing with lay activity in Lutheran union during the forties.

The Historical Institute has very few papers of twentieth-century laymen. Those of A. G. Brauer that remain from the twenties help shed light on the early LLL. The papers of Herbert W. Knopp illuminate LLL district organization and institutional fund raising. E. J. Gallmeyer opened to me a number of personal files he retains on the Lutheran Hour. Miss Marletta Wesche of St. Louis rescued some of the papers of her grandfather, A. H. Ahlbrand, from basement storage in Seymour, Indiana, and called my attention to them. Diligent search has, sadly, failed as yet to turn up files of men such as Henry Horst, Theodore Lamprecht, Fred Pritzlaff, and A. A. Grossmann.

MINUTES AND RECORDS

In this category there are often two extremes, an embarrassment of riches or empty shelves. The records of the triennial synodical conventions since 1900 were an essential source of this study. They include the preconvention *Reports and Memorials* (*Eingaben* in the German edition), retitled *Workbook* in 1965, and the *Proceedings* (*Verhandlungen* in the German edition). These five have been cited separately in footnotes to avoid confusion. They usually do not include minutes of committees or general sessions and thus must be read in conjunction with the synodical press and contemporary manuscript sources to be very illuminating. The essays at district conventions indicate trends of thought, but unfortunately there is no ready guide to them. One is usually reduced to *Witness* reviews for aid. The district *Proceedings* are somewhat less essential in the period after 1945 because of the surfeit of other official and unofficial statements within the synod.

With a few notable gaps, the minutes of the Lutheran Laymen's League are intact. Those up to 1929 are at CHI and are open for scholars; the league retains subsequent records and put at my disposal all save the minutes of executive sessions dealing with personnel matters during the late sixties. Minutes up to the mid-twenties are especially valuable because they include verbatim transcripts of some of the earliest league meetings. Preliminary drafts of minutes in the early twenties are also still extant and are much more revealing than the final version. This is not the case after the late twenties when Cramer retired, and the records of some important sessions are frustrating, to say the least. Taken as a whole this is an impressive set of documents, running to about six shelf feet. The league has retained virtually no correspondence files of historical value, however.

Two other sources ought to be mentioned here, even though they are secondary sources. John Theodore Mueller's typescript "The Story of the Lutheran Laymen's League," completed in 1948, is less a history than a chronology of events and a biographical dictionary of LLL leaders and staff members. Donald A. Prahlow's dissertation, "The History of The Lutheran Laymen's League, 1917–1967" (St. Louis University, 1972), is a narrowly conceived institutional history, apparently undertaken with the misapprehension that my own completed study of the league was unavailable because of LLL action. Rather than continuing the process of duplication of effort further, however, I have here curtailed my own discussion of the details of league organization and personnel with the availability of Prahlow's work in mind.

As far as I know, the minutes of the American Luther League were destroyed. The records of the Ways and Means Committee at CHI give an excellent insight into the first large-scale building fund drive in 1923. Through the courtesy of O. P. Kretzmann, I was able to read copies in his files of mimeographed minutes of Lutheran Men in America meetings during the late forties. Early minutes of the synodical board of directors are at CHI, and I was permitted access to them up to 1929. They are generally spare in reporting opinions and raise more questions than they answer about the relations between laymen and clergy on the board. The early minutes of the synodical school board are open at CHI; I found them interesting chiefly for discussions of and attitudes toward the Sunday school.

INTERVIEWS

When the press was silent, files destroyed or closed, and minutes cryptic, I turned to individuals who might draw on memory to guide me. Usually working with a tape recorder, I learned much from conversations with the people listed below. Harry Barr, Sept. 18, 1966; John C. Baur, May 21, 1963, June 11, 1964, July 9, 1964; Oscar Brauer, Sept. 16, 1966; E. R. Bertermann, Sept. 20, 1966; Richard R. Caemmerer, Nov. 18, 1966; W. C. Dickmeyer, Sept. 24, 1966; Ernest J. Echtenkamp, Nov. 29, 1966; Theodore Eckhart, May 16, 1963, July 16, 1963; Edwin Faster, May 30, 1964; Oscar Feucht, Nov. 18, 1966; John A. Fleischli, Sept. 15, 1966; Paul Friedrich, Sept. 19, 1966, Sept. 21, 1966, Aug. 25, 1970; E. J. Gallmeyer, Sept. 24, 1966; Rueben Hahn, Feb. 27, 1970; A. W. Herrmann, Nov. 28, 1966; Robert Hirsch, Oct. 23, 1966; B. M. Holt, Aug. 21, 1966; William Irving, Sept. 22, 1966; E. C. Jacobs, Nov. 29, 1966; Elmer Kraemer, Sept. 20, 1966; O. P. Kretzmann, July 5, 1966, June 24, 1969; Lawrence Meyer, April 21, 1964; Louis Menking, Sept. 23, 1966; Martin W. Mueller, June 26, 1969; Martin Scharlemann, Nov. 21, 1966; Edgar Witte, June 25, 1969; Marcus Zill, Nov. 22, 1966.

Index

ABOUT THE AUTHOR

Alan Graebner is associate professor of history at the College of St. Catherine in St. Paul, Minnesota. He obtained his B.A. at Valparaiso University and his M.A. and Ph.D. at Columbia University. A number of his articles have appeared in *Cresset, Journal of Social History,* and *Concordia Historical Institute Quarterly.* He is the author of *After Eve: The New Feminism.*